CW01083210

TEARS OF A BALLET MUM

Sabine Naghdi

Grosvenor House
Publishing Limited

This book is published by
Grosvenor House Publishing Ltd
Link House
140 The Broadway, Tolworth, Surrey, KT6 7HT.
www.grosvenorhousepublishing.co.uk

A CIP record for this book
is available from the British Library

ISBN 978-1-83975-837-9

Disclaimer

Any view or opinion expressed in this book is solely mine, and is based on my personal experience and understanding of the training process. They do not necessarily represent those of any institution mentioned. The book is sold with the understanding that the Author is not engaged to render any type of professional advice. Neither the Publisher nor the Author shall be liable for any physical, psychological, emotional, or financial damages, including, but not limited to, special, incidental, consequential or other damages.

Acknowledgements

My husband Kamran; my youngest daughter Tatiana; my dear friends Marianne, Colette, and Deryck; Jacqui Dumont, former Principal of the Outreach Programme; Gailene Stock CBE AM (1946-2014), former Director of The Royal Ballet School; Yasmine's Royal Ballet School teachers at White Lodge: Nicola Katrak, Hope Keelan, Anita Young, Diane Van Schoor; and her Upper School Graduate Year teachers Glenda Lucena and Petal Miller Ashmole.

"The purity of her style is something. It is so crystal clear how she dances, and the musicality with that, and then this extraordinary ease on top of that just makes it a pleasure to watch her."

Kevin O'Hare, Director, The Royal Ballet,
The Times, 10 July 2017.

"As Princess Aurora, Yasmine Naghdi confirmed that she has prima ballerina qualities in abundance."

Graham Watts, Bachtrack, 10 November 2019.

"Looking sensationally glamorous with her dark hair and Mediterranean looks, Naghdi avoided all the Kitri clichés and Spanish posturing in favour of something all together more convincing. She had plenty of technical command for the show-stopper numbers which never spilt into look-at-me bravura and were always, even at their most over-the-top moments, underpinned with intelligent musicality."

G J Dowler, Dancing Times, May 2019.

"Yasmine Naghdi, the archetypical music-box ballerina, is perfect for Aurora as she dances with cut-glass sparkle and silent steely control."

Lyndsey Winship, The Guardian, 8 November 2019.

"Yasmine Naghdi, already an important jewel in The Royal Ballet's crown, makes a superb Terpsichore – serene and wise."

Jenny Gilbert, The Arts Desk, Review,
Balanchine's "Apollo", 8 June 2021.

"Naghdi is simply an ideal interpreter of the role of Terpsichore, her diamantine technique allowing her to trace the art deco choreography with the cleanest of lines. Her brilliance as an artist, however, is how she marries that quality with a powerful sensuality; her use of her arms and upper body is particularly striking and she displays an impressive understanding of how to delay, prolong and extend a move or pose."

G J Dowler, Classical Source, 19 June 2021.

Contents

"Then come on the lights, lovingly painted from the front of the theatre. You realize that every nuance on your face and body will be visible. The spotlight following you burns through your eyes, the bumper lights stage right and left add dimensional color to your arms and legs. You can see absolutely no audience. It is all alternatingly black.

Then you realize it is all up to you. You are the performer. You forget everything you have learned. You forget the intricate process of technique; you even forget who you are. You become one with the music, the lights, and the collective spirit of the audience. You know you are there to help uplift them. They want to feel better about themselves and each other.

Then they react. Their generous communal applause means they like you – love you even. They send you energy and you send it back. You participate with each other. And the cycle continues. You leap, you soar, and you turn, extend, and bend. They clap, yell, whistle, stomp, and laugh. You acknowledge their appreciation for what they see and you give them more. And so it goes and goes and goes."

Shirley MacLaine, from *Dancing in the Light.*

Prologue

Swan Lake

Act III: The Palace

A fanfare announces the arrival of an uninvited guest, and all action on the stage of the Royal Opera House comes to a halt.

Yasmine suddenly appears on the grand sweeping staircase of the palace, wearing an exquisite Black Swan tutu. Her make-up is vamped up and red lipstick applied with precision. Prince Siegfried is taken by surprise when he sees his beloved appearing at the ball. Her beauty dazzles him, but he is unaware that Von Rothbart, the evil spirit in human form, has worked his magic: Odile, the Black Swan, looks exactly like Odette, the White Swan Princess. Odile, however, is icy. She has an air of superiority as she gives Von Rothbart furtive conceited glances. The Spanish, Hungarian, Neapolitan, and Polish princesses and their entourages all dressed in breathtakingly beautiful costumes, proceed to entertain the court, as well as us the audience, with various national dances. Firework solos by Odile and Prince Siegfried follow, culminating in one of the greatest technical challenges in a classical ballerina's repertoire, and the most exposed example of virtuoso technique: the thirty-two consecutive fouettés. The precise execution demands incredible technical skill, control, immense strength, and stamina of the ballerina.

"Don't be nervous, just in case she senses your nerves," I mumble to myself. When Yasmine reappears on the stage soon after Prince Siegfried's solo, I cross my middle finger over my index finger and bury them into my other hand. *Will she make it? Or will she lose*

control midway? Or during her last few fouettés? Will she triumph? I have to remind myself that I am not the one performing. I take a deep breath and I try to relax but to no avail. As soon as I hear the first notes of the score marking the start of the thirty-two fouettés, I freeze in my seat. *Swan Lake* is such a long ballet, and at that point in time I know Yasmine is totally exhausted. *How does she do it?* I ponder, as I am watching her throw her working leg out to the side, whipping her foot in as she turns. In between, she throws in several double and triple fouettés.

My eyes are now focussed on that one tiny spot on the stage where the pointe shoe of her supporting foot meets the stage floor. That quick up-and-down of her foot could send her travelling downstage. The legendary Russian Prima Ballerina Natalia Makarova, the finest ballerina of her generation in the West according to *The History of Dance* (1981, p.210), is said to have struggled all her life with those fouettés. When Makarova was dancing her first Odette/Odile with the former Kirov Ballet in St Petersburg, and progressed through her fouettés, she gradually began to travel backwards, and after just sixteen fouettés she finished in the back wing and totally disappeared out of sight! Dance critics described Prima Ballerina Assoluta Margot Fonteyn's thirty-two fouettés as "a cook's tour" (meaning she was all over the place). Yasmine finally comes to a halt, and I can breathe again. The audience claps and cheers. "*She did it,*" I say to myself with a sigh of relief.

Odette now appears as a vision, and she tries in vain to warn Prince Siegfried of the deceit, but he falls into Von Rothbart's trap and chooses Odile as his bride. When Von Rothbart reveals the truth to him, he is shattered.

Act IV – A lakeside clearing

The swans anxiously await Odette's return. Yasmine reappears on the stage as Odette, now wearing a gorgeous white feathery tutu and a striking headdress. As Odette, she is fragile and vulnerable, and totally broken-hearted. She tells the swans of Prince Siegfried's betrayal and how she is now doomed to remain a swan forever. She must die in the lake in order to free herself from Von Rothbart's curse. The deeply saddened Prince returns to the lake in desperation to look for Odette. With her destiny now sealed, she runs to the top of the cliff and jumps off. Moments later, the Prince is left to embrace Odette's motionless body.

The Royal Opera House crimson curtains, with their gold trimmings, gradually lower on the hauntingly beautiful Tchaikovsky score, and *Swan Lake* comes to a close. The music gets me each time, and I well up. Tears stream down my cheeks from my unblinking eyes. Possibly the most admired and best-loved classical tutu ballet of all times has ended, and thunderous applause ensues.

The curtains open again. Yasmine and fellow Principal dancer Federico Bonelli (Prince Siegfried), still very much in character, bow to the audience. The clapping goes on for a while until the curtains close. When the curtains reopen the corps de ballet swans are all on the stage to receive their well-deserved applause. Soon after, the Soloists join them. The curtains close again.

When they reopen, Yasmine reappears on the stage. She graciously acknowledges the audience seated in front of her in the Orchestra Stalls, and those seated in the Stalls Circle, Grand Tier, and in the Boxes, and gradually she looks up to the audience seated high up in the Amphitheatre and the Upper Slips. She thanks them all. The applause and cheers go on and on. Yasmine now walks towards the left stage wing to invite the Music Director of The Royal Ballet and conductor Koen Kessels to join her and all the other dancers. She thanks him with a deep curtsey and respectfully lowers her head. After she has thanked the Orchestra, the ushers walk onto the stage to lay numerous bouquets of flowers at Yasmine's feet.

Chapter One

Her Dream Was Never Mine

More often than not I go backstage after her performance, but on this occasion, I had agreed with Yasmine that we would meet up by the Stage Door in Floral Street. I walk out of the Royal Opera House on Bow Street. I am still on a high. I turn round the corner into Floral Street, and I am in no rush. I know it will take Yasmine at least half an hour before she will be at the Stage Door.

Once the curtains have finally come down, she has a few words on stage with Kevin O'Hare, Director of The Royal Ballet, and with her coach, followed by meeting invited backstage guests, after which she walks to her dressing room, where staff from the costume and wig department are waiting to assist her in taking off her tutu and her headdress. She will take a quick shower, dress, and pick up as many bouquets as she can possibly carry, before she walks from her dressing room to the Stage Door.

As I walk on Floral Street, I briefly look up at the twisting glass bridge high above the street, called the "Bridge of Aspiration", which links The Royal Ballet School to the Grade I-listed Royal Opera House, home of The Royal Ballet. The glass bridge resembles a twisted concertina and has twenty-three squares with glazed recesses, supported by an aluminium "spinal" column. The squares rotate in a sequenced alignment, "performing" a quarter-turn all over the entire bridge. It is a striking sculpture-like architectural structure and conjures up imageries of the elegance of dance. It had always been the aspiration of Dame Ninette de Valois, Founder of The Royal Ballet and The Royal Ballet School, to unite both organisations. Seventy-one years had passed since she had founded her Company and the Vic-Wells Ballet School in 1931, when her dream finally materialised. The bridge was lifted into position on 6 October, 2002 – a year and a half after "Madam", as she was affectionately known, had passed away at the grand old age of 102.

In passing by The Royal Ballet School at No. 46, I glance at the entrance door, but I do not let my mind drift back to the past, and I continue walking towards the Stage Door. Ballet fans are already gathered inside the entrance area. Their excitement is palpable, and they are eagerly waiting to meet the dancers, exchange a few words with them, have them sign the cast list or their red programme, and take photos with their favourite performers. As I try to make my way through to the Reception area, which is separated from the public by a glass door, I spot a woman holding the hand of a pretty little girl with a bouquet of flowers in her arms. In an apologetic manner, the woman greets me and says, "You are Yasmine's mum, aren't you? This is my daughter and she is training at The Royal Ballet School. She has such great admiration for Yasmine and dreams of becoming a ballerina just like her. Can you give me some advice?"

Sixteen years had passed by since I had been standing there in that same spot with Yasmine, waiting to meet the Principal ballerina after a performance.

Once, ten-year-old Yasmine and I had waited to meet Sylvie Guillem (then Principal Guest Artist with The Royal Ballet) after her performance in *A Month in the Country*. We were first in line to meet her. After congratulating Sylvie Guillem on her wonderful performance, she signed a pair of pointe shoes which Yasmine had brought along with her. Yasmine timidly told Sylvie Guillem that she was a Junior Associate at The Royal Ballet School. Just as Sylvie Guillem was about to turn her attention to the other waiting fans, she took one last look at Yasmine, smiled at her, and said: "*Bon courage*, Yasmine!" As I walked out through the Stage Door, hand-in-hand with Yasmine, I wondered why on earth someone would need courage in order to become a ballerina.

Now I found myself standing in exactly that same spot where Yasmine and I had once waited to meet Sylvie Guillem, but this time I am waiting for Yasmine to come through that door, and I could fully grasp the significance of Sylvie Guillem's all-encompassing words: "*Bon courage,* Yasmine!"

I briefly considered whether I should give the mother a concise or a more in-depth answer, but I swiftly decided that if I were to opt for the latter, I would still be standing at the Stage Door the following year. It took me a moment before I was able to come up with what I felt was a meaningful, yet brief enough answer. "Take one step at a time," I said. "It is an intense and demanding long road. So much can happen, so much can change, and talent alone is just not sufficient. For now, all you can do is try to enjoy the journey with your daughter as much as possible."

I guess the mother was none the wiser, as she had a puzzled look on her face. Perhaps she expected an entirely different answer. Maybe she hoped I would somehow be able to divulge a "formula" for success, or practical guidance. It is such an ambivalent journey, with so many highs and lows, and describing it cannot be condensed into just a few words, sentences, or paragraphs.

This chance encounter made me reflect, and I began to think of all those parents who are at the start of their journey, alongside their young daughter or son. Many parents come from a non-ballet background – just as I did – and they have little or no idea what to expect. There are so many questions to be asked, concerns to be addressed, and so many unknowns. I knew very little about the world of ballet back then, and I had to go in search of all the answers myself. I only wish I had known then what I know now.

I distinctly remember how I was initially under the impression that dancers had day jobs, and that they walked into the theatre early in the evening after their day job was done, to get dressed and perform on the stage. Not surprisingly, dancers are time and again asked what their day job is, or what they really do for a living. At the outset, I had absolutely no idea that many years of intense and demanding training preceded their ability to dance ballet, and that ballet *IS* their real day job, as well as their evening job.

Ever since Yasmine joined The Royal Ballet, friends, family, and acquaintances would invariably say, "It must have been such a hard journey." To which I jokingly replied, "Oh, I could write a book about it." Many have tried to persuade me on numerous occasions to do so. They urged me to share my journey as the mother of a vocational ballet student – one who ultimately became a Principal ballerina of The Royal Ballet.

I have been on an all-encompassing journey with Yasmine, from the moment I walked with her into her first ballet class up to the moment she was promoted to the highest rank of Principal ballerina.

Shortly after Yasmine joined The Royal Ballet in April 2010, Anna Meadmore, Manager of Special Collections and brilliant teacher of Dance Studies at The Royal Ballet School, urged me to keep whatever was relevant to Yasmine's performances, such as dance reviews, interviews, and press articles, whilst she was shaping her career at The Royal Ballet. Initially, the idea greatly amused me, because I felt anything worthy of archiving was only relevant to dancers of Principal status, but many years later I am glad I followed Anna's advice. Pointe shoes in which she has danced notable debuts are wrapped up in tissue paper and kept in boxes; the annual Tour red booklet issued to the dancers, containing flight information, hotel reservations, performance dates, relevant local information such as a list of recommended restaurants, interesting places to visit, are all kept, together with Seasonal performance programmes, cast lists, interviews, and press articles. After eleven Seasons with The Royal Ballet, numerous brown Muji boxes have been filled, and it is truly captivating to now look into those very first boxes covering her corps de ballet years.

Members of the audience and backstage guests I have met in the past often asked me if I had been, or if I had ever dreamed of becoming a ballet dancer myself. The answer is no. Yasmine's dream was never my dream.

I was born in Belgium, and I grew up in the Flemish-speaking part of the country known as Flanders, close to the city of Bruges – often referred to as the "Venice of the North".

I began taking bi-weekly after-school ballet classes at the age of eleven, alongside attending music and drawing lessons. My ballet teacher was a former dancer with the Royal Ballet of Flanders, and her elderly mother would always sit in during our ballet class. As our teacher was taking us through our paces at the barre and centre exercises, her mother would pace up and down the ballet studio like a five-star ranked army general inspecting his (her) soldiers. The piercing look in her eyes scared us to death, but it was her cane, purposefully held behind her back, that we feared the most. Whenever we did not execute the steps correctly, she would hit our leg or poke our torso with her cane, simultaneously shouting out corrections at us. I think my ballet teacher was afraid of her own mother, since she let her interfere all the time. Her mother must have been one hell of a ballet mum.

Nonetheless, I somehow enjoyed standing at the barre with my friends, even if it felt like I had joined the army. I loved it, but I never dreamed of becoming a ballet dancer. I was too conscious of the fact that I did not have a sufficient amount of flexibility. I could not even do a half decent split. Nevertheless, I continued my ballet lessons until I turned sixteen, but it ended there and then. For one reason or another, I had come to fear the prospect of boys laughing at me if I told them that I took ballet lessons.

I was vaguely aware of the existence of a world-renowned ballet company in London called The Royal Ballet, and I knew of the existence of the Royal Ballet of Flanders based in Antwerp, and I had heard of Maurice Béjart, Margot Fonteyn, and Rudolf Nureyev.

My exposure to ballet dancing was limited to watching the annual New Year's Day concert on TV with my parents. It was a firm annual family tradition to watch the concert together. The concert still takes place in the "Goldener Saal" (Golden Hall) of the Musikverein and is performed by the Vienna Philharmonic, presenting nostalgic music from the vast repertoire of the Johan Strauss family and its contemporaries. As a child, I absolutely loved it. I was enthralled by the beautiful music, mesmerised by the beauty and elegance of the Vienna State Ballet ballerinas wearing gorgeous dresses and tutus, as well as by the stunning 17th and 18th century Baroque architecture of the various Austrian palaces and the splendid gardens where they would dance.

By the time I was twelve years old, I had made up my mind that I wanted to become an archaeologist. However, a few years later, I had a change of heart when I became downright gripped by the visual arts, by paintings, sculpture, architecture, and the ancient civilisations of Egypt, Greece, and Rome. This translated into an all-encompassing desire to become an art historian. Ever since I'd started secondary school, I had loved my history lessons. Whilst doing my homework, I would often fantasise about entering a time machine to travel back to medieval times, to walk inside creepy medieval castles, or to watch knights at a tournament riding at each other with levelled lances, or I travelled back to Ancient Greece, being hidden inside the huge hollow wooden horse constructed by the Greeks to gain entrance into Troy during the Trojan War.

When I was sixteen, I also became passionate about opera, and I began to accompany my mother to every new opera performance at the Ghent Opera House (now known as Kunsthuis Opera Ballet Vlaanderen). The Ghent Opera House dates from 1840 and has three elegant salons, forming an impressive ninety-metre long gallery with a magnificent chandelier. The first ever opera performance I attended was *The Pearl Fishers*, an opera in three acts by Georges Bizet. First performed in 1863, *The Pearl Fishers* is set in ancient times on the island of Ceylon (Sri Lanka) and describes a moving tale of friendship tested by love. As I sat there in one of the boxes with my mother, I remember literally falling in love with the fisherman Nadir, played by a very handsome French tenor. "Au fond du temple saint" and the beautifully sung aria "Je crois entendre encore" played in my head all night long. The story, the music, the costumes, and the scenery had such an impact on me, and I'd become hooked on opera ever since, and on our regular Sunday outings to the Ghent Opera House.

Many years later, after I had moved to London in the mid-1980s to carve out my career as an art expert at Sotheby's European headquarters in New Bond Street, I attended my first opera at the Royal Opera House in Covent Garden. I was given corporate tickets to accompany a prominent American art collector to see *Madame Butterfly*. Those were the days when many patrons still dressed up to the nines; some women wore elegant long gowns and pearls, and gentlemen wore a suit and a tie. That evening, I wore my most glamorous dress and high heels, too. It felt incredibly special to walk into the world-renowned Royal Opera House. Even in my wildest dreams, I could have never imagined when those stunning crimson curtains with gold trimmings and ER II crests opened, that one day I would sit there to watch The Royal Ballet, and to see my daughter dance as a Principal ballerina on that very same stage.

During the summer of 2017, I made a tentative start to write the book I had so often talked about in the past, but I had my reservations. I wondered who would really want to read about my journey and my experiences as a ballet mum, and I abandoned the idea. However, in February 2020, during the escalation of the Covid-19 pandemic, and just before the United Kingdom went into the first lockdown on 23 March, I made a second attempt and I decided that I would finish it this time. I finally felt ready to share my journey.

The book is not an intricate account of Yasmine's life at The Royal Ballet School. It is first and foremost about my journey as her mother, though obviously linked to Yasmine's. Furthermore, it is about how her talent slowly found its own way into The Royal Ballet School, about all the physical and mental challenges she faced and had to overcome throughout her training years, and as a young professional in the corps de ballet. The "tears" in the title of my book epitomise the "pain" I have felt at times. They also represent my initial feelings of doubt and serious concerns about my young daughter entering vocational ballet training. The "tears" are about my early indecisiveness and feelings of helplessness, because I did not understand the unfamiliar and complicated world of ballet. Obviously, because of my early misgivings and trepidation I really was not keen at all for my daughter to become a ballet dancer.

My "tears" are likewise about the bewilderment, frustration, disbelief, and occasional resentment I felt during her early years in after-school ballet classes, and later on during her vocational training at The Royal Ballet School. Moreover, they stand for my silent anguish at not being able to wholly comprehend why my daughter would want to put herself through the daily physical hardship of ballet training. The ensuing uncertain future of a life as a ballet dancer further fed my anguish, and I couldn't stop thinking, *What a cruel life awaits her*. It was not a probable path or career I had envisioned for my daughter, but eventually I did come to terms with it, as her passionate love for ballet became so obvious. Ultimately, I became equally impassioned, and so did her father, who is one of her most devoted fans.

Throughout her first year at White Lodge, I felt lost, and I was worried that I would not be able to protect my daughter from feeling hurt, and from the ensuing adversity. I soon realised that my best "weapon of defence" – as I entered the unfamiliar territory of the ballet world – was to educate myself about ballet training, as well as about the world of ballet as a whole. The moment I realised that by aiding the development of her mental strength, thereby giving Yasmine the tools to enable her to get over the many obstacles she would encounter, really ignited the start of my own journey. It sparked my profound desire and intense curiosity to want to comprehend every aspect of her vocational training. That inquisitiveness drove me to read a huge number of relevant books, as well as reading about the history of ballet from its origins in the Italian Renaissance courts and introduced to France by Catherine de Medici in the 16th century, to the history of

Russian Ballet, Diaghilev and the Ballets Russes, and of course that of The Royal Ballet. I basically read every book I could get my hands on. As I gained knowledge and understanding in a relatively short space of time, I soon grasped what ballet training, ballet technique, and ballet dancing was all about. Consequently, I was able to guide Yasmine with great confidence, and certainly when – at the age of sixteen – she went through a solemn crisis in her training.

Ballet is a complex art form, and it often serves up a plate of diverse human emotions – and so does ballet training. Each year that her training progressed, new challenges presented themselves and had to be dealt with: from counterproductive perfectionism, teenage issues magnified by the dance trainee, building up her sense of self-worth and mental strength, dealing with a first injury, confronting physical exhaustion and understanding the nutritional needs of top athletes, to dealing with an earnest crisis, facing the isolating experience of being fast-tracked into the Graduate Year, and becoming a young professional before she had graduated from The Royal School which necessitated the sudden urgency for Yasmine to adapt to life as the newest corps de ballet member mid-Season.

My "tears" subsided once she had joined The Royal Ballet. Her initial years as a dancer in the corps de ballet still presented its challenges, but soon my "tears" dried up and turned into "tears" of joy and immeasurable sense of pride.

Based on the numerous biographies of ballet dancers I had read just before Yasmine embarked on her vocational ballet training, I had drawn my own conclusions, and I profoundly feared that she would never really be able to find true happiness within herself if she was to become a ballet dancer. Therefore, my ultimate aim was for my daughter to get through her ballet training with as much normality in her life as possible, so that she could mature into a well-balanced young woman without any mental hang-ups, and would be able to successfully balance her professional life with her private life. I certainly wanted Yasmine to be mindful that there is also a life to be lived away from the stage. And as far as I was concerned, I hoped that being a ballet dancer was not to become the all-encompassing, be-all and end-all of her existence.

During the writing of this book, there were memories I found hard to have to recall to mind, because I had suppressed them all a long time ago. The past was the past. At times it wasn't easy to deal with some recollections or ill feelings that came flooding back. Opening up one's heart is to expose one's vulnerability, and some may argue that we must show all-pervading strength and courage, and never show any such vulnerability; one is not weak because one's heart once felt heavy. Many years later, I wondered if I had not taken it all far too much to heart or far too seriously. Perhaps I should have felt more relaxed and gone with the flow? I concluded that I could not have done it in any other way.

I took Yasmine's training and her trajectory to the top of her profession very much to heart. She grew used to being tough with herself; I never did. Elite-level ballet training – meaning training at the highest level, with the intention to become a professional ballet dancer – is certainly not for the faint-hearted. Even the most determined and talented students may not be able to reach the finishing line. Many consider dancers to be super-human, and the audience gasps or holds their breath when they see a dancer "fly" through the air, spin around the stage like a top, or "bash" out thirty-two fouettés, or when the ballerina balances in an arabesque for what seems to be an eternity. They don't become super-human without a very strict daily training regime, starting out from childhood, and without having the capacity to overcome many physical and mental obstacles. It is very much like an Olympic Games' steeplechase track race, in which only the very best athletes compete. The sheer physical demands of ballet training itself cannot be made easier. It is the mental approach and support, and having an understanding of the workings of the mind of a dance trainee, by the teachers, the parents, or any other supporting adult, that can help alleviate the highly demanding training conditions, and can thereby greatly assist in preventing potential long-lasting mental health issues and/or eating disorders.

Right from the outset of writing my book, it was never my intention to offer any definitive or all-encompassing advice. I merely wanted to share my experience and observations, and all that I have learned along the way, in the hope that those parents whose daughter or son is about to embark on, or is in, vocational ballet training, will be able to get a better understanding of the various challenges a child in ballet training has to face. Of course, every child will experience their training in a different way, and they will try to cope accordingly. So will the parents or the carers.

Likewise, I hope that those members of the public who are either unfamiliar with ballet or are attending their first ballet performance, as well as the individuals who regularly attend a performance but are unacquainted with the demands of vocational ballet training and the demands of life as a professional ballet dancer, will be able to further increase their appreciation of the ballet trainee and the professional dancer.

Clearly, professional ballet dancing is just not an "evening side-job" as I once naively thought many years ago. It necessitates many years of absolute dedication and strenuous daily training from childhood, before a ballet trainee can become a professional ballet dancer. It takes several more years of professional dancing before a few highly exceptional dancers will reach the highest rank of Principal dancer.

Chapter Two

Firstly, Let's Talk about the Ballet Mum

The mother of a child going to a ballet school is called a ballet mum, but who is she really? Clearly, there are varying degrees of a ballet mum's involvement and intensity of her inter-personal relationship with her offspring, as well as with the training. So, how do we define the ballet mum?

Unsurprisingly, the description "ballet mum" is not listed in the Oxford Dictionary of Dance. However, the US Urban Dictionary defines a ballet mum (mom) as:

"A mother, often a single parent, who has raised her child with one idea: to be a great ballerina in a great ballet company. To achieve this, the ballet mom will do anything to advance her little girl's career. The child herself, while she may love dancing, finds it less and less easy to cope with her training and with her mom. Ballet moms watch what their kids eat down to the last calorie. Famous for hovering around dressing rooms and driving beaten-up old cars, she would never waste money on a new one when point shoes have to be bought, along with leotards, lambswool, ribbons for the shoes, and all the other junk that's required. When she hits sixty, when her little darling hits thirty, it's all over for them both. They are sisters under the skin. The ballet mom is always the poorer sister. Ballet moms rarely have their own career or interests, and they would never ever buy their daughter a cake. For the ballet mom, where others see a cake shop, she sees an empty plot of land with weeds growing on it. One famous US ballet mom was reputed to carry a small handgun in her purse."

Some ballet mums do indeed acquire quite a reputation, and the saying "Hell hath no fury like a ballet mum scorned" or "No mother is ever as dangerous as a ballet mum" springs to my mind. An exaggeration? Or is there a grain of truth in it?

Right from the start, I fervently disliked being referred to as a ballet mum, because the collective noun had such a negative connotation to me, and in no way did I identify myself with any of the mums. I simply did not want to be labelled as a ballet mum. Full stop. One indubitably thinks of mothers such as the one in Darren Aronofsky's movie *Black Swan*, with Natalie Portman (Nina Sayers) in the title role. Nina's obsessive and over-protective mother, herself a former ballerina, exerts suffocating control over her twenty-eight-year-old daughter, and she keeps her child-like. Just seeing Nina's pink soft toy-filled bedroom filled me with absolute horror. I remember watching the movie, thinking how sickening and totally selfish her narcissistic mother was, and how she was mentally damaging her daughter, as well as her career. Or Herbert Ross's movie "The Turning Point", with Shirley MacLaine in the role of the ballet mum, in which the mother is similarly portrayed as an overbearing and all controlling parent. Although excited for her daughter, she is nostalgic about her past life as a dancer; her jealousy and regret rise to the surface, naturally affecting her daughter.

A fascinating and detailed description of a ballet mum is found in Meredith Daneman's biography *Margot Fonteyn* (Viking, 2004). Mrs Hilda Hookham, Margot's mum, must have been a shrewd and tenacious woman. She did everything she could possibly do in order to enable her young daughter to take ballet classes in the best of circumstances and with the best teachers available in Shanghai. Eventually she made the choice of leaving her husband behind in Shanghai in order to take Margot to London for further training. Her decision ultimately affected their family life and resulted in a divorce.

Once they had settled in London, Mrs Hookham did everything within her power to find the best ballet teacher for her daughter.

She managed to persuade Princess Serafina Astafieva – a Russian dancer, and later on ballet teacher – to take on Peggy Hookham (Margot Fonteyn) as her student. Princess Astafieva's house, called "The Pheasantry", still stands at 152 King's Road in Chelsea, London, and an English Heritage Blue Plaque marks it stating: *Princess Serafina Astafieva, 1876-1934, Ballet dancer, lived and taught here, 1916-1934*. "The Pheasantry" is a Grade II-listed building, and it now houses a branch of the Pizza Express restaurant chain. We have fond memories of our regular Sunday family lunch in the courtyard when Yasmine and her younger sister Tatiana were little girls. I was well aware of the remarkable history of the place linking it to Margot Fonteyn, and so was Yasmine.

Once Margot became a professional ballet dancer, her mother was permanently to be found backstage, as well as in Fonteyn's dressing room. She was also very close to Ninette de Valois, then Director of The Royal Ballet. When in June 1973 Margot's mother joined the Company on tour to Paris, she became known as the "Black Queen". The dancers nicknamed Mrs Hookham after the Black Queen in Ninette de Valois' ballet, *Checkmate*. Rather than feeling insulted, Mrs Hookham felt flattered. In my opinion, a better nickname for Mrs Hookham would have been "The Hawk", as she was forever watching over Fonteyn like a predatory hawk ready to swoop down on its prey at any time. No doubt Mrs Hookham did all this with the best of intentions, but to me she really epitomises the ballet mum: total involvement in every aspect of her daughter's life, even after Fonteyn had become a professional ballerina and was an adult woman.

Such an attitude certainly does not allow a dance trainee or a professional dancer to spontaneously develop her own personality, and to a certain extent there is the danger of infantilising the trainee or the professional dancer. Nonetheless, according to the biography, even the constant presence of Fonteyn's mother could not thwart Fonteyn's early sexual encounters. At the age of seventeen, Fonteyn had an enduring affair with the married

Constant Lambert – a British composer, conductor, and Founder Music Director of The Royal Ballet.

I first became aware of the ballet mum "label" when I was watching Yasmine in ballet class at the end of each term during her pre-Royal Ballet School years. Before long, I sensed their competitive side, and it baffled me that some mothers were seemingly rather confident their daughter was going to make it as a ballet dancer. That thought had not even occurred to me, and I found it all somewhat bizarre. I never enrolled Yasmine in ballet class with the intention, hope, or dream, that she would ever become a ballet dancer. I remember feeling uncomfortable and out of place amongst the eager ballet mums. After a while, I also became aware that the conviviality of some was shallow. Later on, when favouritism in the ballet classes became apparent, I decided I really did not want to be part of it, and that it was better for me to stick to being a non-ballet mum. At first, I tried to keep my distance as much as possible. Unsurprisingly...I did get sucked into it all.

Ballet mums meet each other whenever there is an opportunity to watch their child in class, and some ballet mums can be really irritating. They are the turbo charged kind of ballet mums; their determination to thrust their child into ballet stardom from a young age is palpable; they think their offspring is the best, and they become resentful of others. They are super ambitious, controlling, and they think and talk as if the parent and child are one and the same person. They also do not hesitate to criticise the teacher or certain students. Tipped off by the ballet mum, the local newspaper – eager to fill their pages with regional success stories – zealously describe her offspring as a "ballerina" or as a "star".

I recall once reading a headline stating: "*Eight-year-old star ballerina set to join The Royal Ballet!*" What the reporter should have said instead was that the eight-year-old had been accepted as a Junior Associate in one of the nine centres in the UK where children are introduced to The Royal Ballet School's System of Training, before they have the option to audition, aged eleven, for a place at The Royal Ballet School. Said "star ballerina" was a long way away from joining The Royal Ballet.

The frequent casual use of the word "ballerina" in that context is also wrong. According to the Oxford Dictionary of Dance, the term "ballerina", which in Italian means "female dancer", strictly refers to a Principal female dancer in a ballet company, and it is never correctly used in connection with any lower ranked dancer, and with any other form of dance, let alone labelling a young child in training a "ballerina".

Nowadays, it seems that many youngsters also amass a huge social media following. Needless to say, this type of media exposure puts children and teenagers under a lot of pressure. They may be under the false illusion that they have "made it", but once they are to embark on life as a professional dancer – if they have managed to make it through the rigorous training – they are anything but a "star". Taking centre stage is not a place where they will find themselves any time soon. They will stand un-fêted at the back of a company ballet studio as a cover, watching the corps de ballet dancers rehearse.

Surely a child has to be encouraged, but she or he will have to learn that the ability to self-motivate and focus is vital to their ongoing daily practice and learning. Eventually they will either achieve success or they will fail. Talent in the end will find its own way without self-promotion. I remember back in my day, some ballet mums created a website (Instagram or Facebook did not yet exist) for their daughters with the intention of giving their offspring exposure and an early flavour of stardom. The current social media pressure a child in training risks being under is, in my opinion, distracting and does not help them to develop a healthy self-image, nor a balanced mental attitude and self-confidence. Most parents are aware that the excessive use of social media has the potential to be damaging, and how the self-esteem and overall happiness of children and teenagers can be seriously dented by adverse or cruel comments coming from their peers. Luckily, when Yasmine started training at White Lodge in 2004, Facebook was still in its infancy, and her use was limited and rightly controlled by the House Parents, as well as at home. Present-day use of platforms such as Instagram and Tik-Tok were non-existent, and therefore posed no risk of distraction or adversely influencing Yasmine's mind as a ballet trainee.

I once heard the down-to-earth account of a highly esteemed chess teacher and coach telling his new eleven-year-old pupil – who was about to sit down on a chair at the chess table with his coach – to go and sit down on the floor instead. The very talented young boy was puzzled. The teacher told the boy that sitting on a chair at the table with him to practise chess was a right the boy first and foremost had to earn. Too much pride makes one artificial. Humility makes one real. It is all about total focus and complete concentration on what really matters; all the rest pales into triviality. Veritable artists and genuine talent have no ego, and their humility always speaks louder than words (or social media images for that matter). Understanding the importance of humility is to understand the importance of being in a state of maximum concentration, and knowing that no-one can win on talent alone.

I used to compare a group of ballet mums to a pride of lionesses who fight tooth and claw to defend their cubs. Except, in this case, they are not watched over by a coalition of male lions. Those ballet mums don't hesitate to elbow you out whenever they think they have reasons for doing so. One summer, when Yasmine was eleven years old, a year prior to joining The Royal Ballet School, I took her to the Koninklijke Ballet School in Antwerp, Belgium, to attend a week of summer ballet classes. On the second day, just before pick-up time, I was watching Yasmine in class through the window, alongside all the other ballet mums. I noticed the level was really too easy for Yasmine, and I felt we had not come all the way from London for her to attend an easy ballet class, even as we were on our bi-annual family visit in Belgium. At that point in time,

Yasmine was a Junior Associate at The Royal Ballet School, and the purpose of attending the Antwerp Summer School was for her to learn new things and to be challenged. Was I pushy? No. It just made sense: the class was too easy for Yasmine, and she had told me straight after her first day that the ballet class was far too basic, and it was boring.

I spoke to the teacher, Maria Metcharova, and without any reservation she concurred that the class level was indeed too easy-going for her. Miss Metcharova promptly arranged for Yasmine to join a higher-level class with the fourteen-year-old students the following morning. This gave rise to an unexpected confrontation with the Belgian ballet mums. Once they had noticed "that girl from London" had joined a higher-level class, they confronted me and vehemently disapproved of me speaking to the teacher. Needless to say, I was completely taken back at being ambushed by a couple of "lionesses". From that moment onwards, they turned their backs on me each morning when Yasmine and I arrived at the ballet school. The "gang" would give me stern looks as they all stood by the entrance door, and they were no longer on speaking terms with me. In short, I was "elbowed" out of the group. This was my first disagreeable encounter with archetypical competitive ballet mums. For the rest of the week, I stayed far away from them. I entered the ballet school with a poker face, and as soon as I had dropped Yasmine off, I left the building as fast as I could. After all, I had better things to do than to involve myself, and waste my time, with a group of gossipy, green-eyed ballet mums. Luckily, the Rubens House – the *palazzetto* where the world-famous Flemish Baroque painter lived in the sixteenth and seventeenth centuries – was nearby, as were a number of excellent bookshops, museums, and art galleries, to keep me entertained during the hours that Yasmine was attending her daily classes.

Even when done with the best of intentions, no amount of ambition of the parent can turn their offspring into a wunderkind or a highflyer; not even arranging for the child to appear on the front page of a newspaper can do that. The ballet mum may have her own reasons to be proud of her child, but in the end, what is she actually trying to achieve? It is obvious that no amount of self-publicity or gracing a page in a newspaper or a magazine will magically turn a child into a successful graduate, nor does it aid or pave the way for a lasting and successful career as a professional dancer. There is no need to be an overly ambitious or a pushy mother when the child has real talent for ballet; and if the child is not naturally gifted, there is little that can be done about it but to ultimately realise and accept it. This is by no means a reason for not continuing and enjoying non-vocational dancing classes or ballet lessons for as long as the child or teenager loves it.

There is a huge dissimilarity between being a pushy mother and being an encouraging and supportive mother. Yasmine's sister Tatiana enjoyed ballet, jazz, and tap classes until she was twelve years old, but she gave it up of her own accord. I did try to encourage her to continue just for the fun of it, and for the self-discipline it installs in a child, but these rational arguments could not change Tatiana's mind. When Tatiana told me she didn't enjoy it any more and that her pointe shoes hurt too much, I knew ballet classes were no longer a suitable after-school pastime for her. She threw herself into school team sports instead and greatly enjoyed it.

Yasmine, on the other hand, is a case in point of how her talent eventually found its own path. Up until the age of twelve, I simply let Yasmine enjoy dancing as a hobby, without ever thinking ballet dancing might one day become her career. I felt that four hours of ballet classes a week for eleven-year-old Yasmine, as had been suggested by her ballet teacher, was already far too much for her. Yasmine never asked to go to The Royal Ballet School, and we never instigated for her to go. I always left the door wide open so that she felt free to decide for herself, in the knowledge that she could walk away from her ballet classes anytime she wanted to. After she had joined White Lodge, it was imperative that she learned to take full responsibility for her training without feeling any parental pressure whatsoever. Persistence and the will to work hard, combined with intense focus, came naturally to Yasmine.

Take Emma Raducanu, Britain's recent overnight teenage tennis sensation, as an example. She said that her secret weapon is her non-pushy parents. Her mother and father were far more interested in her A-level exam results. Tennis champion Raphael Nadal had non-pushy parents, too, and they provided him with much needed normality, as well as a loving family atmosphere. His mother insisted he must go to university, and his father's sole role was to facilitate getting the young Nadal to his various junior matches all over Mallorca. And that was it. They always played down his winnings, and they never gave much importance to any of his tennis achievements. They rightly wanted to keep him grounded, and so did his formidable uncle and coach Toni Nadal.

In my early days, I really learned a lot by reading the biographies of sports stars. No doubt there must be examples of insistent parents who have achieved results, but I do wonder what the mental cost has been for the child, and its long-term effect.

At The Royal Ballet School, White Lodge, we formed a small group of unperturbed mothers, and we were affably close; we effortlessly bonded in our common cause to support our daughters. The majority of parents lived within one-to-three hours driving distance. Those who lived at a greater distance from White Lodge were mostly absent. We were only all united when we were invited to watch the ballet class at the end of term.

Of course, there were a few unpleasant incidents over the years, and I distinctly remember one such instance when a frenzied ballet mum reported an issue within the girls' year group relating to her daughter. It caused such unnecessary turmoil and it was entirely preventable. This resulted in seriously agitating us mothers, because we felt the matter was ultimately dealt with in an inequitable manner. The ensuing measures taken were beyond the pale, resulting in the entire class being admonished to an exaggerated level, and given the cold shoulder treatment. Feeling powerless as a parent and being unable to alleviate our daughters' ordeal left us mothers fuming. Every evening, for an entire week, the mothers in our group were on the phone with each other to discuss what we as parents could do about the disagreeable situation. We requested a meeting with the Headmistress the following Sunday, to talk about the high-handed measures taken. When we dropped off our daughters that Sunday afternoon, we were snappishly told the issue was not to be discussed any further and the case was closed. Five mothers, including myself, were left standing open-mouthed, flabbergasted, and in total disbelief, right next to Margot Fonteyn's bronze statue. We merely felt like children who had been told to shut up. We felt very dispirited and frustrated, and absolutely dumbfounded how one parent was seemingly permitted to cause such disproportionate pandemonium whereas our parental voice, as a fair counterbalance, was not taken into account at all. A proper, civilised dialogue would have offered a much better solution. There are always two sides to a coin.

Of course, there are stories galore just about anywhere of the disruptive parent, and in the majority of cases it will be a ballet mum. Personally, I have never met an unpleasant ballet dad.

...AND WHAT ABOUT THE BALLET DAD?

Little is ever said about the ballet dad, who is – on the whole – endearing and seemingly not (as) competitive, unlike the ballet mum. The interest he takes in his daughter's or son's ballet training is charmingly looked upon. He usually walks coolly alongside, or right behind, ballet mum whenever they attend a ballet school performance together or watch the end-of-term ballet class. On the face of it, he follows his offspring's progress with a degree of reservation, unless of course he is a former ballet dancer himself. However, the father of the now retired Royal Ballet Principal dancer Carlos Acosta was not a former ballet dancer himself, yet his well-intended paternal interference decided on the future of his son. He steered him away from petty fruit-stealing in the streets of Havana, and just as Carlos was getting into break-dancing aged nine, his father decided that his son should go to ballet school to teach him discipline and to provide him with daily free lunch. The rest is history!

On the other hand, in the field of sports, many fathers do play a very active role in the early coaching of their son or daughter. We only need to look at how tennis champions Serena and Venus Williams were intensely coached by their father, Richard Dove Williams Jr., who started out by giving his daughters tennis lessons when they were four-and-a-half years old; or how Rafael Nadal was coached by his uncle, Toni Nadal, who recognised Rafael's natural talent when he was only three years old; or Earl Dennison Woods, the father of professional golfer Tiger Woods, who coached his son during the first few years in the sport. A noteworthy exception is Judy, the mother of British tennis star Andy Murray – a former Scottish tennis player herself and initial coach for both her sons, before handing over the reins to another coach as their professional career blossomed. Many of the great sports women and men had parental coaching from a young age.

Yasmine's father was no former ballet dancer either, and his familiarity with dance and ballet was cultivated through his attendance of "The Shiraz-Persepolis Festival of Arts", an annual international arts festival held in Persia every summer from 1967 until 1977, under the auspices of Empress Farah Pahlavi, née Farah Diba. It was presented in Shiraz, at the foot of the Zagros Mountains, about forty miles northeast of the ceremonial capital of the Achaemenid Empire (c.550-330 BC) of Persepolis. The festival was an inspired exploration, experimentation, and creative conversation between Persia and the outside world. It unfolded through music, drama, dance, and film, and it was without doubt the most significant performing and experimental arts festival in the world at that time. The local artistic scene shared a stage with the likes of Ravi Shankar, Yehudi Menuhin, Rwandan percussionists, Japanese Noh, Balinese gamelan, and Indian Kathakali performers, as well as creations especially commissioned by the festival by Merce Cunningham, Maurice Béjart, John Cage, Gordon Mumma, Iannis Xenakis, and Karlheinz Stockhausen, amongst many others. Ground-breaking experimental works were created when many of the artists remained marginal in their own countries. The artistic gains were not only beneficial for the Persian culture and arts scene, but it invited distant voices from Asia and Africa to test their own traditional ideas on the very essence and nature of drama, music, and performance. It was there that Kamran saw contemporary and experimental dance performed on music by Stockhausen, where he saw Maurice Bejart's *Heliogabale* and the world premiere and site-specific commission "Persepolis Event" by Merce Cunningham Dance Company.

Yasmine's father was born in Tehran, but his parents moved their young family to Geneva soon after the birth of their fifth child. Kamran and his two brothers were sent to boarding school in England; his two sisters attended schools in Switzerland. Once Kamran had graduated from university, he returned to Tehran to set up his own business. Persia, at that time, was still ruled by the Pahlavi dynasty. However, when the last Shah, Mohammed Reza Shah Pahlavi, was overthrown during the Iranian Revolution in 1979, Kamran had to abandon the business he had built up through so much hard work, and leave everything behind. Kamran had no other option but to return to England in order to escape the oppressive regime.

Many years later, yearning to see all the historical monuments and architecture I had studied at university, we travelled through Persia together with Yasmine. Kamran needed a lot of persuasion before he was willing to return to the country he had abandoned. We visited many splendid archaeological sites, ancient cities, and awe-inspiring Persian gardens that brought to mind the mesmerizing tales of *One Thousand and One Nights*. Yasmine delighted in running around in the Persian gardens with abundant water streams, and she always expressed great excitement at the sight of any fountain – and there were plenty of them. We travelled through the desert en route to visit centuries' old palaces, mesmerizing mosque architecture, and the marvellous Persian gardens in the beautiful city of Isfahan, with its grand boulevards, covered bridges, and the breathtaking Nasq-e-Jaha square with the 16th century Grand Ali Qapu Safavid Imperial Palace situated right opposite the 17th century Sheikh Lotfollah Mosque, its beautiful mosaics making one truly light-headed; and Shiraz, the city of poets, literature, nightingales, wine, and flowers. We travelled to the ancient desert city of Yazd, nicknamed the "City of Wind Catchers", described by Marco Polo as the "Noble City of Yazd", and to the impressive ruins of Persepolis.

Whenever we were in Tehran, I always took Yasmine with me on my numerous visits to the museums. I let her run around – to my own delight – amongst the many architectural treasures in the impressive Archaeological Museum. It was closed to the public, but opened up for me by the Museum's Director after I had contacted him and given the name of my archaeology professor, who was renowned for his extensive research in the north of Iran. Our mornings or afternoons were filled with visits to the striking Glass and the Ceramic Museum, the breathtaking Malek Museum, the magnificent Carpet Museum, and the Museum of Modern Art, created by Empress Farah Diba. We also visited the graves of the world-renowned Persian poets Hafez, Omar Khayyam, and Ferdowsi. Yasmine's father is a great lover of Persian poetry, and he would often recite poems to Yasmine and Tatiana when they were children.

Kamran did more than his fair share as a father, to driving one of our two young daughters to their respective weekly ballet classes in various locations at different times. He used to take Tatiana to her ballet class at the Marie Rambert Studio in Notting Hill, and I took Yasmine to her West London School of Dance (WLSD) ballet lessons, just off Oxford Street, or vice versa. Her father even became a prop during one of the girls' weekend rehearsals of *Little Women* – a ballet based on the novel by American writer Louisa May Alcott. Since Kamran was the only father present at the rehearsal, he was asked to go and stand in the middle of the dance studio and pretend to be a tree, so that the children could dance around the "tree". Not realising that the rehearsal was folding up, Kamran remained "centre stage"... until the teacher noticed and told him the rehearsal had ended and the tree was no longer needed. From that moment onwards, Kamran became a ballet dad.

Chapter Three

Can Talent be Spotted?

"Doing easily what others find difficult is talent; doing what is impossible with talent is genius."

(Henri Frederic Amiel)

One of the questions I have often been asked in the past is how did I spot Yasmine's talent? I did not spot her talent for ballet, because it was not apparent in any distinguishable form until she was about eleven or twelve years old. Her only early discernible features were her hyper-flexibility, her swayback legs, and her highly hyperactive nature. She showed potential, but I certainly did not define it as having an obvious or remarkable talent for ballet. However, by the age of eleven she began to show her innate talent. By the time she was fourteen, her ability to develop much needed mental toughness and intense focus, and to consistently invest great effort to improve during her daily ballet classes, became very obvious. Yasmine's talent for ballet was recognised at the age of twelve by Mrs Jacqui Dumont, then Principal of The Royal Ballet School's Associate Programme. None of Yasmine's pre-White Lodge ballet teachers had ever unambiguously articulated to me that she was outstanding in any way, nor had any one of them encouraged me to audition Yasmine for a place at The Royal Ballet School. In the end, Jacqui Dumont did, and I wondered why.

Had they all a different idea or definition of what talent is all about? What was it that Jacqui Dumont detected or spotted in Yasmine that the others had not?

As soon as Yasmine started her ballet training at The Royal Ballet School, I began to question where her talent might have come from, because I was frequently asked if anyone in our family had been a ballet dancer. As far as I knew, nobody in my or Kamran's family had ever been a ballet dancer. Yasmine's father had always been a very keen and active sportsman, and Yasmine certainly inherited the flexibility gene from her father, as well as his hyperactive nature and physicality.

However, one day a friend of mine who lives in Paris called me excitedly to say that she had discovered an old book in one of the vintage bookstores in the Marche aux Puces de Clignancourt, titled *La Danse a l'Opéra*, dating from 1927. Only one hundred copies had been printed, and Monsieur Louis Laloy, Secrétaire General du Theatre National de l'Opéra, wrote a fascinating text. The book is full of wonderful old photos of dancers at the Paris Opéra Ballet in the 1920s. Amongst them were photos of two sisters who were both Grand Sujet at the Paris Opera Ballet during the time Carlotta Zambelli and Olga Spessivtseva were Danseuse Etoile. Those two sisters not only bore my paternal grandfather's rare surname, but they both had an astounding and striking resemblance to him, as well as to my father. Further research into our family genealogy confirmed that his two nieces had departed for Paris in the early 1920s. Could it really be that their dancing genes had been passed on to Yasmine after three generations?

So, what exactly is talent? Opinions differ, depending on which criteria are being used. I realise that I am comparing apples with pears here, but one only needs to look at what is considered "talent" in the British reality television music competition "The X Factor" or "Britain's Got Talent", and the natural inborn talent of the participants in the Queen Elisabeth Competition, established in 1937 as a springboard for young violinists, pianists, singers, and cellists on the threshold of an international career, or the Frederic Chopin International Piano Competition, or the Prix de Lausanne and Youth American Grand Prix – international ballet competitions for young dancers seeking to pursue a professional career in classical ballet.

Real talent is something one is born with, and it cannot be manufactured. It needs to be discovered, then nurtured, developed, and enabled to blossom. Initially, the talent lies dormant in a child, and it is the direct or indirect stimulation coming from its environment during their initial years that may fuel or induce their passion for ballet, or sport or music, or any other field in which their talent may lie. In the case of ballet, some young children may show a certain degree of musicality, some may be more expressive than others or look more determined or have an early ability to focus, or are extremely flexible, but there is no guarantee that any or all of these qualities will still be present by the time they are sixteen, in readiness for further advanced training.

Talent is by and large defined or described as having a natural ability and possessing the aptitude to stand out and shine, achieved with much more ease than others do. However, talent is not solely about one's "base" ability. Eventually there has to be a staunch innate drive towards an intense desire to do a tremendous amount of practice, combined with multiple factors that will contribute to turning the training into a success. Their inborn talent will become apparent after a reasonable amount of practice, at which point their ability to rapidly adapt and improve will become more discernible. An "a-priori" talent, as well as a "responder" talent, is necessary, further enabling one's ability to achieve competence in an accelerated manner. It is not about how good one is right away, but how good one eventually can and will become. It is said that artistic or athletic talent stems from genetic inheritance, but such talent can only manifest itself through sheer determination, hard work, and many years of consistent practice.

In relation to athletic talent, I really do not subscribe to the "ten thousand hours-practice" concept created by Professor Anders Ericsson, who proclaims that ANY individual can become an elite athlete if they practise for a minimum of ten thousand hours. That, in my opinion, is an all-too-simplistic statement. I rather side with Lee Jun-fan (Bruce Lee, martial arts artist) who said he did not fear the man who has practised ten thousand kicks once, but feared the one who has practised one kick ten thousand times. Ericsson seems to have omitted taking into account genetic, mental, and other physical factors such as body type, muscle fibre type, whether somebody is injury prone or not, as well as bone mass and limb proportion. All these factors will ultimately determine the ensuing limitations to training and performing. Genetic factors clearly have an impact on how one adapts to elite-level training and how far into the training the sports or ballet trainee can advance. Some physiologies do have a ceiling, and some will reach a plateau beyond which they are unable to go for a variety of reasons. Training, be it in ballet or sport, is about trying to realise one's potential, in combination with possessing a strong drive and a high degree of mental toughness. Achieving success in training is also the result of that talent being able to train in the right environment with experienced teachers or coaches. The realization of one's talent and reaching one's full potential is rare and relies heavily on a combination of factors, such as parental or carers' support, strong commitment, self-confidence, high-level motivation, robust mental skills, intensity of learning and practising, strong focus, and physical aspects such as flexibility, agility, coordination, physical strength, stamina, pain tolerance, speed of learning, speed of recovery, as well as overall health and diet. Developing or possessing all the mentioned qualities will allow those trainees to improve at a much faster rate than others. These exceptional qualities will facilitate their capacity to adapt with relative ease to the increasing intensity of their training, and they will develop the necessary skills through which the genetics, combined with the desire to practise, comes together. This will ultimately create a higher ability level in their particular field of training.

Eventually, their unique individual qualities will shape and colour their personality, and this must come to the surface and shine through, enabling the dancer to become a veritable artist. Without a combination of all those skills, the trainee or young professional will not be able to last long enough to ultimately develop the necessary expertise for high level performance quality. The ultimate exquisiteness of dancing ballet lies not solely in the ability of the dancers to dance a series of highly difficult technical steps, but in their ability to move the audience emotionally. It is about the art of making it all look easy, to make the audience forget about the steps and the enormous physical effort it necessitates, and for the dancers to transport the audience from their individual reality into the (ballet) story being told, being able to sweep the audience along with them, deep inside the character they are dancing. Even in the non-story ballets, the exceptional dancer will be able to sweep the audience along solely through the sheer beauty of their movement. A ballet dancer is often considered to be an elite athlete – and they certainly are – however ballet is a performing art form, not a sport.

It takes about eight years of intense training from the age of eleven, and on average another four years of dancing in the corps de ballet with a ballet company, to produce a proficient professional ballet dancer. Some will have that inimitable quality, and they will quickly stand out in the corps de ballet and show potential to become a Soloist. For a Soloist or a First Soloist to set her or himself apart, yet another set of qualities and skills are needed in order to reach the ultimate top rank of Principal dancer. Unsurprisingly, the number of dancers in each rank gets smaller and smaller towards the "top of the tree".

THE TELL-TALE SIGNS THAT IMPLIED YASMINE'S FUTURE

A few months after she was born, Yasmine displayed signs of physical strength, rather uncommon in babies of her age, her paediatrician told me.

She was walking by the time she was barely ten months old, and as soon as she had mastered walking, she would not sit still, ever. She hated sitting on my lap. When she was a bit older, I asked her why she disliked sitting on my lap. She answered that it made her feel as if she was deprived of oxygen. She was an exceedingly hyperactive toddler, and by the time she was eighteen months old, I really had my hands full with her. Most toddlers are active, but she was exceptionally so. She would scale every piece of horizontal and vertical furniture and then jump off, and she teetered on the edge of every windowsill. Thank goodness our chandelier was totally out of reach. She loved climbing on our coffee table whenever she had a chance to attract our attention or the attention of visiting friends and family to show off dance-like movements. Giving my toddler multiple warnings that she could fall off her "stage" simply fell on deaf ears. As a matter of fact, she never fell off the table.

Later on, she also loved climbing up inside the doorframe and staying high up there for as long as she could hold on. She really enjoyed showing off her physical strength. I found her behaviour simultaneously amusing and intriguing. Those were her "Look at me, here I am, see what I can do!" moments. It was as if her body demanded to move, and she was forever skipping, jumping, climbing, or running around the house, in total contrast to her much calmer younger sister who would happily settle on the sofa to watch her sister provide her with all sorts of entertainment. We called Yasmine "Speedy Gonzales" after the Looney Tunes cartoon character. Sitting still at the dining table seemed a waste of time for Yasmine, and she was a notoriously difficult child to feed. In her early years, she only wanted to eat French baguette and pasta.

I despaired, wondering how on earth she would get all the vitamins and minerals needed as a growing child, and in total desperation I took her to the paediatrician. He told me in no uncertain terms that he had never seen a child who had starved itself, and that I should relax and not make a fuss about mealtimes. From then on, I would not ask Yasmine to come and sit at the dinner table; it was of no use. Instead, I turned mealtimes into game times, and I succeeded in making her eat small portions of food "on the go" as I gave my Speedy Gonzales the freedom to run around the house.

Mealtimes with her were time-consuming efforts. She just wasn't interested in food.

Occasionally, when I was watching Yasmine perform on the stage of the Royal Opera House, my mind did wander off to some early foretokens. When I watched her dance her debut as "Odette/ Odile" in *Swan Lake*, my mind drifted back to the day I popped into a coffee shop, after my daily walk in the park with baby Yasmine. I sat down at a table right next to a Japanese lady. I noticed she held a piece of paper with Japanese lettering in her hands, and she proceeded making an *orizuru*, or paper crane – a design that is considered to be the most classic of all Japanese origami. To me, it merely looked like a swan. When she finished, she stood up and graciously bowed to me. She then looked smilingly at ten-month-old Yasmine, who was fast asleep in her pushchair. She put the origami "swan" on Yasmine's blanket, bowed at her, and walked away. I still have the paper swan, and I love to think it is a metaphor of what Yasmine was ultimately to become in her life.

When Yasmine danced her debut as Swanilda in *Coppélia*, and hopped backwards on pointe on one foot, I found myself staring at her foot. My mind suddenly drifted back to the moment, a few hours after she was born, when I noticed her tiny feet had suddenly turned blue. In a panic, I called the nurse, who hurried Yasmine into the emergency room for a paediatrician to check her out. Nothing was deemed wrong. It was "a matter of poor blood circulation", I was told.

Every time we went on our Sunday afternoon family walk in Hyde Park, Yasmine would run ahead of us with her arms spread wide open – like swans open and flap their wings just before take-off – and she would shout, "The meadow!" Clearly, Yasmine had watched Walt Disney's *Bambi* over and over. However, the animated musical fantasy film *The Little Mermaid* was her absolute favourite Disney movie, and she was totally captivated by Princess Ariel's underwater swimming skills. Gradually, we noticed she was at her happiest whenever she had space around her, and when she could move around freely. Sitting still was clearly not her forte, and Yasmine never walked whenever she could run. I also have an evocative memory of one summer holiday in Italy. The sun was setting as I was watching eight-year-old Yasmine wandering all by herself on the beach, slowly walking towards the edge of the sea. I suddenly noticed she started dancing. Facing the horizon, her toes touching the water, she was improvising, and she was clearly in her own world. The sight of her dancing by the edge of the sea at sunset will never leave me.

She wasn't interested in building sandcastles with her younger sister, nor quietly collecting shells; instead, she skipped and hopped and ran on the beach, enjoying the wide-open space, always followed by a swim. She was clearly in her element whenever she was in or under the water. It fascinated me. I guess it was an expression of her inner world, of her desire to move, and also of her happiness at being by the sea. Even today, she is still at her happiest whenever she is by the sea. It is no coincidence that the short black/white film she directed and produced during the Covid-19 pandemic in June 2020, was set by the edge of the sea on the Italian Riviera.

Another occasion that will forever remain engrained in my memory is when I took Yasmine and Tatiana to the 2003 blockbuster "Art Deco 1910-1939" exhibition at the Victoria and Albert Museum in South Kensington. Gallery after gallery was filled with stunning furniture, decorative objects, and numerous eye-catching paintings, jewellery, and ceramics. It was a most glorious feast for the eyes. As I wandered from one gallery into another with Tatiana, I suddenly noticed Yasmine was nowhere to be seen. I walked back to where I had last seen her, and there she stood in the gallery titled "The Exotic".

A black & white film excerpt "The Banana Dance" was showing Josephine Baker (the first black woman to star in a major motion picture, the 1927 silent film *Siren of the Tropics)* dancing in a banana skirt. Yasmine seemed totally absorbed and rendered immobile. The film was shown on a loop, and her eyes did not leave the screen. I was intrigued and wondered why she was so spellbound by this film. Was it the music, or was it the dance, or was it Josephine's banana skirt?

Instants such as these remained engraved in my mind, and they slowly but surely built up to the moment I felt that movement and dance was something that naturally captivated Yasmine, something her body seemed to ask for. She often spontaneously expressed what she subconsciously felt or what she was thinking of during those fleeting instants, and I retained them all. Years later, I considered them all to have been early indicators.

Chapter Four

What led her to The Royal Ballet School?

"The will to win is important but the will to prepare to win is vital. Failing to prepare is preparing to fail."

(Joe Paterno)

Her academic schooling took precedence over her ballet lessons, as they were only a means to an end: to get rid of her excess energy built up whenever she had to sit still in class, which seemed pure torture for her. On more than a few occasions, her teachers told me that Yasmine's restlessness and incessant wriggling on her chair during academic lessons often caused her to fall off her chair, to the great amusement of her classmates. Doing homework and revising the timetables with her at home was ever so challenging, until the moment I told her we would revise the timetables together on her bed so that she could wriggle and roll as much as she wanted to. It delivered the desired result.

Not until the age of fourteen did she express a fervent desire to become a ballet dancer. Yasmine was never the proverbial little girl who would dreamily glance through books, looking at sweet pictures of pretty ballerinas in a tutu, or sit still in front of TV to watch *The Nutcracker* video and tiptoe around the room imitating the dancers. One Christmas Day, her grandmother had bought her a pink tutu as a present. As soon as ten-year-old Yasmine had opened the box and looked at the tutu, it quickly made its way back into the box – neatly folded up – and the tutu has remained in that box ever since. One video, however, did stop Yasmine in her tracks as she was running around the house, and she spontaneously sat herself down in front of TV. I was watching a video of William Forsythe's electrifying and high-voltage ballet *In the Middle, Somewhat Elevated*, created for the Paris Opera Ballet in 1987, commissioned by Rudolf Nureyev, and starring the young Sylvie Guillem. I assumed my little one was simply attracted to the gymnastic aspect of the movements, to the energy and physicality of this ballet, but she said the music scared her.

Aged five, we registered Yasmine at Hill House International School in Chelsea. Lieutenant-Colonel Stuart Townend founded the school in Switzerland in 1949, and in London in 1951. He was Oxford-educated, had excelled at sports and athletics, and he had won the Gold medal in the British Empire Games in Ontario in 1930. He was also known to select his pupils for acceptance into the school solely on the basis of his approval of their mother. We loved the fact that the school gave great prominence to playing a multitude of sports in combination with academics, thereby encouraging healthy competitiveness and self-discipline in the children. The school's slogan "A child's mind is not a vessel to be filled but a fire to be kindled" really struck a chord with Kamran and me. I also liked the fact that, as an English school, they were teaching French to the children from the age of five onwards. I was adamant that school for my children had to be a fun place to be, and without any academic pressure put onto them before the age of eight. Doing half an hour of daily homework before that age was the most I was willing to accept. Hill House ticked all my boxes. Additionally, the school had kept their chalet-style Founding School, and twice a year the headmaster and his wife took a selected group of children to the Swiss Alps.

The selection was based on their sports or academic achievements, and this highly motivated the children to excel in every aspect of the school's curriculum, as well as in the weekly sports competitions. Aged nine, Yasmine was invited, alongside a group of children, to go for two weeks to Switzerland. After their academic lessons in the morning, they would go for long walks or go mountain climbing all afternoon with the Colonel, who steadfastly installed in them that no mountain was ever too high to climb. And he taught the children to persevere whenever they were tired, and to never ever give up. They were also encouraged to be self-reliant. The children walked to the local village to run daily errands – a freedom that did not exist in London.

Back in London, not one day went by without the pupils playing sports in between their academic lessons: mid-morning they would go running on the nearby Duke of York's track on the King's Road or around the Serpentine in Hyde Park; they would also play a variety of ball games in Hyde Park, or go swimming in the Chelsea Town Hall, or go rowing on the Thames. The school was just perfect for Yasmine, as throughout the day she had plenty of opportunities to be outdoors, and was able to get rid of all her excess energy. Every Friday morning at 8am sharp, come rain or sunshine, ten-year-old Yasmine and her classmates went running around the Serpentine in Hyde Park.

The weekend started at noon on Friday, and Yasmine would eagerly await her end-of-week running time result, ceremoniously pinned onto a wall-mounted board by the Head of Sports teacher. I distinctly remember Yasmine's first run, and she had finished in 12th position. When I picked her up, the first thing she said was, "Next week I'll be in the top five! I'll do anything as long as I don't have to sit still." By the time she finished her eleven-plus exams (a test of verbal and non-verbal reasoning, also offering papers in mathematics and English), she had been introduced to a great range of sports.

I had also enrolled Yasmine in a pre-primary ballet class at the Vacani School of Dance – a ballet school near Victoria Station, founded in 1915. Mary Stassinopoulos, Cecchetti Fellow and holder of the Enrico Cecchetti Diploma, was the head of the school. After picking Yasmine up from primary school, and with her three-year-old sister Tatiana strapped in the back seat of my car, I drove her to her weekly ballet class. As Yasmine was kept busy at the barre, I walked around in the area with her little sister, or I sat out the hour-long ballet class in a nearby coffee shop, reading children's' stories to Tatiana. At the end of the term, the parents were allowed to watch class, and I didn't see anything exceptional in six-year-old Yasmine; she obediently executed all the steps, albeit with a little wobble here and there. In December 1997, she appeared on the stage for the very first time, at the Commonwealth Institute (now The Design Museum) in Kensington. She was cast as a Toy Soldier in *The Nutcracker,* and on the day of the performance we proudly took our seats in the auditorium, taking along her little sister. Yasmine's appearance was brief. She only had to march around on the stage for a while. I remember dressing her up in the children's dressing room, and she suddenly developed a stage fright and started crying. "I don't want to do it!" she said, covering her eyes with her hands. I reassured my five-year-old that all would be ok, and that it was going to be great fun. I continued dressing her up in a turquoise-coloured soldier's costume, put on what resembled a Moroccan fez hat, and off she went.

By the end of that school year, Yasmine took her first ISTD (Imperial Society of Teachers of Dancing) Classical Ballet Cecchetti Method Examination, and she passed with "Special Merit". Sarah Powell, the Examiner, comments on the certificate: "*A most promising examination. Yasmine worked well with a good sense of application, and she strongly used legs and feet throughout. Expressively danced hand and arm movements with especially good 'butterfly fingers'. Beautifully danced steps and dancing to the music was well moved. Clearly danced with assurance.*"

In addition to her weekly ballet class, Yasmine was also taking gymnastics lessons at the Kensington & Chelsea Sports Centre, just off Ladbroke Grove. Every Saturday morning, I drove her to the Sports Centre, where she would take a two-hour gymnastics class.

She loved all the challenges and enthusiastically learned new skills such as balancing on the beam, jumping on the trampoline, swinging on the parallel bars, balancing on the vault, and rhythmic gymnastics. She became increasingly daring, and began to execute full backflips. One Saturday morning, when watching her at work in rhythmic gymnastics, her reckless back flips made me anxious, and I feared she would injure her back.

When Yasmine's best friend joined the West London School of Dance, her mother urged me to also enrol Yasmine. It was the only non-vocational ballet school in London at that time to offer performance opportunities to children, she told me. In 2000, right after the Easter holiday, eight-year-old Yasmine started out at the West London School of Dance, and her weekly one-hour Friday evening ballet class took place at the Marie Rambert Mercury Studio in Notting Hill. Yasmine was frequently referred to as a "butterfly" and she often seemed "to be away with the fairies".

By the time she was ten years old, her ballet teacher suggested that Yasmine should increase her once-a-week class to four lessons per week. I remember feeling rather baffled by the idea. "Why increase the amount of ballet lessons? Surely one lesson per week is enough to keep her busy and active?" I queried. After all, she was already doing so many sports activities. In the end, I went along with it, and from then on Yasmine took four hours of after-school ballet classes per week. I considered that to be a huge amount. She never had any private lessons.

Yasmine had her first stage experience with the West London School of Dance, dancing in the annual *The Nutcracker* at the Bloomsbury Theatre in Gordon Street. She was cast as an Angel. Over the following years she would progress to dance as a Party Girl, as a Snowflake, in the Waltz of the Flowers, and as Clara's Best Friend – the last role she danced with the West London School of Dance before she joined The Royal Ballet School in September 2004.

For one reason or other, the rehearsals increasingly became a source of frustration for young Yasmine. All she wanted to do was dance, and not what she considered "wasting her time" standing at the back waiting for a possible chance to dance. Unknown to her was the fact that years later, as a new corps de ballet member of The Royal Ballet, she would initially do just that: stand at the back and watch the older dancers rehearse. On numerous occasions, I picked her up after a rehearsal and she would voice her feelings of frustration; her outburst of exasperation would last until we arrived back home. I would never say anything back to her, and I would let her "waterfall of words" stream freely without showing any reaction. She was eager to make her mark and to get an opportunity to prove herself, but it felt as if she was constantly fighting an internal battle. It was rather intense.

Every year, by mid-September, the casting for the annual Christmas show, *The Nutcracker,* went up, and dancing the title role of Clara was the ultimate dream of many girls in her year group. Eleven-year-old Yasmine had dreamed all summer long to finally dance the role of Clara and her hopes were high. When the casting went up and she found out that someone else had been chosen over her, great disappointment manifested itself. Her summer dream came crashing down. However, a few months later, the tide completely turned for Yasmine when she was invited to join The Royal Ballet School. Instead of dreaming once more of dancing the role of Clara with WLSD the following year, Yasmine would instead dance on the stage of the Royal Opera House with The Royal Ballet in *Swan Lake*, and she never looked back. Her early frustrations were ultimately translated into an immense inner drive during her training years at White Lodge.

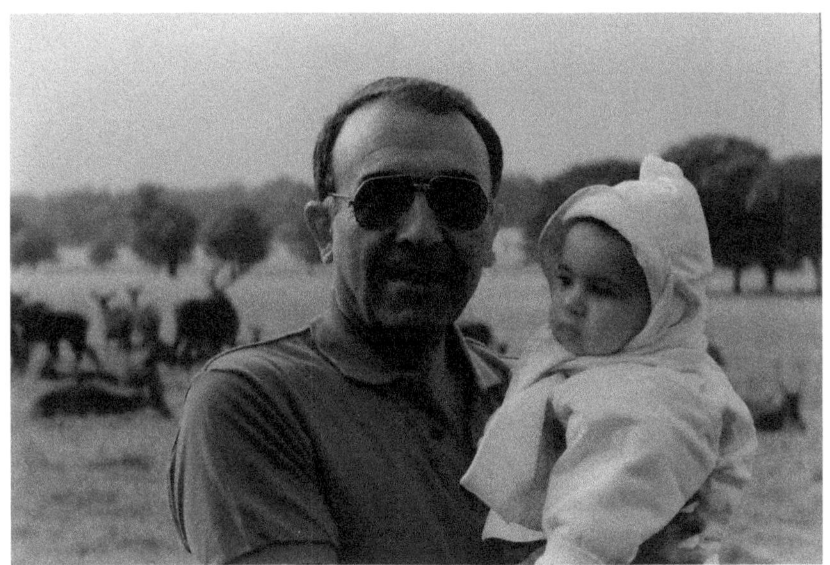

Yasmine and her father in Richmond Park, London.September 1992.

Visiting the ancient ruins of Persepolis. Close inspection of the Persian soldiers on the eastern wall of the Apadana Hall. Persia. April 1995.

Walking down the stairs of the Palace of Darius the Great.

In the entrance of the Tahara Hall.

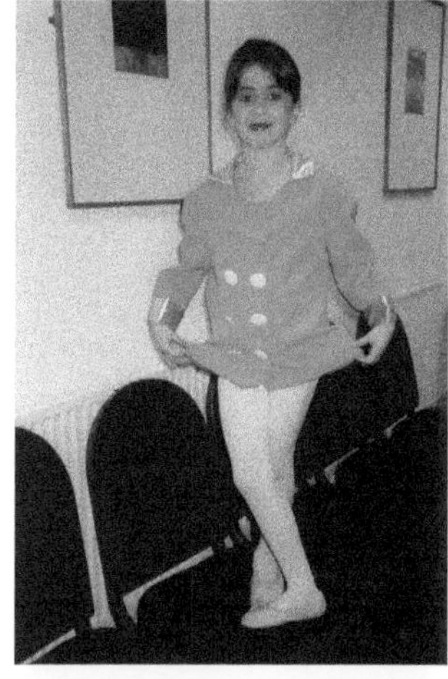

Her first stage appearance. Toy Soldier in The Nutcracker, Vacani School of Dance. The Commonwealth Institute, Kensington, London. December 1997.

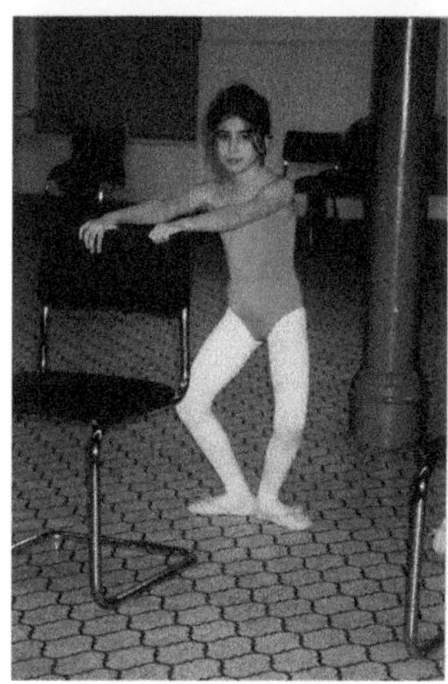

Seven-year-old Yasmine in ballet class. Vacani School of Dance. Bayswater, London.

A daily routine: climbing inside a doorframe.

Eight-year-old Yasmine practising the trapeze on holiday in Turkey.

Yasmine and her sister Tatiana performing in Little Women with the West London School of Dance. Commonwealth Institute, Kensington. June 1999.

On her ninth birthday, by Enzo Plazotta's bronze sculpture of a Young Dancer. Opposite the Royal Opera House.

The Royal Ballet School's annual White Lodge Summer Fair. Yasmine as a Junior Associate. June 2003.

"I want to go home!" In a pensive mood, after performing with fellow Junior Associates.

Dancing with The Royal Ballet as a Spring Page in Cinderella. Mid Associate. December 2003.

Student photo. Year 8. The Royal Ballet School, White Lodge. September 2004.

Dancing with The Royal Ballet in Swan Lake as a Little Swan. December 2004.

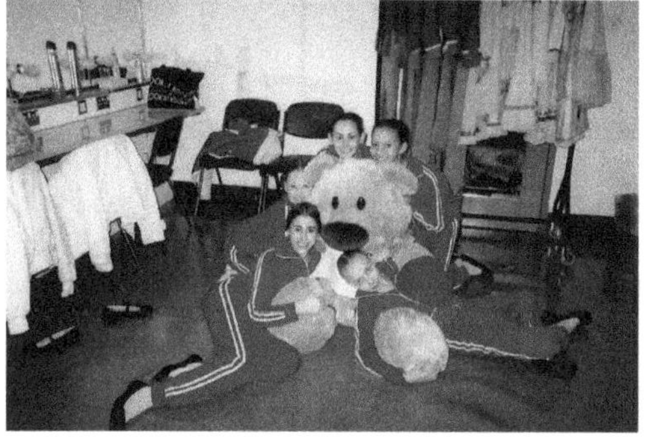

The Royal Ballet School. Year 8, (clockwise) Yasmine and classmates Aimee Higgs, Mitzi Arshamian, Francesca Hayward and Rachel Ware, after their last performance in Swan Lake. January 2005.

At Heathrow airport before departure to St Petersburg, Russia. February 2007. (L to R): Francesca Hayward, Yasmine, Shiori Kase, White Lodge Ballet Principal Diane Van Schoor, Claire Calvert, James Hay, Benjamin Ella, Vadim Muntagirov, Sergei Polunin, William Bracewell, amongst others.

Yasmine and her classmates in Year 10. A fancy dress party at White Lodge.

Graduation ceremony Year 11. Coming down the staircase at White Lodge. Gailene Stock (then Director of The Royal Ballet School) to present her Lower School Graduation Certificate. June 2008

Graduation lunch at White Lodge.

Yasmine, after winning the First Prize in the 10th Young British Dancer of the Year competition, with Mrs. Ricki Gail Conway (Sponsor) and nine previous winners: Jamie Bond, Lauren Cuthbertson, Anniek Soobroy, Joseph Caley, Aaron Robinson, Ruth Bailey, James Hay, Sergei Polunin, William Bracewell. March 2009.
Copyright: Johan Persson

Chapter Five

A Year as a Junior Associate

Two years before Yasmine joined White Lodge, I came across The Royal Ballet School's website, and I learned that they ran an Associates Programme. I had never heard of the Programme before. It was established in 1931 as a means of identifying children with an aptitude for ballet, with a view to taking them into full-time training if they showed enough potential. A Junior Associate (JA) programme was developed training young children aged eight to ten; older children join the Mid (MA) or Senior (SA) Associate programme. Tens of thousands of children from all over the country audition each year and, according to the statistics at that time, about 10-15% were selected to start in the Junior Associate Programme. I was curious to find out more, so I called The Royal Ballet School and asked them to send an application form to my home address.

However, when I took Yasmine to her Friday evening ballet lesson the following week, I noticed the teacher was busy distributing Junior Associate application forms to a select group of girls. Arrangements were promptly made by her to take audition photos of all those girls. I didn't understand why or how this had happened. Evidently The Royal Ballet School had sent a pile of JA application forms directly to Yasmine's ballet school. By late April, I received a letter from The Royal Ballet School, stating that Yasmine had been accepted as a Junior Associate, and on 7 September, 2002, ten-year-old Yasmine began her weekly Saturday morning ballet class at Barons Court.

In 1947, the Sadler's Wells School of Ballet had moved from Sadler's Wells Theatre to No. 45-46 Colet Gardens, Barons Court, in

West Kensington. There, the final three years of ballet training for the older students continued, after having finalised their early training years at White Lodge in Richmond Park. Up until 1999, The Royal Ballet also rehearsed in the building, after which date they moved out of Barons Court and into the newly refurbished Royal Opera House in Covent Garden, thereby separating the Upper School from the Company. This old building, comprising eight terraced houses – designed by architect Frederick Wheeler – was notable for its double-storey windows and stood on Talgarth Road, seemingly lost, albeit full of Royal Ballet memories. I had driven past this building on countless occasions, unaware it had once been the seat of The Royal Ballet Upper School and the Company.

Yasmine was too young to grasp the full historical significance of the place we entered that Saturday morning. It was a timeworn building, it felt stuffy, with lots of dark brown wood, and it felt like I was walking straight into a museum. Time seemed to have stood still in there. I could sense as well as smell – just like the woody, smoky, or earthy aroma of an antiquarian library – all its past glory. As we entered the building, I gave Yasmine's name to the receptionist, who reminded me of an elderly guard in a museum. He briefly looked up from his newspaper, lifted up his chin, pointing it into the direction of the large wooden staircase. "First floor, turn left, second room on your right," he said.

Stepping onto the very same staircase former celebrated Royal Ballet dancers had walked on filled me with huge respect for its past. It felt as if I was treading on sacred ground.

A room, filled with desks and chairs, was assigned to us mothers, and in there we helped our daughters to get ready for the JA ballet class. The girls wore a white leotard and a blue elasticated waistband, and their hair had to be done up in the appointed Junior Associate hairstyle: two plaits, horizontally crossed over at the back of the head, with a tiny blue ribbon pinned to either side. Precisely five minutes before class was due to start, their teacher Miss

Fairbairn arrived and greeted her pupils. Fourteen little girls stood quietly in a neat line ready to follow Miss Fairbairn into the ballet studio. Seven became professional dancers: Yasmine and Francesca Hayward became Principal dancers with The Royal Ballet; Hannah Grenell joined The Royal Ballet's corps de ballet in 2014, and Sophie Allnatt in 2018; Karla Doorbar is currently a Soloist with Birmingham Royal Ballet; Abigail Prudames a Principal Soloist with Northern Ballet; and Roseanna Leney a Soloist with Scottish Ballet.

I felt ill at ease in this environment. I soon became aware of how the mothers were reserved as well as economical with their words. Whenever I asked them a question, the answer was very brief or vague, which gave me the impression they didn't want to give too much away. It felt like I had joined a secret society. Some seemed keen and hopeful to get their daughter into White Lodge. I was the odd one out. Nonetheless, it was noticeable that we all felt a great sense of pride. All the mothers knew each other well, since their daughters had joined the Associates Programme the previous year. Yasmine was the new kid on the block.

I listened discreetly to their conversations, and it made me very conscious of the fact that they knew a hell of a lot more than I did. By the end of the first term, they began talking about auditioning their daughters for entry into White Lodge the following September; they also discussed participating at local competitions and festivals, summer schools and physiotherapy sessions. It felt like "them" and "me", because I had not even considered it to be an option for Yasmine to audition, let alone attend White Lodge full-time. I seriously began to wonder what in fact Yasmine and I were doing there. What was the purpose of attending those JA classes if her father and I were not considering letting Yasmine train at the School full-time?

During their ballet class, we were allowed to wait downstairs in what was once the School and Company canteen. Rudolf Nureyev, Margot Fonteyn, Alicia Markova, Svetlana Beriosova, Anthony Dowell, Antoinette Sibley, Darcey Bussell, and so many other great

Royal Ballet dancers – as well as the renowned Company choreographers Sir Frederick Ashton and Sir Kenneth MacMillan – had often taken their break from rehearsals in the basement canteen. Framed black and white photos of many of those stars hung on the walls.

Four months later, in January 2003, the Associate classes transferred to The Royal Ballet Upper School in Floral Street, Covent Garden, where Saturday morning class would take place from then on. Every Saturday morning, Yasmine and Tatiana would get up at 7:30am, organise their dance bags and arrange their hair in readiness for their respective ballet classes. Dad would take Tatiana to her ballet, jazz, and tap classes at Danceworks, and I walked with Yasmine to the nearby bus stop to catch bus No.9 to take us to The Strand. As it was early in the morning, the Covent Garden Piazza was still devoid of weekend tourists. The streets had the pungent smell of beer. We passed by street sweepers who were cleaning up after the partygoers who had filled the bars and pubs the previous night.

Once inside The Royal Ballet School, I would meet the other mothers as we all stood waiting in the corridor for a sign by the receptionist to tell us that our daughters could go upstairs to prepare for their weekly ballet class. I would exchange a few words with some of the mothers, after which I made my way to my favourite coffee shop in Seven Dials. They always played glorious opera music in that coffee shop. I was often their only client at that time of the day, and I loved spending some quiet time all by myself, enjoying my coffee and reading The Arts Newspaper. By 11am I would walk to the Royal Opera House, and always popped into the shop to check out any new ballet-related book publication, the ballet and opera magazines, videos, and DVDs.

Yasmine's class finished at 12:30pm, and upon leaving the School we would often see The Royal Ballet dancers walking across the street towards the Stage Door. On several occasions I was totally star-struck when crossing paths with Carlos Acosta, Tamara Rojo,

Alina Cojocaru, Johan Kobborg, and other dancers. I was still totally ignorant about the life of a professional ballet dancer, yet their world – which I perceived as mysterious – fascinated me. *Who are those superhuman 'creatures', able to defy gravity on that stage, and dance with seeming ease and so much grace?* I wondered. I looked at them with great admiration.

By mid-January we were given a form to fill in and indicate if we wanted our daughter to audition for White Lodge entry the following September, or to continue as a Mid-Associate. Surely the last option, the Mid-Associate box, was the only one I should have ticked… but I ticked both boxes. I remember feeling really audacious, because Yasmine going to White Lodge was not under any parental consideration. I really felt like a naughty child who had done something I was not supposed to do. I recall reasoning: *Well, why not test this out? If it is a "yes", I can always say "no".* However, I did not tell Yasmine or Kamran. In early February, we received a letter stating:

> *Dear Mr & Mrs Naghdi,*
>
> *With reference to Yasmine's Preliminary Audition for The Royal Ballet Lower School, we are sorry to tell you that she was not successful. All candidates are assessed on their suitability for Classical Ballet training at this School. It is the policy of the School not to enter into any correspondence concerning the results of the audition. Her result for the Mid-Associate Course will be send at the end of March.*

I had also ticked the box to apply for a place at the White Lodge Summer School, and in late April I received another letter from The Royal Ballet School, saying that Yasmine was not accepted to attend the Summer School. *So, that is it then,* I thought. *End of story.* Yasmine had received a "no" for the White Lodge pre-final audition, and also a "no" for the Summer School. She was blissfully unaware, and now I had peace of mind.

Seven of her JA classmates made it into the Final Audition, and subsequently they were all accepted for entry into Year 7 after the summer. However, having watched them all in class, I really could see no reason why Yasmine had not also been invited to at least the Preliminary Audition alongside those seven JA pupils who had gained a place. Yasmine never expressed any desire to go to White Lodge, nor did she seem bothered when she heard seven girls were going there in September. She thought it was a choice they had made, and she was happy to continue as a Mid-Associate after the summer holiday. As far as I was concerned, I had tested the ground and I gathered, based on the "No" letters, that Yasmine just didn't have "it". I simply assumed The Royal Ballet School didn't see any future for Yasmine in classical ballet.

Now I could fully focus on Yasmine's academic schooling, and I hardly gave it any further thought. In fact, I felt relieved that I had eliminated the prospect of a potential future in ballet for Yasmine, and to me the "No" letters had proved that vocational ballet training was no longer an option to be considered. Many years later, when I was talking to Gailene Stock (then Director of The Royal Ballet School), she wondered why Yasmine had been overlooked for entry into Year 7.

In the end, it simply didn't matter. Yasmine joined The Royal Ballet School one year after all the others did, finished the eight-year training course in five-and-a-half years, crowned by a contract with The Royal Ballet, and she joined the Company seven days after her eighteenth birthday.

In April that same year, all the parents were told the Junior Associates were to perform a character dance, taught by their teacher Tania Fairbairn, during the annual June Summer Fair at White Lodge. The Royal Ballet School's Summer Fair traditionally opened the much-anticipated end-of-year School performances at the Linbury Theatre, and the Matinee on the stage of the Royal Opera House. The open-air Summer Fair took place in the garden of White Lodge, and it was meant to be a display of national folk and character dances. A character dance is a wide-ranging term that refers to either national dances like Polish, Spanish, Italian, Russian, and Hungarian, or to folk, ethnic, and rustic dances. They provide divertissements in the story ballets. It is a specialisation that is part of a classical ballet student's curriculum. These dances can be seen in *The Nutcracker* with its Chinese, Spanish, Arabian divertissements, and Polish mazurka, as well as in *Swan Lake* with the Neapolitan and Spanish Dance, Czardas, and Mazurka. Folk dance had always been close to Ninette de Valois's heart, and she integrated it into the School's curriculum. She said that to study folk dancing is to study a country's style of natural movement. To Ninette de Valois, it was a fundamental part of their ballet training to aid with rhythm and musicality, to promote good teamwork, concentration, and vitality. In Katherine Sorely Walker's book *Ninette de Valois, Idealist Without Illusions*, she writes about de Valois, saying, "...although many people believed in the inherent artificiality of ballet, nothing could be further from the truth; in fact all ballet's fundamental steps are derived from folk dances of Western Europe and they can be traced from the Basque country to the Highlands of Scotland..."

I was far more excited to attend the White Lodge Summer Fair than Yasmine was. After all, we had never been to White Lodge, besides catching occasional glimpses of the stately former Royal Hunting Lodge whenever we would go walking, biking, or picnicking in Richmond Park. Many years before Yasmine attended White Lodge, I had read in a magazine that there was a Ballet Museum at White Lodge (this was years before the School opened the White Lodge Ballet Museum and Resource Centre in February 2009). One day in August, after our family picnic in Richmond Park, I suggested we drive up to White Lodge and visit the Museum. On arrival, the gate to White Lodge was wide open, and we cautiously drove into the car park, expecting to be told off any minute for trespassing. We walked up to the windows and gazed through. I could only spot some antiquated furniture, a framed photo of Princess Margaret – the School's then President – a Ballets Russes framed poster, some 19th century Romantic era lithographs of the ballerinas Fanny Essler, Carlotta Grisi, and one of Marie Taglioni.

It was on a sunny Saturday morning in June 2003 that I drove with Yasmine and Tatiana to White Lodge. The parents of the current White Lodge students, as well as the parents of the Associates, all stood in a designated cordoned-off area in the grounds as we waited excitedly for the various year groups to commence their performance. The Junior Associates, dressed in their character skirts, opened the Fair, and Yasmine stood last in the line-up. The girls were patiently waiting for a sign from their teacher to start dancing. After their performance, they quietly returned, in a two-by-two line, to the Dining Hall to take off their costumes. After a while, all the Junior Associates re-joined their parents, and those who had been given a place to commence in Year 7 were talking to their future ballet teacher Nicola Katrak. Yasmine, on the other hand, was nowhere to be seen.

I stretched my head out above all the visitors, and suddenly I spotted her walking all by herself, lingering near the Dining Hall, dragging her feet through the grass. She seemed in no rush either to rejoin her classmates or to mingle with anybody else. She appeared to be in her own world, and only once did she get distracted, looking up into the sky when a skein of noisy geese flew over. I wondered what on earth she was thinking.

When she finally joined me, all she said was, "I want to go home!"

"You want to go home?" I repeated, raising my eyebrows and giving her a surprised look.

"What for? For once, you are at The Royal Ballet School, so I think you should use this opportunity to talk to the teachers, have a chat with the current students, ask them questions, learn, and be curious," I said, gradually raising my voice, irritated by her total lack of interest. Even the beautiful Georgian villa didn't impress her.

"Let's walk around a bit," I said, trying to persuade her.

"I want to go home!" she repeated, this time more insistently.

I looked at her and I did not reply. Standing face-to-face with her in silence, I waited for her further reaction, hoping that she would change her mind. But it was no use.

"I don't want to walk around! And I don't want to talk to anybody! I just want to go home!" she said, now frowning, her inner eyebrows giving me an angry and irritated look. Eleven-year-old Yasmine had made her point, and I was rather frustrated by her apparent lack of interest. Reflecting on that day, perhaps she did wonder why she wasn't joining her seven JA classmates after the summer.

I took her sister Tatiana by the hand, and Yasmine quietly trailed behind us as we made our way back to the car. When I drove out through the White Lodge entrance gate, I said to Yasmine, "Look, if this is your attitude to life, it will get you nowhere, so don't even think you can ever become a ballet dancer if this is what you are thinking of." Her unresponsiveness and seeming indifference exasperated me.

All of a sudden, Yasmine sank right down between my driver's seat and the back seat. Curled up in a ball, she started crying uncontrollably. I had never heard her cry like this before. She was inconsolable and cried non-stop between Richmond Park and our home in West London. *Why was she crying so much if she didn't care about White Lodge? What made her so upset?* I really couldn't figure it out and I felt sorry for her little sister, who had to put up with Yasmine's crying all the way home. All hell and fury broke loose. I had never seen Yasmine so distraught. It came deep from within her, and nothing I subsequently said could comfort her.

As I crossed the Hammersmith Bridge, I pondered whether her crying was perhaps an affirmation of her unexpressed or concealed desire to become a ballet dancer. *Was she crying out of frustration, or was she indeed feeling rejected? Why was she so upset?* When we recalled the incident many years later, we could laugh about it, but Yasmine clarified that she had felt that I had no faith in her at all, and what I had told her that day had made her very cross. Whereas I had wanted to encourage her to be less timid and to be more inquisitive, she had felt that my statement had decided her future: that she was never to become a ballet dancer.

That summer, I purchased my first biographies of illustrious ballet dancers such as Margot Fonteyn, Rudolf Nureyev, Maria Tallchief, Maya Plisetskaya, Mikhail Baryshnikov, Tamara Karsavina's' *Theatre Street* and *The Memoirs of Alexandra Danilova*, *Winter Season* by Toni Bentley, as well as Richard Buckle's *Diaghilev*. Those books were real eye-openers for me, and I learned so much about the world of ballet and a dancer's life. I was totally absorbed and spellbound, but the more I read, the more I became deeply concerned about my daughter's potential future. *How was I to allow, facilitate, and encourage her towards leading a life of – what I then perceived as – hardship, unhappiness, and nastiness, based on all the books I had read?* Never could I have imagined that the life of a ballerina was so complicated and so hard, despite all the glamour surrounding it. I had sombre misgivings and mixed feelings, and I felt very uncertain about whether I should encourage Yasmine to take any further ballet lessons. *Should she not choose her own path in life?* I wondered.

I had also purchased Gelsey Kirkland's autobiography *Dancing on my Grave*. Kirkland was an American ballerina who joined New York City Ballet in 1968 at the age of fifteen, at the invitation of George Balanchine. As one of the most astounding ballerinas of her generation, she enthralled audiences all over the world. She was promoted to Soloist in 1969, and to Principal ballerina in 1972. This book really made me dither even more, and I continued wondering whether I was not unwittingly encouraging my daughter to take an erroneous path in life. The highly pressurised world of ballet drove Kirkland into drug addiction – she even performed high on cocaine, before collapsing in the wings – into eating disorders, undergoing plastic surgery, and ultimately it drove her into suicidal despair. Reading about Kirkland's agonising descent into her cocaine addiction, suffering anorexia at the height of her career, being plunged to the haunts of drug dealers, and finally confinement in a mental institution, couldn't have been more wrong for me to read at that stage. I had a vivid imagination, and I was still trying to understand what the life of a ballerina entailed. What I had read in all those books was way too much for me to digest, and frankly the world of ballet began to seriously frighten me. After I had finished reading that book, I concluded: Why on earth would I want to let my daughter become a ballet dancer? It all sounded plain misery to me, with very little joy and rewards attached to the enormous efforts needed, huge sacrifices to be made, and so many difficulties to have to overcome. At that point in time, I did not yet comprehend the tremendous pleasure dancing and performing gives a dancer, no matter how hard it is.

After having read all those biographies, I followed up with a book titled *Dance Technique & Injury Prevention* by Justin House. The book's chapters covered Anatomy and Physiology, Injuries – Pathology, Causes, Treatment, and Prevention – as well as Nutrition, Specific Injuries to Technical Faults and Anatomical Variations. The book gave me the opportunity to make further reflections, and I did devour the book like one would go through a pack of crisps. It was a page-turner for me. I began to understand what an immensely complex thing ballet training is, and how difficult it is to fine tune the human body which by nature is not made for dancing classical ballet. I began to question how anyone could possibly get through such a rigorous training regime, and how my own daughter's growing body would be able to cope. My admiration for intensive ballet training steadily grew, but in the end I was still really torn and full of doubts.

That evening, when I put *Dance Technique & Injury Prevention* on my book shelf next to all the biography books I had read, I decided there was no way that I was ever going to allow Yasmine to go through all of that. Combining Gelsey Kirkland's autobiography with a book on injury prevention was certainly not the best of ideas to make me enthusiastic about ballet training. Moreover, the more I learned and understood, the more I felt that the chance of her making it through White Lodge and into the Upper School, let alone get into The Royal Ballet, was so very slim.

A YEAR AS A MID-ASSOCIATE

Nonetheless, for some totally inexplicable reason, I went against all my misgivings and let Yasmine continue in the Mid-Associate programme. In spite of feeling highly sceptical, I adopted a wait-and-see attitude instead of acting instantaneously and with compulsion on my misgivings by precipitously taking Yasmine out of her ballet lessons. Deep down, there was somehow a puzzling hesitancy towards any form of maternal intervention with the direction that my young daughter's life seemed to be gradually taking, even if it went directly against my maternal instinct of wanting to protect her. In the end, I reasoned that life would show her the way. *What is meant to be is meant to be*, I thought.

In September 2003, with seven of her former JA classmates now at White Lodge, Yasmine carried on as a Mid-Associate as well as taking a daily after-school ballet class. By November, Yasmine's Mid-Associate teacher Sylvia Hubbard announced that The Royal Ballet was holding an audition, as they needed a few girls to perform in *Cinderella*. They were requested to be at the Royal Opera House midweek for the audition.

On a dark November evening, I took Yasmine through the Stage Door, and a chaperone picked her up. I was asked to come back in an hour's time. I aimlessly wandered around Covent Garden and returned to the Stage Door at the requested time. A few girls had already come back and told their parents it was a "no" for them. Yasmine walked out as one of the last ones. She did not say anything except, "Let's go!" She firmly grabbed me by the hand and pulled me away from the other parents. I was sure she had been told "No", and I assumed that if she wanted to talk about her disappointment, she would surely do so later on. As we walked out of the Stage Door, intending to cheer her up, I chatted about the Christmas fun coming up and the presents. Once we had turned around the corner of Floral Street into Bow Street, walking in the direction of our bus stop on The Strand, she suddenly stopped, looked at me, and said as if revealing a secret, "Mummy, we really didn't have to do much, you know. We were just asked to walk around in a circle, and we kept walking around and around until out of nowhere a man walked up to me. He put his hand on my shoulder and he said, 'This one will do!'"

That man was Christopher Carr, and many years later Yasmine and Christopher had a good laugh about that audition. So then it was decided that Yasmine was to be a Spring Page in *Cinderella*. I received a letter the following week, stating that Yasmine would be needed by The Royal Ballet throughout the Festive Season, as well as on New Year's Day, further specifying that she had to be at the Royal Opera House by 10am on that day. I truly pitied myself and thought gloomily, *Now we are not able to travel to Belgium and Switzerland to see our families for Christmas and New Year.* I really had not anticipated that this would affect our Christmas and New Year's family get-together.

I found it an odd idea to have to sacrifice Christmas with our family only because Yasmine had been selected as a Spring Page. All she had to do was to walk forward at the right time, hold a lamb in her arms, and walk back again, and I had visions of Yasmine falling down on the stage as she walked backwards. *Well*, I sighed to myself, *we have come this far now, and we are not going to tell Yasmine she can't be a Spring Page because we want to celebrate Christmas with our family.* I dutifully followed the instruction by The Royal Ballet School to apply for a Performance Licence for Yasmine – as is required by the Children and Young Persons Act 1963, and the Children

Performance Regulations 1968 – issued by the Child Employment Officer at our local council.

We decided that Kamran would go and see his family in Switzerland, and I would stay behind in London with the girls for the entire Festive Season. I now faced a stumbling block, as I would need to ask the stern headmistress of Yasmine's academic school for permission to be absent on particular days throughout November, as well as early December, because Yasmine had to attend some of The Royal Ballet's rehearsals. My request was met with great disapproval. The headmistress did not like me taking Yasmine out of school for ballet rehearsals, not even at the Royal Opera House.

"Is she going to do ballet or study academics?" the headmistress asked severely, looking me in the eyes.

"I don't know," I replied. "All I can do is give Yasmine the opportunity as it comes along."

The headmistress grudgingly agreed on this one occasion, but cautioned me this could not continue.

New Year's Eve felt more like an ordinary evening for the three of us: bedtime by 10pm for a wake-up call at 8am. The next morning at 9:40am, I jumped in a taxi with Yasmine and Tatiana, and we arrived at the Royal Opera House by 10am. I dropped Yasmine off at the Stage Door, leaving her in the safe hands of The Royal Ballet School-appointed chaperone, Miss Kim Allen. I now had two hours to kill until the start of the Matinee. Tatiana and I strolled around Covent Garden Piazza for a while, but the surrounding streets were not at all a pleasant sight. Plenty of drunken New Year's Eve revellers were lying around, with broken glass strewn everywhere. Seven-year-old Tatiana was not amused, and the sight of drunken rough sleepers scared her, while the pungent smells as a result of their excessive drinking revolted her. Not only had she had to wake up early, but she was bitterly complaining she was totally bored walking around the Piazza. Nothing was open, and we had no choice but to sit and wait inside the Royal Opera House until it was time for the performance to commence.

Tatiana loved *Cinderella*, but she found the Prokofiev score scary, and at times she would cover her ears. Luckily, there were Anthony Dowell and Wayne Sleep as the Ugly Sisters to amuse her. I very much enjoyed watching Alina Cojocaru as Cinderella and Johan Kobborg as the Prince, as well as Yasmine's five-minutes of fame when she appeared on the stage in Act I, innocently holding a lamb. In Act II, when all the Guests arrive and a fanfare heralds the arrival of the Prince, mysterious music follows, announcing the arrival of Cinderella in her magic silver "pumpkin" coach, with a boy page sitting on top of it. When the coach suddenly swung onto the stage, I was totally taken by surprise to see Yasmine making a second appearance on the stage, but this time she was sitting on top of Cinderella's coach. *It can't be*, I thought, because I knew a JA boy was meant to be sitting on top of that coach. But the child looked so similar to Yasmine. After the performance had finished, I collected her at the Stage Door, and when Miss Allen handed her over to me, Yasmine told me excitedly, "Mummy, you will never guess what happened. The boy who was meant to be sitting on top of the coach fell ill all of a sudden, so Miss Allen quickly dressed me up in the boy's costume, put a funny triangular hat full of feathers on my head, and I was put on top of the coach. Before I realised, the coach got onto the stage, and as it was making a big circle, I was nearly swung off the coach because I have never rehearsed that role."

I burst out laughing. This was Yasmine's very first experience in taking over a role unrehearsed and at very short notice.

ACCEPTANCE INTO THE ROYAL BALLET SCHOOL

With the *Cinderella* performances now behind us, life could return to normal, and Yasmine's Saturday morning Mid-Associates classes resumed. It was during my "mother-on-duty" morning at the end of January that I noticed the teacher was discreetly preparing a pupil in Yasmine's class to audition for a place at White Lodge. I took this as yet another affirmation that obviously something was not right with Yasmine, since the teacher had not suggested that she should audition. Interestingly, the pupil was not offered a place at White Lodge that year. On the other hand, Yasmine was.

It was Jacqui Dumont who recognised Yasmine's aptitude for ballet, and in doing so she had spotted a future Royal Ballet Principal ballerina. On Saturday morning, 5 June, 2004, Jacqui Dumont appraised Yasmine's class to assess who would benefit from a further year of training and who wouldn't. The following Monday at precisely 9am, the telephone rang at our home. As I picked up the telephone, I instantly recognised Jacqui Dumont's voice. My first thought was that she was going to tell me Yasmine had been assessed out and could no longer continue her weekly ballet class the following year.

Instead, she said, "Mrs Naghdi, may I ask you *why* Yasmine is not at White Lodge?" Jacqui stressed the why, and I was totally flabbergasted.

"*Why* is Yasmine not at White Lodge?" I heard myself repeat in astonishment. "Well, she is not at White Lodge because last year Yasmine was not invited to attend the pre-final audition, so we let her continue in the Mid-Associate classes, and this year I was not advised by her teacher to audition Yasmine. I reckon she just doesn't have it, does she?"

Following my answer, Jacqui Dumont asked if I could immediately take Yasmine to White Lodge on Wednesday for Miss Stock, then Director of The Royal Ballet School, to see her in a ballet class alongside the current Year 7s.

I had already incurred the wrath of the headmistress of her academic school back in December, and since Yasmine was in the middle of her end-of-year academic exams, I told Jacqui I couldn't possibly take her out of school that week.

Jacqui enquired if I could bring in Yasmine the week after next, once her exam week was over.

I glanced at my diary and replied, "Oh, Yasmine has a school trip that week, and she will be in Scotland."

Jacqui sounded increasingly annoyed. "Well then, how about in three weeks' time? But that's really the very last Wednesday this year that Miss Stock will have time to see Yasmine."

Still staring at my diary, and without even thinking, I replied, "Ah, but on that Wednesday Yasmine has a school trip to the London Zoo."

As soon as I heard myself saying this, I could have slapped myself in the face. I realised how plain stupid, annoying, and unexcited my answer must have sounded to Jacqui. I quickly gathered that she must be fed up with me by now and would hang up the phone.

I hastily corrected my answer and said, "But I am sure I can tell her school that she is ill, so she can skip her trip to the London Zoo and I'll take her to White Lodge."

Jacqui wasted no time in replying, "That's it then. Miss Stock will be expecting Yasmine on Wednesday, 23 June. Goodbye." And she hung up the phone.

I was thunderstruck, and simultaneously worried that I must have sounded either totally indifferent or totally stuck-up. But this had come so out of the blue, so totally out of nowhere. After two years of attending Associates' classes, and four years of after-school ballet classes at the West London School of Dance, we were all of a sudden being asked – with insistence – by Jacqui Dumont, to take Yasmine for a private audition to White Lodge.

Yasmine's father asked me who had called, and I told him all about my conversation with Jacqui Dumont. He raised his eyebrows and said, "Yasmine going to The Royal Ballet School to train full-time in ballet? To become a professional ballet dancer? What about her academic education?"

A long conversation ensued, as I tried to persuade him that we should at least let her try it out. I hoped to be able to convince him, by saying that if she didn't make it through the training, she would at least have acquired great self-discipline, and this would assist her to achieve success in whatever profession she would choose later on. Kamran responded by saying he seriously needed to think about it, since he was keen for Yasmine to continue her academic studies and go on to university.

On Wednesday morning, 23 June, I emailed Yasmine's academic teacher to say that she was unwell and would be unable to join her class on their day out to the London Zoo. Yasmine had arranged her hair in a bun, had put on her navy-blue Mid-Associates leotard, and Kamran and I drove her to Richmond Park by 8am. She didn't show any excitement as she sat quietly in the back of the car. I think she was more concerned about missing out on her day trip to the London Zoo, so the consequences of a possible decision that morning completely passed her by.

As we drove through Roehampton Gate to enter Richmond Park, she asked, "So what exactly am I supposed to do at White Lodge?"

I told her that all she had to do was to join in with the current Year 7s in their ballet class, and that Miss Stock would have a look at her.

We parked our car near the main entrance, and as we stepped out, we could hear the sound of a piano through an open window, and the commanding voice of a teacher putting her pupils through their paces. At precisely 8:25am, Kamran and I walked up to the front door with twelve-year-old Yasmine and rang the doorbell. The receptionist welcomed us and requested us to sit down and wait. After a few minutes, Aimee, who had been with Yasmine in the Junior Associate class, appeared. They greeted each other and swiftly walked off through the double doors leading into the Salon. We were asked to come back in about two-and-a-half hours' time.

Kamran and I drove to nearby East Sheen high street, and at the local coffee shop we discussed what we would say in case Yasmine was accepted at White Lodge. We were anxious about having to make a commitment there and then. At 10:30am, we drove back to White Lodge and, upon entry into the reception area, we were asked to sit down and wait for Miss Mary Goodhew, then Ballet Principal at White Lodge. I was becoming rather nervous. I felt that since Jacqui Dumont had been so insistent for us to take Yasmine to White Lodge for a private audition with Gailene Stock, it could only have been because she was sure our daughter would be given a place.

Yasmine had still not returned by the time the receptionist told us to go and see Miss Goodhew in her office. We entered a beautiful, elegant room, formerly called the Blue Room. This small drawing room used to be Princess Mary Adelaide's boudoir. It felt rather palatial, and the rich history of the villa penetrated every place and corner. After we greeted Miss Goodhew, we were asked to sit down on the opposite side of her desk. She then informed us that Miss Stock had been very impressed with Yasmine, and that she was offering her a place in Year 8, to commence after the summer holiday.

"But what if Yasmine gets assessed out after a year?" we asked. "She is currently attending a day school in London, and it will be impossible for her to join Year 9 in that school again."

"Oh, don't you worry. That will not be the case," Miss Goodhew replied reassuringly. "Yasmine is already cast as a Little Swan, and she will be performing with The Royal Ballet this coming December and January in *Swan Lake*."

The scenario must have looked hilarious. We were full of reservations, but then again, being told that our daughter not only had a place at White Lodge but had already been cast as a Little Swan following this morning's ballet class, offered us a lot of encouragement. "Yasmine hasn't even started, and she is to dance with The Royal Ballet in *Swan Lake* as a Little Swan?" I queried, as if to reassure myself that I had understood Miss Goodhew correctly. I felt a bit overwhelmed by it all, but any pre-existing doubts began to evaporate. I instantaneously conjured up images of ballerinas in beautiful white tutus. It had worked.

We thanked Miss Goodhew for her time and asked her to pass on our thanks to Miss Stock for offering Yasmine a place, then we left her office. As we walked towards the reception area, we could see Yasmine sitting quietly on one of the rattan chairs, her feet dangling and barely touching the floor, unaware of the outcome.

As we approached the car, I asked Yasmine, "Do you have any questions?"

"Well, do you know anything?" she responded.

I told her that she had been offered a place to start in September, to which she coolly replied, "I like the school uniform."

That was it. "She likes the uniform!" I chuckled. Little did she realise what a journey was waiting for her.

On 29 June, 2004, we received a formal letter confirming that Yasmine had been offered a place at The Royal Ballet School, to commence in Year 8 in September that year. Kamran and I certainly did not take our final decision lightly, and we did weigh up all the pros and cons. We were conscious of the importance of making the final decision that this was likely to become our daughter's professional future. In the end, we agreed that if later on Yasmine felt this was not what she ultimately wanted to do, she could always change. After all, the academic education at White Lodge was of a high standard, so we accepted the offer of a place at The Royal Ballet School.

On reflection, there was always some sort of a surreptitious pull towards her destiny – a destiny she and we were not aware of. We basically enabled her to take ballet lessons after school, but we never initiated full-time training at The Royal Ballet School. We could never have anticipated Yasmine's invitation and subsequent entry into The Royal Ballet School, and it happened so unexpectedly, in the space of just three weeks. Most pupils attending White Lodge are likely to have been encouraged to audition at The Royal Ballet School by their local ballet teacher, but that had not been the case with Yasmine. Had I not discovered the existence of The Royal Ballet School's Associate Programme, and Jacqui Dumont spotting Yasmine's inherent talent for ballet by bringing her to the attention of Gailene Stock, our daughter might never have gone to The Royal Ballet School. In the end, ballet found her.

According to The Royal Ballet School's Annual Report of 2003-2004 – the year that Yasmine entered White Lodge – a total of 193 girls in the UK had auditioned for entry in September 2004. The Year 8 group Yasmine was joining had twelve girls, and she was the only addition to the group. Following her acceptance, she was also promptly given a place to attend the Summer School at White Lodge. On the last day of the Summer School, she met Dame Monica Mason, then Director of The Royal Ballet, for the first time when she presented Yasmine with her Summer School certificate.

Less than six years later, Dame Monica Mason would offer Yasmine a contract to join The Royal Ballet.

Chapter Six

Life at The Royal Ballet School – her White Lodge Years

"Progress, not perfection"

The Royal Ballet School is recognised as one of the leading classical ballet schools in the world, and it is at White Lodge that they teach students aged eleven to sixteen. White Lodge is situated in Richmond Park, in the London Borough of Richmond-upon-Thames, and it has been the home of The Royal Ballet School's Lower School since 1955, when the Sadler's Wells Ballet School was allowed the use of White Lodge on a permanent basis. The School was later granted a Royal Charter and became The Royal Ballet School in 1956. White Lodge is a Grade I-listed Georgian villa, an architectural example of the neo-Classical Palladian English style, and was initially built as a hunting lodge for King George II in 1727. That was the year following the debut of the 'first ballet dancer' Marie Camargo at the Paris Opéra, and the building's history continues to weave in and out of the fascinating history of classical ballet. A wonderful early connection between White Lodge and the world of classical ballet was established in 1874, when Princess Victoria May of Teck received her dancing lessons there from one of the great ballerinas of the Romantic era, Marie Taglioni (1804-1884). The rich history of White Lodge is likewise intricately linked to the history of the British Monarchy, as well as its politics. In 1805, Admiral Horatio Nelson, one of Britain's most heroic figures, came to dine at White Lodge as the guest of Viscount Sidmouth, and this is where Admiral Nelson plotted out his forthcoming naval campaign, the Battle of Trafalgar – often regarded as Britain's greatest naval victory. That room is now called the Nelson Room, and the School's teachers gather in there during their breaks.

Entering the private world of The Royal Ballet School was – and still is – a source of mystery and intense curiosity to the general public and prospective parents. There is a feeling of grandeur, of Royal Family history, and of White Lodge's notable Royal residents from King George II to Queen Victoria to Queen Elizabeth II (she spent part of her honeymoon at White Lodge), as well as the remarkable ballet history.

In many ways, The Royal Ballet School is just like any other secondary school. In Year 7 to 9, the students follow an academic programme which includes English, Maths, Science, Languages, Humanities, and the Arts. In Year 10, work begins towards their General Certificate of Secondary Education (GCSE) exams and coursework, with final GCSE examinations taking place in the summer of Year 11. However, the study of classical ballet is central to The Royal Ballet School's education. Acceptance to the School is solely based on talent for classical ballet.

The School still has its original fine rooms in the main villa, and the six state-of-the-art ballet studios are all located in the adjacent buildings. The brick-lined tunnels, dating back to the 1760s, connect the main villa to the classrooms and ballet studios. The Georgian kitchens – now the School's library – and the Victorian stable blocks are where the School's academic classrooms and science lab are situated. Mealtimes are held in a beautiful, airy dining hall. The students live in boarding houses in the grounds of White Lodge, and their dormitories are separated by gender and year group, supervised by House Parents. As is expected in a boarding school, mealtimes and bed times are strictly regulated during the weekdays, but there is more flexibility at weekends, when students also have a chance to go home if they live not too far away from the School, while the others can take part in activities and outings organised by the staff and the House Parents.

Monday morning, 6 September, 2004, marked the start of Yasmine's first term at White Lodge. She was wearing her new Royal Ballet School uniform – a Scottish chequered navy blue and green skirt, white blouse, and navy-blue blazer with The Royal Ballet School's Coat of Arms embroidered on it. Her Majesty Queen Elizabeth II had granted the crest in October 1956. On top of the crest stands Terpsichore, the Muse of the Dance, who plays her lyre. To the left is shown the Falcon, symbolising Strength, and to the right the Swan, symbolising Grace. The "zigzag" partition is heraldry and called a *dancetty*. The pattern divides three fleurs-de-lys, representing the House of de Valois and Lilian Baylis (she was an English theatrical producer and manager who managed, amongst others, the Old Vic and Sadler's Wells).

If Yasmine was excited about this new chapter in her life, she certainly did not show it. After all, over the past twelve months so much had happened to her. She had successfully finished her eleven-plus academic exams. She had left her friends at primary school to join a new group of girls in her secondary school. She had continued as a Mid-Associate, with half of her former classmates having gone to White Lodge, and she had performed with The Royal Ballet as a Spring Page and as a Coach Boy in *Cinderella*. She had been teased and laughed at while at her secondary school, and name-called a "bun head", a "Nut [cracker] head", and "monkey legs", only because she took ballet lessons after school. The media often cites boys being bullied or laughed at because they take ballet lessons, but they never mention that girls can be bullied too, although it happens to a far lesser extent.

The headmistress had not been very encouraging, and after Easter she had basically given Yasmine an ultimatum, "Are you or are not going to go to a ballet school? You better make up your mind, as I won't accept any further if you are to miss any academic lessons because of your ballet rehearsals."

Driving up to White Lodge along the narrow winding road, I could see the early morning mist hovering above the grass. A herd of grazing female deer was watched over by a male deer with imposing antlers. It was a picturesque scene, and entering this gorgeous nature reserve felt as if we had entered another world. Richmond Park is an area of two thousand five hundred acres, and is the largest of the London Royal Parks. It was created as a deer park in the 17th century by King Charles I, and is now home to over six hundred and fifty deer. The nature reserve looked so perfectly peaceful.

When we arrived on the steep driveway, the automatic gate to enter the private grounds of White Lodge opened, and we drove in. I parked my car in the semi-circular parking place, very near a single tree marking the spot where the ashes of Dame Ninette de Valois lie buried. When I rang the doorbell, I could never have anticipated that barely five-and-a-half years later Yasmine would start her professional career with The Royal Ballet.

Miss Sheila Gresswell, the senior school secretary, welcomed us and informed Yasmine that one of her classmates would come and fetch her. As we sat waiting, we glanced at the antique make-up table and chaise longue on display that had once belonged to the legendary 20th century Russian ballerina Anna Pavlova (1881-1931). Eventually, the tall double door leading to the Salon opened, and Yasmine was met by Eloise, one of her classmates. I could just about spot Margot Fonteyn's bronze statue through the open double door. The statue was created by Maurice Lambert (the older brother of Constant Lambert and Founder Music Director of The Royal Ballet), and it is featured in the BBC documentary "Looking for Margot". Perfectly graceful *en pointe*, the statue of The Royal Ballet's Prima Ballerina Assoluta captured the lyricism of her poise as well as his obsession with Fonteyn. Seen up close, *Margot Fonteyn*'s bodice bares zodiacal emblems in tribute to Constant Lambert's ballet score for *Horoscope* (1938), yet the motif also shows a couple nestled close to *Margot Fonteyn*'s heart: a male figure resembling Maurice. The statue could well have been inspired by Edward Degas' *Little Dancer Aged Fourteen,* which also incorporated muslin for the tutu and silk for the hair ribbon. Any student passing by her statue will never fail to touch Margot's left hand middle finger for good luck, and as a result, over decades, the fingertip now has a gleaming patina. Her fingertip has been touched by so many great dancers of the past, as well as by the current Royal Ballet Principal dancers who attended White Lodge.

I effectively began my journey when Yasmine embarked on her first year in vocational ballet training, and I had little or no idea what The Royal Ballet School's System of Training entailed. I only had a very rudimentary knowledge of ballet technique, and I certainly had no understanding at all of the physical and mental challenges that come with vocational ballet training. I realised early on in her training that there was next to nothing I could contribute to her technical training. However, in the course of her first year at White Lodge, I swiftly understood that it is not sufficient to train a child in the technicalities of ballet dancing, but that it is crucial that the training is supplemented by a fundamental understanding of the psychology of the child in training. Of course, every child is different, and a sensitive approach to each individual is needed, as is frequent positive encouragement, simultaneously leaving room for personal development.

I shall never forget my chance encounter with an elderly Russian woman as I was standing at the bar during the interval of a ballet performance at The Coliseum. I was waiting for my glass of wine to be served, and she struck up a conversation with me. She said she used to be a ballet teacher in Moscow many years before. When I told her that my twelve-year-old daughter had just started her ballet training at a professional ballet school, she coldheartedly replied, in no uncertain terms, "Oh, but those kids in vocational ballet schools are all trained up to join the corps de ballet, and their characters are broken in order to reset them. Just like they break the character of horses when they are trained."

Upon hearing this, I was absolutely horrified and shocked. The image of the ever-present mother of my own ballet teacher, walking around in our ballet class with a cane permanently held behind her back, drifted back into my mind. The statement of that Russian former ballet teacher made me even more determined to want to protect my daughter in any way I could during her ballet training.

As soon as I became aware of the first physical challenge twelve-year-old Yasmine was facing, learning how to deal with, and control, her hyper-extended knees (also called "sway-backs"), I bought several books on ballet teaching and ballet technique. In an old book on ballet physique, I found a chapter on limbs, discussing three most common variations on alignment: knock-knees, bowlegs, and over-extended knees. I learned that hyper-extended knees naturally occur in anyone who is loose-jointed and hyper-flexible, and Yasmine was indeed extremely loose-jointed as well as hyper-flexible. Swayback legs, however, do give the most pleasing aesthetic line in the legs, especially in arabesque, and they are considered by many to be the most beautiful leg shape for any classical ballerina to possess. The problem with having hyper-extended knees is that they extend beyond neutral, and Yasmine's knees pressed too far backward, leaving her ligaments at the back permanently overextended and the front of her knees too flat or almost hollow, with a bulge above. The placing of her body was completely upset, as her weight was falling on the heels. Any pulling-up of her thighs increased the problem, and this also led to working with her arm line too far back. Moreover, there is the tendency to be a poor breather because of the faulty trunk posture, so Yasmine would breathe from her upper chest, and this caused tension in her trunk. Swaybacks are also always associated with weak feet, so a lot of attention needed to be given to simultaneously strengthen her feet. Her speed and elevation were likewise affected. Yasmine needed to prioritise working on correcting several physical aspects, simultaneously increasing her overall muscle strength. There was a hell of lot to think about and to correct with each and every move she was practising in ballet class, starting from a simple plié at the barre.

When I first read about the challenge to train a hyper-flexible child with a swayback posture, I was really concerned that those would be challenging modifications for her to deal with. She basically needed to retrain her brain. Applying all those changes made her feel as if she was leaning, or was about to fall, forwards. For Yasmine, to master all those fine tunings meant working twice as hard in class, and in a holistic way. She needed the watchful eye of highly skilled ballet teachers. It is to the great credit of all her White Lodge ballet teachers, combined with her own intelligence on how to use and apply their expert knowledge and guidance, that she learned to correctly use and place her body at the same time as gaining great muscle strength. This is just not achieved overnight.

As a result of her White Lodge ballet training, Yasmine has never had any serious injury, and she can look back on her first professional decade with The Royal Ballet as being injury-free: from corps de ballet to Principal ballerina, not one performance has been missed due to a dance injury.

Ballet is not a natural activity for the human body. The body is not made for ballet: walking and dancing turned out, hip sockets fully rotating with a high degree of joint flexibility, dancing on pointed toes with feet squeezed into pointe shoes supporting the full body weight, and all the pounding and jumping, demands a strong and solid bone composition. It is true that anybody can learn ballet; shape and age are not at all a restriction. But when it comes to elite-level ballet training, it is an entirely different matter. The natural weeding out process during many years of training ultimately delivers a relatively small number of young dancers who will be able to start a professional career.

By late October, the rehearsals commenced for Little Swans, and they took place after her academic and ballet classes had finished. The Royal Ballet performances were scheduled throughout the Festive Season and until the end of January. *Swan Lake* was reprised in May. Once the studio rehearsals with The Royal Ballet dancers commenced, the selected girls would board the School bus at 8.30am, and the daily journey to the Royal Opera House took well over an hour. Ballet teachers accompanied the students, and an appointed chaperone looked after the young students' wellbeing, to ensure the children ate on time and had proper breaks and resting time. As soon as the rehearsals finished for the day, the children dressed in their red and white tracksuits, boarded the waiting School bus and were driven back to White Lodge. After a long day of rehearsals, they still needed to do their homework before bedtime at 10pm. Those were very demanding days for children aged twelve, but it was all part of their training. After the last performance of *Swan Lake*, the Little Swans found a giant teddy bear in their dressing room as a Thank You present from then Director Dame Monica Mason for all their dedication and hard work.

Just before the start of the Christmas holidays, I had my first parent/teacher meeting with Yasmine's ballet teacher, Miss Nicola Katrak. Meeting the ballet teacher once a term was the only chance to find out about progress, or lack of progress, and to discuss any issues there might be. I assumed there would be little to say, since this was only Yasmine's first term in training. During the meeting, I recall proudly telling Miss Katrak what a perfectionist Yasmine was. I thought this was a very good quality to possess, but I was taken aback when Miss Katrak told me in no uncertain terms that while, to some extent, perfectionism was a good trait to possess, it could also be a detrimental one.

"What do you mean perfectionism isn't always a good thing?" I asked, giving Miss Katrak a baffled look.

In the end, her explanation made sense, and it was a total revelation. It really opened my eyes and prompted the start of my earnest endeavour to increase my understanding of the mental aspects of ballet training. Once I understood the unproductive consequences of perfectionism on a dance trainee, I assisted Yasmine in easing her out of it. Perfectionist traits in an individual are often believed to derive from conditional parenting, but not in our case. I think Yasmine's perfectionist traits came from my genes. I vividly remember how, as a seven-year-old, I had been a little perfectionist, too. As a child, Yasmine could not stand to have even a minor stain on her T-shirt, in total contrast to her younger sister who didn't care a hoot if felt tips or the juice of a watermelon had stained her clothes. "People will think it's a Jackson Pollock!" she would exclaim.

When Yasmine came home for the weekend, ballet talk on Saturdays was totally off limits. It was time out for her as well as for us. However, in the late afternoon on Sundays, before Kamran would drive her back to White Lodge, Yasmine and I usually had our chat, during which we addressed any issues she might be struggling with. One of the first issues that needed to be tackled was her overly perfectionist nature. She had to liberate herself from that self-limiting "corset" she had unknowingly put herself in. Perfectionism is often guided by harsh self-criticism, and it is an unhealthy mental state. If not dealt with, it can lead to many psychological problems. The attention to detail becomes an obsession as the ballet trainee tries to avoid making even the smallest of mistakes, resulting in mental fear of being a poor performer.

I helped her to realise that perfectionism is a disadvantageous trait, and that she was at risk of developing an over-sensitive eye and distorting her own alleged flaws.Perfectionists are hardly ever happy with what they accomplish, and this in turn can lead to depression, anorexia, bulimia, or debilitating anxiety. They set themselves disproportionately high standards, combined with a propensity to make overly disparaging self-evaluations. Their mind is powered by fear of what they consider to be a failure. This impedes their learning, as well as their advancement. Such an adverse mindset made it difficult for Yasmine to forget about errors, and the images of those errors continued to control her mind. In addition, she was also at risk of being overly self-conscious. Instead of focussing on the task ahead of her, she concentrated too much on the "self" and her perceived flaws. She was afraid of looking bad, and as a consequence she would slow down her technical progress. She needed to understand that there is a real difference between trying to achieve technical perfection and the detrimental perfectionist demands she put onto herself. One focuses on the physical aspect; the other on the mental aspect. She needed to understand how to differentiate between the two.

Elite-level ballet training does not run on the notion of happiness, and a trainee needs to learn how to rely on her (or his) self-confidence in order to induce a state of happiness and to find fulfilment in what they do. No-one can do this on their behalf when they remain obsessed with their own flaws, so they need to learn to let go. A ballet trainee with overly perfectionist tendencies will, likewise, never be happy with her or his own physique.

For example, the young Gelsey Kirkland was exceptionally gifted, yet she never seemed happy with herself or with any of her achievements. Instead, she desired to look and dance like fellow ballerina Suzanne Farrell, and it took years for Kirkland to be able to accept her own body and its brilliance. Rudolf Nureyev ardently wished his legs were longer, and he worked devilishly to get the appearance of length. Every dancer has some gripe about her or his "instrument": some are built in and are an unchangeable issue of their anatomy, proportion, or silhouette, that keeps their idea of physical perfection just beyond reach. The ability to let go of perceived imperfections is far more productive. Yasmine's perfectionist inclination was not placed on any physical imperfection, but it was all about her drive to achieve technical perfection. She needed to learn to pace herself, be more self-forgiving whenever she was dissatisfied with herself, learn to move on and not linger on her mistakes or temporary technical flaws, to be more patient, and above all learn how to love herself. After all, she still had many years of training ahead of her.

I told her, "Your strongest muscle and worst enemy is your mind. Be in charge of training it well!"

It all came down to guiding and encouraging her to take responsibility towards building her mental strength, and to ameliorate her mental state in order to find fulfilment in her training, through increasing her self-belief and easing her out of her hyper self-criticism. This cannot all be left to the teacher, who already has a multitude of responsibilities. The student, supported by parents or carers, needs to take responsibility for her or his training.

My advice urged Yasmine on. I guided her, or I berated her, but in the end, it was Yasmine who had to put my words into action. That's where my work ended and hers began.

Soon after my first parent-teacher meeting, Yasmine's end-of-term ballet report arrived. It indicated that she had settled in admirably quickly, but it had taken her longer to adapt to the demands of a professional training. She had a lot of catching up to do, and a lot of hard work lay ahead of her. That didn't seem to faze or bother Yasmine at all, and with enthusiasm she embarked on her second term, having danced throughout the Festive Season as a Little Swan in *Swan Lake* at the Royal Opera House.

In January, Miss Keelan (then Assistant Ballet Principal) took over as their teacher. She was an impressive and dedicated teacher, with a strong convivial personality and an unwavering self-assured presence. She was very strict but equally fair. She also had the task to prepare the girls for their first Royal Academy of Dance exam. Miss Keelan would firmly raise her voice with a couple of decibels whenever Yasmine would not get the exercise right. I jokingly compared her to a general having to train the new recruits, and this was the only way to get them all in line and prepare them for the next level of their training. As a parent, I had complete trust in her. As a teacher, she was able to get the balance just right between firmness and toughness, whilst also showing an appropriate amount of motherly care towards her twelve-year-old pupils. Yasmine felt good in her skin with Miss Keelan. She always loved strict and highly demanding teachers who were simultaneously fair and displayed no favouritism.

Over the Christmas break, I had read *Winter Season* by Toni Bentley, who at the age of eighteen became a dancer with New York City Ballet. Her candid account of what it feels like to be a dancer off and on stage further intensified my lingering trepidation. As a result, I became concerned by the prospect that Yasmine would not be left with sufficient room to develop her true personality. The words of the Russian ex-ballet teacher I had met during the interval at The Coliseum kept resonating in my mind. *If what that Russian ballet teacher told me is indeed the case, then I do not want my daughter to fit into a mold,* I thought determinedly. I had accepted there was next to nothing I could contribute when it came to the technicalities of her ballet training, and I recognised that in ballet class Yasmine "belonged" to her ballet teacher. I never questioned nor challenged a teacher whenever Yasmine moaned or uttered a complaint. I would always talk it through with her, and I would make her see the other side of the coin. I never let Yasmine get away with moaning or complaining, as more often than not such complaints were trivial and very short-lived anyhow; they were often simply a way to let off steam and to get frustrations out of her system. Yasmine soon realised that moaning and complaining wasn't going to get her anywhere, and that it was far more useful to direct her energy and mind onto herself, and to get on with things. Reacting impulsively as a parent doesn't help them built a strong character, and they must learn that not everything can or will go their way. However, I was determined to remain in charge of Yasmine's emotional growth and her mental health, and to assist her in the firm shaping of her personality.

As her mother I had the choice to sit back and watch, to let it all happen and hope for the best, or to be pro-active so that I would be able to appropriately guide and advise her. Through our regular Sunday afternoon conversations, I learned a lot just by listening to her. I always guided her in such a way that she would be able to come up with her own conclusions or solutions. I made her think things through and look at situations from various perspectives, which in turn empowered her and gave her the feeling that she was taking charge of her struggles, of her perceived setbacks, and of her frustrations. I never wanted to give her the feeling that I was on top of her, because I was very aware not to let her become mentally dependent on me. I merely wanted her to know that I was right there behind her.

Training the mindset is as important and vital as training the body; one cannot do without the other. Yasmine's adverse mindset in her early training years was also the result of her own dissatisfaction whenever she felt she wasn't achieving her goal(s) fast enough, and she was at risk of digging herself into a hole. It is a paradox, but wanting to go faster would make her go slower. Ever since she was a little girl, Yasmine ran instead of walking, and as soon as she started her vocational ballet training, she wanted to run again before she could walk. She was forever impatient with herself. But she was at risk of slamming the door on her own growth and progress. Impatience is a great obstacle to success, and I told her, "Whenever you rush, you are no longer in your zone. And the more you hurry, the later you'll get."

She needed to learn how to physically and mentally pace herself instead of trying to constantly "race", and to remain firmly in the "here and now".

A trainee also needs a training environment in which she or he is allowed to thrive and blossom, so that their true personality can surface. Their character has to be positively shaped, and their desire, dedication, determination, and daily self-discipline have to be nurtured, so that they can use all these qualities to achieve the desired success. Ultimately, they have to become an expressive artist, ideally free from any mental constraints, and a teacher's unequivocal demand for strict discipline must be based on unaffected care and not on callousness. For any ballet student, training in an environment of fear or encouraging a "survival of the fittest" approach will not assist her or him to become a balanced, self-confident, and expressive artist.

The ancient Chinese proverb "*The teacher opens the door, you walk through it yourself*" expresses remarkable wisdom and reverberates a valuable life lesson about taking responsibility for oneself. But how does a ballet teacher open that door for her or his students? Is it done without restricting the student's inquisitiveness and eagerness? Have they awakened their artistic soul and strengthened their mind that will transport the student throughout her or his career? It is an incredible challenge and a constant balancing act for any ballet teacher to merge the body, the mind, as well as the soul of a ballet student, all into one. The most remarkable ballet teachers are in a sense like ancient Greek charioteers: they have to hold multiple reins at the same time as steering their students towards –- and hopefully over – the finishing line. Those teachers who do have that extraordinary gift to combine them all are the most memorable teachers.

On her last day in Year 8, Yasmine wrote in her diary: "*I think what I have learned this year is to love dance for its own sake as opposed to wanting to just become a ballet dancer. As soon as I hear the piano music, something deep inside me is ignited and I just have to move around. I have always loved moving around, there is nothing more I love to do!*"

HOW DID IT AFFECT OUR FAMILY LIFE?

Looking back on Yasmine's first year at White Lodge, it was our family life that underwent the most drastic change. As we lived not too far from the School, we initially enrolled Yasmine as a day pupil. The weekdays were long for her, though, as she faced, at best, an hour-long drive back home in the evening. The twenty-five-minute car commute at 7:30am would often take well over an hour-and-a-half in the evening traffic.

Kamran took it upon himself to pick her up every evening, and this meant he had to plough twice through the heavy evening traffic. Getting twice around the Hammersmith Roundabout and crossing the historic Hammersmith Bridge during peak hour – on a daily basis – was no easy feat for him. Nonetheless he enjoyed the precious time he spent with his daughter on their way back home. They were often stuck in a traffic jam, and singing provided entertainment. The *Anastasia* song track – sung by Anya, who is reminiscing about her forgotten past as the Grand Duchess Anastasia Romanov – became a firm favourite and they both knew the lyrics by heart.

Dancing Bears
Painted Wings
Things I almost remember.
And a song someone sings
Once upon a December.
Someone holds me safe and warm.
Horses prance through a silver storm.
Figures dancing gracefully across my memory.
Someone holds me safe and warm.
Horses prance through a silver storm.
Figures dancing gracefully across my memory.
Far away, long ago,
Glowing dim as an ember,
Things my heart
Used to know
Things it yearns to remember
And a song someone sings
Once upon a December

Kamran would let Yasmine sing her heart out, and until today it has remained their song whenever they reflect on those commuting days. It more than made up for the daily hassle, he said. Full kudos to Kamran for putting up with it.

On Saturdays, her ballet class finished at 1pm, and after Kamran had picked her up, they would always drive down to East-Sheen to buy her favourite pepperoni pizza. This became a firm start-of-the-weekend ritual that she always looked forward to, and the Saturday pepperoni pizza remains one of her most cherished White Lodge memories. There was a sigh of relief when she arrived home for the weekend, not only because it gave us a twenty-four-hour break from the daily commute to and from Richmond Park, but also gave us precious time together as a family. Without fail, as soon as she stepped through the front door, Yasmine would walk straight to the piano in our drawing room and play for about an hour, often improvising. She clearly needed that time to be alone.

However, two terms into her first year at White Lodge, Yasmine told us she wanted to become a boarder after the Easter holiday. The School was very understanding, and they accommodated her mid-year request. She felt she was missing out on all the evening fun and social time with her classmates, and the daily commutes were also weighing heavily. We desperately missed Yasmine, but not the daily commute.

Tatiana, her nine-year-old sister, was oblivious to the changes that had taken place in Yasmine's life. She realised that her sister was away for a week on end, that on Saturdays her sister was suddenly around, and that by late afternoon on a Sunday she was gone again. Tatiana often complained that ballet had taken her sister away from her. Some siblings take it all naturally in their stride, but others struggle as Tatiana did, and this raises the issue of the sibling of a talented sister or brother.

There were never any ill feelings towards her sister. Tatiana's antagonism was directed towards us, and this lasted well into her teenage years. Inevitably, our attention went to Yasmine as soon as she arrived home, and somehow this affected Tatiana. Giving her my undivided attention after picking her up from school, assisting her with her homework, or taking her to after-school ballet classes, somehow could not convince Tatiana that we loved her as much as her sister. In an attempt to make her feel better, we ensured that whenever Tatiana was present, we did not have any conversation relating to ballet, and the subject was deliberately avoided. When occasionally we did talk about ballet, she would roll her eyes as if to say, "*Oh no, not ballet talk again!*" She would separate herself from us and withdraw to her bedroom. This really created such a constrained atmosphere, until I eventually had had enough. I sat down with Tatiana and explained that – whether she liked it or not – ballet was now part of her sister's life and ours, and that the subject of ballet could not continually be avoided. In the end, I concluded that the best approach was to let it run its course and to just let her be.

Ballet wasn't something Tatiana was ever really interested in pursuing. It was something she just did, alongside her sister, as an after-school activity on Fridays and on Saturdays. Jazz and tap dancing were far more her style. Her jazz dance class on Saturday mornings preceded her ballet class, and a tap class followed. But it was at her academic school that Tatiana thrived the most, and she really enjoyed all the sports and games they played. In that environment, she flourished and felt most confident as a child, not in ballet classes. When she finally gave up ballet and her other dance classes at the age of twelve, it was not really an unexpected decision. I had seen it coming for months. I initially encouraged her to continue for a few more months, and urged her to think before making a final decision. We had made it very clear that she did not have to be like her sister, in case this was self-styled pressure she had put herself under. We encouraged her to develop her own interests, but nothing we said could change Tatiana's attitude. Even throughout Yasmine's early years in the corps de ballet, Tatiana would often decline to join us at the Royal Opera House. Years later, Tatiana explained that once her sister had gone to White Lodge, it had changed our family dynamics just when she felt she needed stability the most. She felt our family life had always been full of "colour" and that ballet had turned it into many "dark shades of grey". It was her way of coping with that "loss", I guess.

When Yasmine came home for the weekend, all attention was unavoidably on her, and Tatiana now accepts that it was only natural that, as parents, we paid extra attention to Yasmine after not having seen her all week. In a recent conversation with Tatiana, I was interested to hear how she now reflects on all those years. She said she feels a degree of annoyance with herself because she didn't appreciate it all much sooner. She definitely did not understand at that time what her sister was going through from a very young age. Although those years were, no doubt, difficult for Tatiana, she can't help but feel that it was all part of what made her into the person she is today. She knows that if she had had all the attention, she probably wouldn't have been as independent and free-spirited as she is now. She certainly would not have had the incentive or the courage to want to travel to Australia and Japan all by herself when she had barely turned eighteen. She needed and wanted to prove things to herself, and everything happens for a reason.

"It wasn't easy at that time, but for a person to grow stronger one has to walk through mud," she said.

Tatiana is, of course, incredibly proud of her sister, even as she unintentionally changed the dynamic of our family life when she was little. "It is a surreal feeling whenever I attend a performance by my sister," Tatiana explained. "The all-pervading feeling of seeing her dance on the stage of the Royal Opera House is something indescribable. I am in total awe of my sister. Yasmine is such a light in my eyes, and I am beyond proud of her and how far she has come, because I know what it took her to get to the top. I always cry or get tears in my eyes when it comes to the curtain call, and to see her standing there acknowledging and thanking the audience. My noisy 'woops' during curtain call is my way of expressing my love and great admiration for her. It always gives me the shivers. Looking back on all those years, it all turned out for the best."

Tatiana eventually managed to turn the tide for herself after she left the secure environment of her home and family when she was eighteen. For Tatiana to travel all by herself to the other side of the world was very hard for us to digest, especially since she had not set a return date. On the day of her departure, she did not want us to drive her to the airport; not even to the nearest tube station. She said she was going to do it all by herself, all the way to Australia, and was starting by walking to the tube station. That afternoon, she put on her rucksack, opened the front door, and she walked out. She didn't want us to hug her or kiss her goodbye for fear we would all get too emotional.

As I closed our front door, it was one of the most painful moments I had ever felt since the day I became her mother. I knew deep down that Tatiana needed to do this for herself, and to be able to prove whatever it was she wanted to prove. She called me just before the plane was about to take her far away from me, and not knowing when or if I would see her again, I sat down, poured myself a large glass of wine, and I re-read a poem from *The Prophet*, by the Lebanese-American writer and poet Kahlil Gibran:

"Your children are not your children.
They are sons and daughters of Life's longing for itself.
They come through you but not from you.
And though they are with you yet they belong not to you.
You may give them your love but not your thoughts,
For they have their own thoughts.
You may house their bodies but not their souls,
For their souls dwell in the house of tomorrow, which you cannot visit,
not even in your dreams.
You may strive to be like them, but seek not to make them like you.

For life goes not backward nor tarries with yesterday.
You are the bows from which your children as living arrows are sent forth.
The archer sees the make upon the path of the infinite, and He bends you with His might that His arrows may go swift and far.
Let your bending in the archer's hand be for gladness.
For even as He loves the arrow that flies,
so He also loves the bow that is stable."

In the end, Tatiana succeeded in abandoning all her ill feelings, and she used them to her advantage. As Yasmine's sibling, she certainly suffered, but Tatiana ultimately drew great strength out of it all, and that in itself is her very own distinctive success.

When Yasmine embarked on her second year of training in September 2005, work had just commenced on the redevelopment of The Royal Ballet School's facilities. This included two new dance studios, the extension of a third studio, state-of-the-art boarding accommodation for the students, a new dining hall, and major restoration work to the original 300-year-old villa. The grounds resembled a building site. Benefactors, "Knights of White Lodge", Donors, Patrons, Friends of White Lodge, as well as the parents, enabled the School to raise 80% of the extensive £22million, three-year redevelopment. Recreational facilities at White Lodge incorporated an indoor heated swimming pool, a tennis/netball outdoor court, and a small football pitch. The students' common rooms provided darts, snooker, table tennis, video games, and television. In one of them there was even a drum set. There are six ballet studios, one of which is the Fonteyn Studio Theatre, named after Prima Ballerina Assoluta Margot Fonteyn. That studio can convert from a fully equipped theatre with a 250 seating capacity into one large ballet studio – said to be nearly the size of the Royal Opera House stage – or two smaller ones.

Soon after the start of the Autumn Term, I told Yasmine that if at any time she had doubts or wanted to change direction and stop training, she must know she had that choice. I think I simply sought her assurance that this was what she really wanted to do in life. She resolutely answered back, "Mum, if you tell me once more that I can change direction whenever I want to, then it simply shows you do not have any faith or confidence in me. Never ask me this question again!"

I was momentarily taken back by her forceful reply. Once and for all, she had put me firmly in my place, and I never ever questioned her choice again.

Miss Anita Young, former Soloist of The Royal Ballet (joined in 1968) was the teacher in charge of this challenging age group: teenage girls with a changing physical appearance and behaviour. For teenage girls in ballet training, the bodily changes can pose a real threat to their self-image and self-confidence. It is a time when a girl has to accept her physical maturation, but for the young female ballet trainee the physical changes can psychologically work against her. The female trainees are likely to look at the gradual development of hips and breasts as an obstacle, and those physical changes are perceived as undesired changes over which they have no control. A girl aged eleven may have the perfect physique for classical ballet training, but once she reaches puberty, her physical appearance starts to change and her anxieties may increase. The risk she will begin to hate her body is a worrying prospect. From her point of view, her body, as well as her individuality, are to be rejected because she considers her self-identification as a dancer to be at risk.

Any teenage girl is acutely aware and highly self-conscious of her appearance, and she is at risk of low self-esteem. This is no different for the teenage ballet trainee. She will become hypersensitive to remarks, and any comments open for misinterpretation or having the potential to be negatively perceived will automatically be magnified. The teenage girl's longing for dancing can be in direct conflict with the changes her body is going through. Some will simultaneously go through a growth spurt and their bones grow faster than their muscles; some will feel they are losing their flexibility or stability; others will feel a loss of their strength. It will feel as if they are stagnating, and this can cause a great deal of frustration and anguish in the teenage trainee. It is a most delicate and challenging stage in their training, and any teacher in charge of this age group needs to be very sensitive about rash remarks made in class. It is of utmost importance that teenage girls in ballet training are supported in accepting their physical changes, based on the reassurance that a career as a ballet dancer will not stand in their way for that reason.

Now, what is considered to be an ideal female body for elite-level ballet training? Apart from aesthetic considerations, a well-proportioned body is absolutely necessary. It will withstand the stresses and strains of the training with greater ease, compared to a body in which there is a disparity in length of the legs, torso, width to length of the body, or size of shoulders to hips. Ballet reference books define an ideal female ballet physique as: "A slim body of average height, with a long neck, a short to medium length torso, long legs with complementary long arms, and a high instep." It is true that an elite-level training physique needs to conform to certain standards in order for the body to withstand all the demands and rigours of the training, but a professional dancer can come in all shapes and sizes, because it is their ability to dance that is most important.

From a personal point of view, contemporary dance does not necessitate having a perfect (classical) ballet physique, nor do some 20th century ballets. But when it comes to dancing the title role in the highly classical ballets such as *Swan Lake*, *The Sleeping Beauty*, The Sugar Plum Fairy in *The Nutcracker*, *Cinderella*, *La Bayadère*, or *Sylvia*, I prefer watching a ballerina with a "textbook" ballet physique, who possesses long lines and has all the necessary facilities to enable the greatest possible agility, grace, lightness, speed, exquisite extensions, and superlative technical control. When it comes to aesthetic appreciation of a visual art form, there is still truth to be found in the Latin adage "*De gustibus non est disputandum*" (meaning, in matters of taste, there can be no disputes).

Parallel to their physical concerns comes a greater need to feel independent and to rebel, but the latter is totally impossible in this highly disciplined and strict training environment. Punctuality, dedication, focus, self-discipline, obedience, observing strict rules, teachers' and House Parents' supervision at all times, combined with the demands of their academic studies, their choreographic work, as well as their ballet training, is an enormous load to deal with for a teenage ballet trainee. Risking any form of rebellion or disobedience results in reprimand. Their behaviour and appearance must adhere to strict rules, so there is understandably no room whatsoever for any form of non-compliance. They are in a specialist training environment, after all, and anyone deciding to take such a path knows there are necessary rules and self-discipline to stick to. This strict vocational training environment does not suit every child, but Yasmine thrived in such a setting.

Teenagers love to express themselves in a variety of ways, but White Lodge was not a place to show any eccentricities: no colouring the hair blue or pink; no piercings or tattoos; no arriving in class with a creative hairstyle or wearing an "outlandish", un-kempt or casual outfit. The pupils wore the School's uniform of a dark blue suit, white shirt and tie for the boys, and a Scottish chequered skirt, a white shirt, and a navy-blue blazer for the girls during their academic lessons, or a red and white tracksuit worn on top of their leotard for the girls, and shorts and a white T-shirt for the boys when they attended ballet classes.

They also had little privacy, although from the age of fourteen the girls were allowed to spend time in the boys' common room (but not vice versa) on Saturday evenings. Before each half term or term break, the House Parents organised a disco for the fourteen-to-sixteen-year-old age group. The disco party was always highly anticipated, and the girls planned their fashionable outfits weeks in advance. It goes without saying that alcohol and cigarette smoking were not allowed on the premises.

Some Saturday evenings, Mr Green, their fabulous maths teacher, would set up a big screen in one of the ballet studios, and he organised a "special edition" cinema night. Those evenings felt very special for the students, and surely the few teenage couples relished a night out at the movies. On the other hand, they were generally content to slouch on a sofa in their common room on a Saturday night, as the physical demands of the training made them too tired to do much else.

Living in the middle of Richmond Park, nine miles (15km) driving distance to Central London and at a considerable walking distance to the nearest train station, did not allow Yasmine and her classmates to have an external social life. Their non-ballet training peers, in comparison, could enjoy far greater freedom and had a multitude of opportunities to meet within the peer group: their school days finished early, they had no classes on Saturdays, they occasionally rebelled against parents and teachers, they could go out on a Saturday night, and they had the opportunity to date and establish their first relationships. But above all, they are not physically exhausted. For obvious reasons, teenagers in vocational training do not have much free time, nor do they live in an environment where less strict freedoms are conceivable. Ballet trainees are also limited in their social interaction with non-ballet training peers, as there are rarely any opportunities to meet anyone outside the Lower School environment. For that reason, they mature in a different way to their non-ballet training peers. This can result in a certain degree of social immaturity or gullibility, and risks making them more vulnerable once they have to function in the adult world and have to carve out a professional career.

The only free time outside White Lodge that Yasmine and her classmates had was on a Saturday afternoon. As soon as the morning ballet class was over, they could hang up their school uniform for the weekend and change into their own clothes. They were permitted to leave the School grounds and walk to nearby East Sheen, accompanied by their House Parents. Once they reached the high street, they could go shopping or go to their favourite pizza restaurant unsupervised. By 5pm, they reassembled and walked back to White Lodge in time for their evening meal. On Sundays, they could lie in, and in the afternoon, weather permitting, they would sit in the garden or play games. There was a designated area in the garden that was exclusive Year 11 territory, allowing the sixteen-year-olds to have their own space and privacy away from the younger students. The rest of the day was taken up by doing their washing, changing their bed sheets, studying, and preparing for the week ahead.

Having addressed her overly perfectionist tendency which had resulted in inner conflicts during her first year in training, new issues began to surface during Yasmine's second year. Besides the common teenage girl issues, I had a new concern to deal with. I realised that thirteen-year-old Yasmine allowed her sense of self-worth to depend far too much on feeling accepted by others, be that her ballet teacher or her classmates, and that in itself was hindering the development of the second phase of her self-esteem: self-esteem build up during the puberty years. Her sense of self was merely based on the feeling that she existed in the minds of others. She relied far too much on the need to receive daily praise from her ballet teacher, and what shaped her sense of self-worth was based on her teacher's words, attitudes, and opinions expressed. Whenever she felt her teacher did not convey confidence in her abilities and efforts, she would internalise self-defeating thoughts. That mental dependency had to be stopped, and I began to wonder how to change not only her sensitive disposition but also how to steer her through the next stage in the development of her personality. I realised that if it was not corrected at this stage, it could become a serious hindrance in the development of her personality and her technical progress. This could cause lasting insecurities, to be carried with her throughout her training, and likely into her career as a ballet dancer.

It was a most critical stage, and it needed my urgent attention. She certainly was not the only trainee who struggled with this issue. Sure, she was now a teenage girl in training – and I took that fully into account – but I became intrigued by which aspects of ballet training could inadvertently influence her sense of self-worth. I wanted to understand and find out what lay at the origin. Where did it come from? Where and when can it go wrong?

Yasmine's sense of self had been firmly established before she began her ballet training. When she was little, we had praised her whenever we felt she deserved it, without ever over-praising. We always made time to listen to her, she was always spoken to respectfully, she received plenty of attention and hugs, and she had experienced success in sports and academics – all ingredients a child needs in order to develop a firm basic sense of self. Why then was she suddenly struggling with that? I began to question whether the very nature of ballet training could have triggered her lack of self-esteem and had weakened her sense of self.

There are two vital components of healthy self-esteem: the sense of personal worth, and a sense of personal competence. Children – and adults – who are highly motivated will as a rule have a high self-esteem, and this indicates positive self-regard. Although Yasmine was highly motivated, I wondered why she had such a low self-regard. It is a fact that the sense of self evolves throughout life, as we build an image of ourselves through various experiences with different people, countless activities, and achievements. *So,* I wondered, *what caused Yasmine's issue?* I came to the conclusion that there could be a number of reasons. To begin with, I wondered if it was depression. When that happens, self-esteem can be hit pretty quickly. *Or was it insecurity?* If she didn't feel happy about something in her surroundings, and she didn't know what to do about it or how to change it, she could feel insecure. Not feeling good about her surroundings would not be a very nice thing to have to face, and it would make her feel the same way about herself if it went on for too long. *Or was it mental or emotional misapplication? Or was it because of her misperception of "failure"*? Feeling she was failing at her objectives would make her feel like she could not achieve what she wanted to achieve, and that in itself would create a feeling of being worthless, and useless. *Or was it criticism?* Criticism is something she might have well been misinterpreting or misunderstanding. Sometimes a teacher criticises a student for something she or he has done, but it might just be because she or he did something that could have been done better. But if criticism is taken the wrong way, it is equivalent to someone telling themselves that they have failed. On the other hand, self-worth and self-confidence can also be damaged if a student is persistently told that she or he is 'not good enough' or is 'below average', without any supportive explanation. Or if noticeable favouritism exists in class, that can put a considerable hindrance on some students' progress, and it creates friction and an unnecessary mental obstacle.

Thus, there could have been a variety of reasons why her basic sense of self was out of balance and why she had been unable to confidently develop her new sense of self within the context of being a teenage girl in intensive ballet training, not only within her training environment but also amongst her peers. A teenager's mind will identify both positive and negative aspects of her or his traits and emotions as they begin to integrate their perceptions of their attributes to form generalisations, and compare themselves to their peers. With increased maturity and experience, teenagers begin to identify themselves in a more discerning way. They will see themselves as more competent or proficient in some domains than in others. The extent to which their self-perception in specific areas affects their overall sense of self-worth will be influenced by how important they consider those domains to be.

Eventually, I concluded that her wrongly perceived sense of failure and her misunderstanding of criticism had caused the insecurity. Good self-esteem is important, because it helps you to hold your head up high and to feel proud of your accomplishments and abilities. It gives you the courage to try out new challenges and the power to believe in yourself. It allows you to respect yourself, even when you make mistakes. Having good self-esteem enables you to make the right choices. With good self-esteem, you know that you are smart enough to make your own decisions.

Yasmine swiftly understood where she was going wrong in her thinking. Right from the start of her training, she'd had a startling ability to not only process what we evaluated together, but also to apply it instantaneously. So I urged her to place a much higher value on herself and not to continue making the mistake of tying her sense of self-worth to perceived failures and her dependency on positive feedback from her ballet teacher. Focussing on her unquestionable competence and skills should enhance her sense of self instead of diminishing it. If a particular routine showed her increased competence but the teacher did not acknowledge it, her delight in what she achieved lessened, and she would perceive it as if it wasn't good enough. She needed to learn to self-evaluate and not internalise corrections perceived as criticism, but use them as a positive tool to improve. The dance trainee may perceive the frequent corrections and guidance of a teacher as negative criticism, but she or he must learn how to deal with it – as long as the criticism is not soul-destroying or counter-productive.

The inherent nature of elite level ballet training can give cause to a lot of hurt, as well as affecting the sense of self-worth. It is my opinion that the firm foundations to building mental strength and resilience need to be laid down in the early years of ballet training, and it must be built on continuously, so that by the time the trainees are fifteen going on sixteen they have full confidence in themselves, thereby allowing them to accelerate their training with a stronger sense of self. It is an ongoing process, but if mental resilience is not fittingly set up from a young age, they are potentially at risk of continuing to struggle mentally and having to fight various avoidable battles. Internalising detrimental thoughts and feelings, and dragging them through their training, can cause lasting and affecting mental obstacles, ultimately taking them along into their professional career. This only results in the trainees carrying extra, avoidable, weight on their shoulders.

At the same time, I realised that to a certain extent it could be counterproductive to want to protect Yasmine from feeling hurt, so I had to tread a fine line. Overprotecting children does not set them up for life, nor does it teach them how to be resilient. Yasmine had to learn how to recognise when her mind was at risk of misinterpretation, and how to deal with that. Elite level training – be it in sport or ballet – is ruthless, and developing a very thick skin is a must, as long as it is not fashioned on belittling. Yasmine's adverse self-perception was the result of internalised issues that had made her think she wasn't good enough. Over a period of time, she had come to believe that and I recognised that she had to unknot that disparaging belief. Some dance trainees, as well as some professional dancers, are always positive and upbeat, and they intuitively know or think they are good, strong, and competent. What one believes to be true about oneself can determine their eventual success. Yasmine's thoughts controlled her too much; they influenced her emotions, and they became an obstruction to her natural progression.

She needed to create her own reality with positive self-images of her abilities and strengths. If she saw herself as weak or incompetent, it would manifest itself in her training. She had to create a positive intent and decide what it was she wanted to believe about herself – even the seemingly impossible. I explained to her that what she was thinking, what shape or state her mind was in, was what would make the biggest difference of all. I advised her to dump anything that was dragging her down and made her realise that believing in oneself is paramount to achieving success.

At the same time, she also had to learn how to deal with micro-failures. Any ballet student has to overcome this every day; if not, it chips away at her or his mental development and happiness, and ultimately on their technical progress. A missed pirouette, or a class where she had felt invisible to her teacher, or a perceived negative comment was uttered, would affect her. She was overly sensitive. She needed to realise and accept that daily ballet class was there for her not only to improve her technique but also to learn from her mistakes, how to overcome her weaknesses, and to further build her strengths. Class was not meant to be a display of absolute perfection. It is an attempt at doing so, and only after many years of practice can a dancer try to achieve perfection or near-perfection. I remember reading an interview with Jonathan Cope (former Principal dancer of The Royal Ballet), and he was asked how many performances he felt he had danced to perfection or had felt really happy with. He answered that he could count those on one hand.

During one of her weekend visits, Yasmine told me that her class had been rehearsing for the upcoming solo evening performance – a bi-annual event eagerly anticipated by all the parents. The students in her class had been told that if anyone felt they had not had sufficient rehearsal time, they should let the teacher know. Towards the end of the rehearsal, Yasmine had walked up to the teacher and said she felt she had not had enough rehearsal time. Soon after, Yasmine was told to go and present herself in the Ballet Principal's office, where she was severely reprimanded. She was completely taken back and totally confused.

The sheer thought of her being reprimanded for asking something the students had been told to ask made me very cross. *How is a fourteen-year-old student supposed to process this? How can this possibly contribute to building up her self-confidence?* I wondered, whilst trying to make any sense of the situation. It was a fact that some were bellowed at, whilst others had a far easier path. Some never had to deal with disapprobation, and as a result they easily blossomed. Besides feeling really irritated about the incident, I was puzzled, and I wondered if this was not all intentional. I guess I was looking for an acceptable explanation or justification of the incident.

I had been yelled at by some of my schoolteachers; it was nothing unusual decades ago. I even remember when, as a seven-year-old, I had a chunk of my hair pulled out by a screaming Catholic nun, who told me to sit up straight as I was learning to write. Luckily, current teaching methods have changed, but one thing was sure: punishment for the slightest disobedience, for answering back or not following the rules, was standard practice then. Punishment could be in the form of standing in a corner with our hands on top of our head for as long as the teacher wanted us to, or to write five hundred times the same sentence apologising for what we did wrong, or we were excluded from playing with our classmates during the mid-morning or afternoon break. We were "publicly" humiliated by having to stand right next to the scary nuns, feeling very sorry for ourselves, so that all our schoolmates were made aware of our punishment, or we were being grabbed by the ear by the nun who dragged us to a solitary seat at the back of the classroom, where we had to sit for the remainder of the morning or afternoon. We never really questioned such practices, and whenever I told my mother of my ordeal, she would simply say that I surely must have done something wrong to deserve it. She always sided with the teachers. Parents never questioned teaching practices or punishments back then.

In the end, I drew my own conclusion – rightly or wrongly – as to why Yasmine had been called into the Ballet Principal's office to be reprimanded: a corps de ballet dancer would not ask for more rehearsals. They have allocated rehearsal times and, ready or not, when it is time for curtain up, the dancer has a responsibility to know the steps. This was clearly demonstrated the following year when Yasmine was preparing for her first participation in the Young British Dancer of the Year competition. During the last scheduled rehearsal of her two solos, she asked if she could have just one more rehearsal. She was justifiably told she could not, and that she must learn to fully trust herself when going on stage to perform. A precious lesson learned, I guess. As a professional dancer, she has found herself in countless situations being asked to perform barely rehearsed roles, or to take over a role from another dancer at very short notice. Of course, by that time she had acquired the necessary self-confidence to go on stage and perform a role with minimum rehearsal time.

Within a matter of two years, I had gained considerable knowledge and understanding of the psychology of the dance trainee, but one way or another I felt it was still not enough. I wanted to dig further and deeper into the workings of the mind of the accomplished performer. I was unable to find any relevant or helpful information in the ballet literature, so I began searching for answers on the internet. One day, I came across sports psychology – a division of psychology I hitherto wasn't aware of. Determined to understand what made an elite sports person get to – and stay – at the top, I walked to my local library in search of books in which I hoped to find the answers I sought. A few hours later, I arrived back home with a pile of books I was very eager to get my teeth into. As soon as I realised that sports psychology tied in with Yasmine's ballet training, I felt I had found the right tool with which to assist her in further developing her mental strength and control, and to take it to the next level. It was a subject that seriously fascinated and absorbed me. Sports psychology is also called the "Science of Success", and it studies how successful individuals control their mind through targeted mental training, combined with having the ability to instantly apply the coaching information. But this requires constant mental practice. The topic of mental health and mental development of the ballet trainee was not really discussed fifteen years ago, and it certainly was not a priority concern. Ballet training back then was still very much conducted behind semi-closed doors, and any relevant practical literature for the uninitiated like myself or any academic research or report was relatively limited, so I had to turn to American research papers. In the USA, sports psychology and research in relation to the mental health of athletes was already far more advanced in 2005 because of their excellent colleges and university sports programmes, compared to research done in the UK. I fervently began reading about the psychology of athletes and how their coaches worked with top sportsmen and women. In addition to reading academic studies and sports psychology books, I also read the biographies of many elite sportsmen and women, from celebrated tennis stars, to golfers, marathon runners, and Olympic Gold medal winners.

An intriguing world opened up for me, and I was totally gripped. I was curious to know what all those elite sports people possessed and what set them apart from the others. I wanted to understand what performance success entailed, so I further explored the topic of inner training for peak performance in sports. What all those successful elite sportsmen and women had in common was their work ethic and total control of their mind; in other words, it was their mental strength that gave them the greatest power. Equipped with this new information, I felt more confident than ever that I would be able to support Yasmine further by making her aware that she needed an entirely different set of mental skills in order to achieve an altered attitude towards her training, as well as an improved mindset. We had already established that she would need to control her ineffective way of thinking once and for all, alongside her direct mental response not only towards herself but also towards her ballet teacher and her training environment. She was wasting valuable energy on futile things that distracted her from what really mattered, and she invested too much of her energy in the wrong places, therefore she was not using her potential to the full. At times, she seemed to be her own worst enemy.

She had to use her strong drive in a progressive manner, and not depend on – or be affected by – external and uncontrollable factors. Even when at times she was right to put the blame somewhere outside herself, this was not going to be helpful. Blaming is nothing more than a set of excuses, but excuses are known to be the crutches of the untalented, and they are fatal to progress. She had to get out of her comfort zone, stop being afraid of making mistakes, afraid of failing, or feeling she wasn't liked or that she wasn't good enough. She was creating unnecessary obstacles for herself, and her doubts and fears stood in the way of her progress. If she proved incapable of starting to feel good about herself, she would be at risk of diminishing her chances to succeed.

One day I was chatting to Yasmine about some of my favourite sportsmen and women and how many had gone through a personal battle and suffered in order to achieve success, well before they became successful. I further explained to her that success for the top elite sportsman or woman rests on their capacity to "suffer" (coping with the hardship of physical training) and to draw strength out of that "suffering". One detects that capacity in the greatest, and it separates the champions from the merely talented. That capacity is directly related to a winner's mindset, and as they demonstrate their endurance, their head becomes stronger.

"If things come easily your way, you won't really value them, but when achieved through your own efforts and hard work, you'll value them much more. The greater the effort needed, the greater the value you'll attach to your success," I told her.

With a determined look in her eyes, as if she was ready to go on a warpath, she replied, "Well then, MAKE me suffer!"

Her response fascinated me. I did counter that as her mother I could not make her suffer, but that no doubt she would experience suffering at some point in the future – be it during her training or during her professional career – and that I hoped she would remember our conversation at that point.

Favouritism in ballet class is yet another aspect the trainee has to (learn to) deal with. Ideally, a teacher is impartial, giving all the students equal opportunities and refraining from openly picking favourites in class. Favouritism has a very negative influence on the ballet trainee's mind and progress. After all, they need assistance in helping to build their self-confidence, not having it hindered or delayed. However, preference or subjectivity is something they will encounter throughout their professional life, too. In any ballet company, the choreographer will pick his or her favourite dancer(s), the dancers the choreographer feels a personal connection with, or dancers they feel inspired by. His or her selection of dancers is entirely personal, hence it is a totally subjective choice. Apparently, it is called "artistic inspiration". Working with a choreographer means that every move or artistic expression is in his or her hands, and directs how the steps have to be performed. Individual artistic expression or interpretation may or may not be left up to the dancers. A choreographer will have several casts, but he or she will create on the first cast. It is possible that after several months of working at the back of a studio, copying the first cast, the second or third cast doesn't even get a chance to perform what they too have rehearsed for months. Sometimes their name may not even be on the final cast list. It is often soul destroying for those dancers. Students will, therefore, need to learn that once they become a professional dancer and the casting goes up on the casting board, they will inevitably have to accept that some will be picked for particular roles and others won't. They will need to accept that there are certain dancers who will often be in the first cast, and others will be in the second or third cast. It is the nature of the game.

By early November, the rehearsals for *The Nutcracker* were in full swing, and Yasmine was in the first cast, dancing as a Party Girl alongside four other classmates. By now everyone had a pretty good idea where they stood in the pecking order; the same selection of pupils who had danced in *Swan Lake* in Year 8 danced again in *The Nutcracker* in Year 9. The same girls had also been selected to work with Darcey Bussell as part of the BBC documentary "The Magic of Swan Lake". Two future Royal Ballet Principal dancers were in that select group: Yasmine and Francesca Hayward. Darcey Bussell presented the documentary in which she tells the viewer the story of the most popular ballet of all time. Using extracts from the Mariinsky Ballet's (formerly The Kirov Ballet) classic production, which was especially recorded for BBC1, Darcey explains how the romantic music, combined with captivating dancing and dramatic choreography, brings to life a fairy tale of love and heartbreak. There are verbal contributions by the Mariinsky Prima ballerina Ulyana Lopatkina, world-renowned Russian conductor Valery Gergiev, choreographer Matthew Bourne, dance critic Judith Mackrell, *Angelina Ballerina* author Katharine Holabird, and fourteen-year-old Yasmine. At the end of the BBC documentary, Yasmine expressed her dream to one day dance the dual role of Odette/Odile in *Swan Lake*. It would take Yasmine twelve years for that dream to come true, when she danced her debut as Odette/Odile in The Royal Ballet's new *Swan Lake* production in June 2018.

Yasmine passed the annual appraisal in February – an all-important first milestone. Year 9 was the year in which they could be assessed out of their training and asked to leave the School by the end of the year. Her entire class had been offered two further years of training up until their next decisive appraisal in Year 11, which meant auditioning for a much-coveted place at the Upper School in Covent Garden.

Don't neglect your mind.
You have to train it as hard as you train your body.
It can stand almost anything
but it is your mind you have to convince.

Her third year in training marked the year in which everything changed for Yasmine. She was fourteen going on fifteen, two full years into her training, technically she had caught up, and she had succeeded in building a much stronger sense of self. We had basically ironed out any mental issues that could obstruct her further progress or cause long-term mental imbalances. It was the year during which she made the transition from compliantly taking daily ballet class to taking direct responsibility for her individual approach to her training. Her mental attitude had progressively changed for the better, and she was now more driven than ever before. She also understood how to set long-term and short-term goals.

High levels of commitment grew out of her increased positivity and love for what she was doing. She felt more in control, as she had realised it was all about ongoing personal growth and learning, and that making mistakes was indeed the only way to learn. She had turned her initial daily frustrations into a learning process, and she controlled her overly perfectionist tendency. Unmistakably, she shifted from "driving" in second gear to "driving" in third gear.

The pace of the training increased, and Yasmine and her classmates had less than two years to prove their competency, besides simultaneously studying for her academic exams (GCSEs) the following year. She studied History, Science, Maths, French, English, Music, and Expressive Arts.

Diane Van Schoor, then Ballet Principal at White Lodge, was to become their ballet teacher for the next two years. She was born in South Africa and is an expert in the Cecchetti method of training. It is a method devised by the Italian ballet master Enrico Cecchetti (1850-1928), and is defined as a style of classical ballet, and style of ballet training that seeks to develop essential skills in dancers, as well as flexibility and strength.

Miss Van Schoor, as her pupils addressed her, ran the ballet department with an iron fist. She demanded total discipline at the highest level. Making excuses was totally unacceptable, any lateness in class was severely reprimanded, one hair out of place and she spotted it. She could command the entire class with her intense blue eyes alone. She was extremely firm, and she tolerated no shortcuts. She insisted on impeccable behaviour and 200% focus. After all, Miss Van Schoor was preparing her cohort for possible entry into the Upper School. The students were no longer addressed as "girls", but as "ladies". They had the highest respect for her but equally feared her. It was unusual to have the same teacher for two years in a row, but the students certainly benefitted. By the time they graduated two years later, the result was discernible: they were beautifully trained, accomplished student-dancers, and they were well prepared to tackle the next stage of their advanced training at the Upper School.

For a while I continued working on the concept of training the mind, being in the "zone", being present in the "now". Yasmine developed a much stronger focus, and she learned not to look too far ahead in the future but to concentrate instead on her daily progress. We also discussed setting a variety of goals, enabling her to achieve what she set out to achieve. Goal-setting provided her with a "road map", be it long-term or short-term. Keeping up her motivation was never an issue; she considered the repetitiveness of training exercises as challenges, never as tedious. The effort involved in training the body is long and unrelenting, and in many instances, it can also be painful. The effort to maintain the technique is gruelling, but Yasmine always found great satisfaction in the discipline of daily training. She understood progress could be slow at times and that she should not become dispirited. She typically progressed up until February, then felt that she stagnated until after Easter, only to "reappear" re-energised and fully on top of herself and her training during the last few months of the school year. It was as if she would plateau for a while in order to digest all that she had learned. That process, the very paradoxical nature of ballet training resulting in feeling a lack of progress, exasperated Yasmine. I explained to her that she should use that time as a breather, and to pace herself, in order to facilitate hitting the highest possible point by the end of the year. I compared it to mountaineers attempting to reach the summit of Mount Everest. They, too, take a "breather" at various base camps, to rest and recover during the multiple stages en route to the top.

At this stage in her training, I was acutely aware not to overload her, and I was very mindful of the fact that she could begin to resist my guidance because of her need to feel more independent. After all, she was a fifteen-year-old girl, and I was conscious she needed to feel that she was independent, so I deliberately created a distance between her and me. I would not make any contact with her during the week, and I left it entirely up to her if she wanted to speak with me, or not at all. Whenever she was at home for the weekend, ballet talk was totally off-limits, and I never initiated chatting about her past week. The weekend was time out of ballet and a chance to see her primary school friends who were by then all talking about their ambition to go to university. She felt the odd one out amongst them. Their life as a teenager was very different to hers, and she often listened to their stories in disbelief.

As far as I was concerned, I had put her on the road, and I had given her the necessary mental tools. She now needed to learn how to figure things out by herself. As caring and loving parents or carers, we are often tempted to want to protect our children, but trying to solve all their issues on their behalf, or at least without directly involving them, undermines the growth of their independence. At that stage, I gave her time to digest and merge all that she had learned and to balance her intensity of learning with the demands of her training.

Yasmine was always under-impressed with herself, and she didn't believe that she had any exceptional talent. She was rarely satisfied with any of her achievements and she frequently dismissed them as unimportant. It was very obvious that as soon as she had achieved or reached a pre-set goal, she never lingered on it. She was always very keen to move on to her next goal, and to overcome new challenges. I also noticed that the harder or tougher things became, the more she thrived, and only when she felt totally exhausted after class was she truly satisfied. Feeling physically exhausted became her measurement of hard work. Later on, she learned the importance of pacing herself. I had told her to remember that whenever she felt in a rush it meant she was no longer in her zone, and no longer in the present. The only way to "run faster" was through efficient use of her energy and physical efforts.

During her third year in training, Gailene Stock had, unknowingly, the greatest impact on Yasmine's overall transformation. She had selected a small group of sixteen students – seven White Lodgers and nine Upper School students – to travel to St Petersburg. In the group were four future Royal Ballet Principal dancers, Vadim Muntagirov, Sergei Polunin, Yasmine, and classmate Francesca, as well as future First Soloists James Hay, Claire Calvert, William Bracewell, and Soloist Benjamin Ella. Others in the group included Delia Mathews (ex-Birmingham Royal Ballet Principal) and Shiori Kase (English National Ballet Principal). The purpose of the trip was to take daily classes with Russian teachers at the world-renowned Vaganova Ballet Academy, and to present a joint performance with the Russian ballet students at the end of their trip, with each world-renowned ballet school showcasing their method of training and strengths.

On 4 May, 1738, by Imperial Decree of Empress Anna, the Vaganova Ballet Academy in St Petersburg was founded, and as a result the first Russian School of Theatrical Dance was established. Known as the Imperial Theatre School, it was established through the initiative of the French ballet master and teacher Jean-Baptiste Landé. Twelve girls and boys began to study "the foreign steps" on one of the upper floors of the Winter Palace. The Vaganova Ballet Academy has graduated a galaxy of illustrious dancers, such as Anna Pavlova, Vaslav Nijinski, George Balanchine, Altynai Asylmuratova, Ulyana Lopatkina, Diana Vishneva, and Svetlana Zakharova, amongst many others. It was in the late 1950s and 1960s that three Vaganova Academy graduates attracted international fame and recognition, after they began their professional dancing career at the Kirov Ballet (now The Mariinsky Ballet): Rudolf Nureyev, Mikhail Baryshnikov and Natalia Makarova and it was the much-admired former Russian Prima ballerina Natalia Makarova who coached Yasmine in 2018 when she prepared to dance her debut as Gamzatti in *La Bayadère* at the start of The Royal Ballet Season 2018-2019.

The evening before her departure to Russia, I had arranged with the School to pick Yasmine up at East Sheen Gate, one of several entry gates to Richmond Park. It was in the depths of winter, and the various gates to the park closed at 4pm so I couldn't drive up to White Lodge for the 5:30pm scheduled pick-up. I parked my car right in front of the tall, wrought iron gate, and switched off my engine and headlights. All I could do was sit and wait in near darkness and total silence until the School's minibus would eventually arrive. Staring into the dark, the vast expanse of the nature reserve was eerily lit by a full moon and a few twinkling stars. Bit by bit, my mind started drifting off, and I travelled back to February 1980. Memories resurfaced of my History of Art study trip to the USSR, as the Russian Federation was called up until the collapse of the Soviet Union in 1992, during the post-Stalin period. Political tension was very palpable at that time, and the authoritarian and xenophobic ideological attitudes inherited from the Stalinist era made it impossible for any Westerner to enter the Soviet Union. However, the USSR Embassy in Brussels issued special permission to university students to travel to the USSR. Our presence as Western students was looked upon with great suspicion, and we were prevented from visiting certain museums and particular buildings of architectural interest, nor were we allowed to speak to any Russian citizen or to freely wander around in the city. Foreigners were forced to stay in a hotel on the outskirts of St Petersburg and Moscow, and the uniformed agents of the KGB (translated in English meaning Committee for State Security, which was the main security agency for the Soviet Union from 1954 to 1991), wearing a cap with an oversized khaki high crown with cornflower blue band and piping, and a five-pointed red star (symbol of communism) in the centre, stood visibly by the entrance of our hotel: two inside, and two on the outside. They looked threatening and constantly monitored our whereabouts.

We had an Intourist-appointed guide who accompanied us everywhere on a daily basis. We could clearly feel we had entered an alternate universe. We only felt "safe" inside our hotel rooms, but we had no doubt there were listening devices hidden in the walls. As foreigners, we were shielded from the vagaries of Soviet life, and we were under constant surveillance. There were clear barriers put up between us and the uncomfortable truths about the Soviet Union. My keenness to see as much as I could of St Petersburg got me into serious trouble with the Soviet Intourist guide, when I stubbornly insisted that I wanted to visit a particular museum that was not on our itinerary. That afternoon, on our way to the Peter and Paul Fortress, which I wasn't remotely interested in visiting, I grabbed the opportunity to break loose from our group and set off on my own to see the museum I was not allowed to visit by the Russian authorities. I was never one to take no for an answer!

As I strode along the banks of the Neva River, I met a Russian student in European History, and we struck up a conversation. He invited me for dinner at his home, where he lived with his girlfriend and *babushka*, and he asked to bring along some fellow students. That evening, the brutally restricted freedom Intourist imposed on us was no impediment for me to dodge the KGB agents positioned at the hotel entry. A fellow student and I managed to evade them, and we escaped through the backdoor staff exit and ran as fast as we could into the barely lit, deserted street. I vividly remember seeing just one functioning lamppost.

We waited about half an hour for a bus to come along, during which time we nervously kept scanning the vast open space between our bus stop and the hotel, expecting a KGB agent to arrive any minute, arrest us, and take us to prison. After an anxious wait for what seemed like an eternity, we boarded a rusty, old, diesel-fuelled bus and headed off to the centre of St Petersburg. I had agreed to meet up with the Russian student on the square right in front of the Hermitage at 7pm.

He was already waiting for us when we arrived at the snow-covered, deserted square. He intentionally led us through barely lit back streets, where our guide would never have taken us. We encountered beggars, snowploughing elderly women, drunken people, and motionless bodies lying in the snow, evidently frozen to death. It was a shocking sight. Clearly, the Russian student wanted to show us what Western visitors were not supposed to see. He was very hungry for information about the West and to hear all about how we Western students lived. Our conversations on various political and historical subjects descended into a feverish debate. We knew it was very risky to be in his home, and his girlfriend was livid that he had invited us. She feared a tip-off from a neighbour would be sufficient for the KGB to come knocking at their door any minute. She begged us to whisper as we were talking. When we left, he pleaded to keep in touch once we were back in Belgium.

Two weeks after our return, I received a letter from him. I promptly replied... but I never received any further correspondence from him. I had no doubt that he had been arrested and imprisoned for having been in contact with us Westerners. The only time I saw Russians with a big smile on their faces was at the Moscow Domodedovo airport, as we all carried Communist propaganda posters on our return journey. As Art History students, the Communist designs fascinated and amused us.

My reminiscing was suddenly interrupted when I finally spotted the lights of the School's minibus in the distance, driving down the winding road from White Lodge towards East Sheen Gate. At 5:50pm Yasmine stepped off the minibus and walked through the rotating side gate towards my car. I could sense her mood just by looking at her! She looked exhausted. I had brought along some food, as I knew she would be starving, and indeed she gobbled it up in no time. I knew better than to engage in any conversation until after she had eaten. After about ten minutes, she began talking about the afternoon rehearsals in preparation for their trip to Russia, and she complained about how her toes were hurting, how her big toenail was bruised, and on top of it all she had three blisters on her feet and all her muscles hurt badly. I drove her straight to the Sports Medicine Clinic for an hour-long deep tissue massage. As I sat on the side and the Sports Therapist took care of her, I looked at her and all I saw was tiredness on her young face. I desperately wanted to hug her, to hold her in my arms, but I knew she just wouldn't take it. Whenever she was tired or in pain, she did not want me to feel sorry for her, ever.

The following morning, I drove her to Heathrow airport at 6:30am. In the Departure Hall, the group of sleepy-looking students were standing next to Ballet Principal Miss Van Schoor, who was dressed in a warm fur coat and with her hair neatly done in an elegant French roll, and Mr Jay Jolley, then Assistant Director to Gailene Stock. They had all come well prepared and ready to face the freezing Russian weather conditions of -20 Celsius (-4 Fahrenheit). With the images of my trip to Russia still on my mind, I hugged my daughter and kissed her goodbye.

On arrival at Pulkovo 2 Airport, a waiting coach drove them to the centre of St Petersburg and Mrs Vera Dorofeeva, the Principal of the Vaganova Ballet Academy, warmly welcomed The Royal Ballet School students. So there she was, at the School where Anna Pavlova, Vaslav Nijinsky, Rudolf Nureyev, Natalia Makarova, Mikhail Baryshnikov had all trained and graduated.

A page in Yasmine's diary reads: "*Walking through the corridors of the Vaganova Ballet Academy on my way to my daily ballet classes, I see delicate paintings of some of the greatest Russian ballerinas decorating the walls. I arrived punctually in ballet class where Professor (as teachers at the Academy are called) Kovaleva was waiting for us. I had to adjust to the raked studio floors and the different way of teaching. I watched some Russian students in their character dance class and I was amazed by their expressiveness. We will have further opportunities to observe the Russian students and this will give me a better understanding of what Russian ballet and Vaganova training is all about.*"

Their daily ballet class started at 10am, after they had consumed a Russian breakfast of dry rye bread or *butterbrot* (open-faced sandwiches), tasteless sausages, and watered-down scrambled eggs, soured potatoes, *kasha* (cooked buckwheat), and *tvorog* (similar to cottage cheese). The day also included rehearsing in the evening for their upcoming performances.

Yasmine was cast to dance Dance of the Mirlitons from *The Nutcracker*, Dance of the Fiancées from *Swan Lake*, and Tarantella from *Napoli*. Rehearsals would take place well past 10pm. One evening, she called me to tell me all about her day, and how exhausted she was. After supper they had all gone into the dormitory to rest, but it had been decided that further rehearsals were needed, and they all had to dress again and walk back into the studio. *How can this possibly be just?* I thought. *She is totally exhausted, yet she has to get out of bed again to rehearse until well past 10pm?* It may seem harsh, but it was the only way to prepare them for their future professional life and to build their stamina; tiredness or exhaustion was never to become an excuse.

A visit to the lavish Winter Palace – now the Hermitage Art Museum – and a city tour to see buildings of different architectural styles and eras, from Baroque to Classicism to Stalinist architecture, was also on the programme. They attended an evening performance of *Cinderella* by the Mariinsky Ballet at the Mariinsky Theatre and met up with the dancers backstage after the performance.

On their last day, they performed at the Musical Comedy Theatre, and afterwards they were all invited to attend a Grand Ball to celebrate Maslenitsa (Shrove Tide), also known as Mardi Gras. Maslenitsa began as a pagan ritual and has since been absorbed into the Eastern Orthodox religion. Maslenitsa serves many purposes and signals the end of winter and heralds the arrival of spring. As part of the pre-Lenten celebrations, it is also a pre-emptive strike to the upcoming fast, because meat and dairy would traditionally be forbidden. Maslenitsa is the time for feasting, especially on pancakes and blinis.

At the Grand Ball were ladies and gentlemen beautifully dressed in historical costumes and wearing elaborate ball gowns; it could have been a scene straight out of *Onegin*. They danced and listened to opera singers, and they also watched the Mariinsky corps de ballet waltz and gallop. The following day, they were taken for a bit of shopping on Nevsky Prospekt before heading back to the airport.

It was on the flight back to London, looking out of the window as the plane was circling high above St Petersburg, that Yasmine unequivocally decided she wanted to become a ballet dancer. Any occasional reservations she had had in the past now seemed to have vanished.

Back at White Lodge, preparations commenced straight away for her first competition in the Young British Dancer of the Year 2007. She was the youngest semi-finalist selected amongst the thirty-two candidates, including Sergei Polunin who performed Basilio's Variation from *Don Quixote* – Act 3, as well as Brandon Lawrence and William Bracewell. For the semi-finals, Yasmine performed Lilac Fairy from *The Sleeping Beauty* Prologue. Of course, there was no use competing against Sergei Polunin, who won that year. For Yasmine, it was all about the preparations and experience of taking part in her first ever ballet competition.

It was around that time that Yasmine became peevish about her lack of freedom and leisure time. Pressure was up on all fronts, and I sensed she was lacking in focus. I think she was seeking what any ordinary teenager was looking for, and she started moaning about missing her old school friends, who were by now all going out in London on Saturday evenings. I had to have a serious conversation with her right before she competed in the Young British Dancer of the Year. Actually, I wrote her a very stern email, in which I asked her to think about what she was most desperate for: free weekends to go out, or was she hungry to dance?

I further told her that on her talent alone she was not going to get anywhere, unless she was prepared to consistently and continuously work really hard. There was no place for any external distractions now. There was no middle way. It was giving it her all, or nothing.

"You know the choice is entirely yours," I said.

To be a great champion you must believe you are the best.
If you are not, pretend you are!"
(Tiger Woods)

When I look back on all those years, Year 11 at the Lower School and her 1st Year at the Upper School were physically and mentally the toughest and certainly the most challenging for Yasmine for a variety of reasons, but it was precisely during those two years that the foundations were resolutely laid down for all her future successes. "*When the going gets tough, the tough get going!"* was certainly most pertinent in her case. When things are easy, you do not learn how to cope with encountered difficulties; when there are no setbacks, you don't develop coping mechanisms; and when everything is served on a silver platter and all comes easily one's way, it creates laziness, because it does not necessitate situational problem solving, and it barely creates a fighting spirit.

"Always remember that hard work beats talent any time when talent doesn't work hard!" I told her.

She now entered her last year at White Lodge, and Miss Van Schoor started preparing them straight away for the Royal Academy of Dance "Vocational Graded Examinations in Dance – Advanced Level 1". On 28 November, Yasmine and her classmates were taken to the Royal Academy of Dance in Battersea, and Frank Freeman was the examiner. The students were judged on their ports de bras, centre practice, pirouettes, adage, allegro, free work, pointe work, musical timing and rhythm, responsiveness to music, performance, and dance technique. A few weeks after the RAD examination, the results were announced and Yasmine was awarded "Distinction with 100%". She had received a 10/10 mark for every aspect of her RAD examination. The year could start on a high.

However, barely a few months later, she hit a low when she began to suffer serious pain in her lower leg, and by November she had her first encounter with a dance injury: she was diagnosed with shin splints. This type of pain concentrates in the area between the knee and the ankle. It is a cumulative stress disorder caused by repeated pounding. The daily practice of grand jeté – a high leap in the air with one leg stretched forward and the other back, involving a full leg split in mid-air with the weight pushed slightly forward, giving the dancer a gliding appearance – had caused high stress on her bones, muscles, and joints of the lower legs. The excessive force caused her muscles to swell, and this increased pressure on the lower leg bone, leading to pain and inflammation.

However, shin splints can also result from stress reactions to an existing bone fracture, as the constant pounding can cause minute cracks in the bones of the leg. The body can normally repair the cracks, if given time to rest. On the other hand, if the body does not get sufficient time to rest, the tiny cracks can ultimately result in a complete fracture or a stress fracture. At first, I thought rest over the Christmas period, combined with targeted specialist sports massage, would aid the healing of her shin splints. I was totally unfamiliar with dance injuries at that stage, because Yasmine had never before suffered any injury during her training. I also feared this could jeopardise her chance of getting into the Upper School; worse, it could mean the end of her training. I could neither understand nor accept why she was continuing her daily ballet class, as well as rehearsing her Gamzatti solo she was so adamant to dance at the upcoming YBDY 2008.

"How can you possibly dance in pain?" I asked her.

When she casually replied that she was learning to dance through her pain, and that being in pain was part and parcel of ballet dancing, I literally flipped.

"You must be mad to think you should dance through your pain," I objected. "This has to be sorted out immediately by a medical specialist," I countered. "Dancing in pain? What for? Dancing should be a joy, not having to cope with pain."

It is true that professionals sometimes dance with a minor injury, but they know how to deal with it and how to cope. They are adults, whereas she was still a growing teenager, and she had no idea yet how to deal with an injury, or how to pace herself and how to adapt her exercises in ballet class, which I felt she would not be allowed to do anyhow.

After the Christmas holidays, her pain did not subside, and by mid-January I received a telephone call from Miss Van Schoor, who informed me that she had decided to send Yasmine for an MRI scan at Wimbledon Hospital the coming Saturday. She wanted to start pushing Yasmine again in class, but she needed to know precisely what was the cause of her pain.

I was seriously worried. I called the School's physiotherapist, who thought the problem was caused by her shin muscle being attached to her bone. Her bones had grown, one leg was longer than the other, and she needed an MRI scan in order to decide on the right treatment for Yasmine. She reassured me that she would be up and running at full strength after Easter.

"What do you mean AFTER Easter? But what about her participation in the YBDY competition in March?" I queried. She replied that she wasn't too sure about that.

Later that evening, Yasmine called me at home, and she was totally worked up. "Who decided to do this MRI scan on Saturday afternoon?" she complained. "There goes my entire weekend. I only have the weekend to look forward to, you know, and have a bit of freedom. Why did you insist on being there for the MRI scan? All my classmates had their scan during the week."

"All your classmates had a scan during the week?" I queried.

"It's nothing special that scan, you know. They all have something wrong with them, or it is an issue with their lower back, or a painful ankle, or a painful hip joint, or a painful knee," she answered.

"So you are not the only one in your class with an injury?" I further questioned.

"You must be joking, mum. We all have something that bothers us! An MRI is nothing special, and all dancers have it. And don't expect me to be in a good mood when I see you on Saturday, and

I won't be coming home with you after the hospital visit. I can't study at home with all of you around me."

"But the gates to Richmond Park will be closed by the time we leave the hospital. How will you get back to White Lodge?" I asked.

"Drop me off at East Sheen Gate and I'll walk back in the dark to White Lodge," she replied.

Having just listened to the tirade of my teenage daughter, I became rather wary that something else was going on. Why was she so upset that her Saturday afternoon outing to East Sheen was going to be lost? Why was she so insistent to return to White Lodge on Saturday evening? *Hmmm, there surely must be a boy on the scene*, I thought.

The School did not permit us parents to seek a second medical opinion, but I was having none of it. I looked up who was the Consultant Orthopaedic Surgeon at The Royal Ballet and I promptly made an appointment with Mr R. Lloyd Williams in his London Orthopaedic Clinic. I was determined to get to the bottom of it, to fully understand what was the matter with Yasmine's shin splints and what had caused it.

His first abbreviated assessment stated: "A diagnostic MRI scan showed marked bone marrow oedema in the medial half of the distal epiphysis of the tibia also involving the medial malleolus. There is evidence of fluid in the tendon sheaths of the Tibialis posterior, FDL, and FHL. Wasting of the soleus and lateral gastrocnemius in the calf... the knee in genu varum... Tibialis posterior painful over the periosteal attachment... tendons showed hypo echoic areas... did not show features of hypertrophy or thickening... Power Doppler failed to highlight neovascularisation... needs to address abnormal biomechanics and poor muscle development in her lower leg with expert physiotherapy input..." The report went on and on.

Now, what is all that supposed to mean? I thought.

When a week later I received a detailed two-page clinical report full of medical and diagnostic terminology that I didn't understand,

I felt it was time to learn more about medical language. I bought a couple of books on dance injuries, and I looked up the meaning of each and every word in the medical report from Mr R. Lloyd Williams. The terminology in his diagnostic statement petrified me, and I wanted to understand every detail, what it all meant, and what exactly her injury was all about.

A week later, I met up with the School's nurse. She smiled reassuringly at me and said,

"Mrs Naghdi, most dancers cope with one or another injury throughout their career. You should see The Royal Ballet dancers. There is always someone who is injured."

"Always someone who is injured? Does this mean dancers dance with injuries?" I asked her.

"Some do," she replied. "It all depends on the severity of their injury, of course. An injury is very rarely career ending, and specialist revalidation will get a dancer 'up and running' again."

A fascinating new topic, that of Sports Medicine, opened up for me, and bit by bit I learned a new "language" – the medical language relating to sports injuries.

I also felt that I would need to interfere with her training for the very first time, which was something I had never done before. It was time for ballet dad to come onto the scene. I felt that if I were to call Miss Van Schoor, I would be looked upon as an overbearing, overprotective, overreacting, and interfering ballet mum. But if ballet dad were to call, it would be taken seriously. So, Yasmine's father called the School and asked to speak to Miss Van Schoor. Kamran asserted that Yasmine must stop practising grand jetés in class, and he asked for her YBDY solo to be changed from the jumpy Gamzatti solo to a non-jumpy solo.

Kamran told Miss Van Schoor, "Yasmine is adamant she wants to dance the Gamzatti solo for YBDY, but I doubt whether she has told you about the pain she is suffering in her shin. Her muscles and bones are just not ready yet to take on the intense and continued jumping." Endearingly, he felt very protective of his daughter.

Yasmine finally stopped resisting, and she accepted that if she continued to rehearse the Gamzatti solo, it would further aggravate her shin pain and eventually result in a bone fracture. That would have been worse. She reluctantly accepted to dance the Bluebird Variation instead. Interestingly, this was the very solo she danced years later in 2020, as a Principal ballerina, for the worldwide live cinema relay of *The Sleeping Beauty*.

At last, with the full diagnosis now behind us, she could resume her ballet classes and rehearsals, and the recovery process was supported by daily physiotherapy. We could breathe again. She knew how to tape her leg in order to increase the blood flow in the injured area, which also supported the affected area and simultaneously took some of the workload off her muscles, thereby aiding and speeding up the recovery of her injury. In a very short space of time I had learned a lot about injury management, and also about aiding the healing process through adapting nutritional needs, about managing and adjusting her training programme, and how to deal with the mental challenges that come with being injured.

Besides dealing with her injury and getting ready for the YBDY competition in March, as well as studying for her GCSE exams, she was also in the midst of preparing for the final appraisal class, taking place in February. The appraisal would decide if she was to continue her training at the Upper School or not. Although Yasmine was one of the top students in her class, we weren't at all sure if she was going to be offered further training at the Upper School.

Soon after the appraisal ballet class was over, Yasmine and her classmates assembled in the Salon, formerly used as a ballet studio but now used as a reception room. The Salon overlooks the beautiful far-reaching vista and grand avenue called the Queen's Ride. The atmosphere was, as to be expected, very tense; in fact, it must have felt like being inside a pressure cooker. In the meantime, the parents back home were nervously waiting for the result. One by one, the students were called into the office of the Ballet Principal Diane van Schoor, where Gailene Stock delivered the good or the bad news. It was organised in such a way that each pupil entered through one door and left via another door, so as to not encounter any of their waiting classmates.

It was late in the afternoon, around 5:30, when Yasmine called me. All she said was, "Hi mum, it's a yes for me. I am so happy. It's very hard over here and there is so much drama going on. I want to shout out my joy and skip around the garden of White Lodge, but I can't do that right now, not when half of my class got disappointing news."

Eight out of the fifteen girls had received a "yes", and unsurprisingly they each walked out of the Ballet Principal's office with a big smile on their face. However, they felt ill at ease being confronted by the classmates who had not been offered a place at the Upper School. It was a lesson in self-effacement. Once they had all reunited in the dormitory after supper, tears of sadness were shared with tears of joy. It was hard for both groups, but even more so for the few who had received a "maybe". Their future was still in the balance.

A few weeks later, the international students had to audition, and they joined in a ballet class with those eight female students who had received a confirmed place. That year, forty-five pre-selected girls from the UK, USA, Australia, Japan, and Europe auditioned for five available places. The few White Lodgers who had received a "maybe" also joined in that audition class. Those who in the end did not make it into the Upper School had their hopes squashed and their dreams seemingly destroyed. Clearly, this did not mean the end for them, as they could try to gain a place at other UK ballet schools, such as Elmhurst School of Ballet, or the English National Ballet School, Central School of Ballet, or any other ballet school they had selected. The division in the year group became very palpable as those told "no" and those told "yes" stuck together in their own groups. The dynamic within the year group became awkward.

Once the nerve-racking appraisals were behind her, Yasmine could concentrate on the Young British Dancer of the Year 2008 competition. The semi-finals took place at The Royal Ballet Upper School in Floral Street on Saturday afternoon. Yasmine danced the Bluebird Variation in *The Sleeping Beauty*, but something was amiss; something was lacking in her. I could see that very soon after she had come on stage. She looked tense, and she was far too restrained in her dancing. Nevertheless, she made it through to the Final. The following Sunday evening, the Final took place at the Linbury Theatre at the Royal Opera House, and First Year Upper School student William Bracewell won the First Prize.

The Easter break couldn't come soon enough as Yasmine and her classmates were beyond exhaustion. However, the Easter break was not really offering her a proper holiday; she had to study in preparation for her upcoming GCSE academic exams. It was a gruelling marathon of a year on all fronts – training-wise and academically.

On Saturday, 28 June 2008, the long-awaited White Lodge Graduation Ceremony took place. An official invitation letter had been sent out to all the parents, and this very special day was celebrated with a performance in the Margot Fonteyn Theatre. The performance lasted an hour and fifteen minutes, during which all the Graduates were able to show their level of achievement. Yasmine danced Mirlitons from *The Nutcracker* alongside four of her classmates, as well as the Dance of the Stars from *Cinderella* and Ashton's *Les Rendezvous* pas de six. After the performance, an open-air champagne lunch in front of the Dining Hall took place, and the female students changed into elegant cocktail dresses. It was a joyful and very proud moment for all the students, their teachers, and parents.

It was an established tradition that the female students wore a long gown and the male students a suit and tie – colour matched to the gown of their female "partner" – during the final presentation of their Graduation Certificate. Months before her big day, Yasmine had set her heart on a flowing, dusty pink and lilac silk organza gown, but we could not find her tiny size 4 in the UK. No other dress would do it for her. I called a family friend in Los Angeles who came to the rescue. She bought Yasmine's dream dress in the designer's flagship store on Rodeo Drive in Beverly Hills, and duly shipped it to London. A ballet mum's job description is endless.

Around 3pm, all the parents began to assemble on the lawn, facing the dual winding staircase at the back of the villa, waiting for their daughter or son to walk through the double doors of the Salon and onto the balcony terrace. At 3:15pm sharp, triumphant music played through loudspeakers, and one by one the female students appeared on the balcony. Their waiting "partner" bowed and handed over a long-stemmed rose, after which the "couple" slowly descended the winding staircase. Once they had reached the bottom of the staircase, they graciously curtseyed to Miss Stock, who gave each one of her students their Graduation Certificate. It was a highly emotional moment.

After Yasmine had received her Certificate, she walked towards Miss Van Schoor, curtseyed to her teacher of two years, and posed for photos to be taken. Kamran, Tatiana, and I were so proud of her, but I knew the real challenge would start now. Getting through the White Lodge training was one thing; getting through the Upper School training was an entirely different ballgame.

Twelve female students initially stood at the starting line in Year 7. Yasmine joined in Year 8 and two more students joined in Year 9, making up a total of fifteen female students. Eight of those fifteen made it into the Upper School – a record number in those days, so I was told. Those who continued into the Upper School had now only one goal: to get into The Royal Ballet.

When Ballet Principal Miss Van Schoor addressed her students in a goodbye speech, she said, "If you think your training in Year 11 was hard, you have no idea yet what hard means!"

That didn't seem to faze them, and they looked forward to the next chapter in their life. In a motherly and caring gesture,

Miss Van Schoor presented her students with a beautifully wrapped cookery book, *Delia's How to Cook*, and in her handwritten dedication she encouraged them to take good care of their health and nutrition.

On Saturday, 6 July, the annual Matinee Performance at the Royal Opera House took place, and Louise Bennett choreographed a new work especially created for the students of the Lower School. Patricia Williams, writing for *Dance Expression* magazine (September 2008) captured the atmosphere: "Ballet school children everywhere aim to entertain their parents at end of year school shows, and noisy is the hum of keen audience anticipation in the school halls up and down the country. But to perform for your nearest and dearest on the stage of the Royal Opera House is something else indeed. The excitement tinged with anxiety was tangible before even the curtain rose upon final year White Lodger Yasmine Naghdi. The huge weight resting upon her young shoulders as being the dancer to open the Matinee must have seen sleepless nights for her in the run up to 6 July. *Concerto in Red*, the opening ballet, is a specially choreographed story-less beautiful work to piano music of Scriabin by Louise Bennett, herself a former Royal Ballet School pupil. The admirable precision and unison of her dancing was remarkable... Indeed such was the polish and flair I had to keep reminding myself I was watching children perform."

After the Matinee at the Royal Opera House, all the parents returned to White Lodge. It was time to pack up and move out. Our car was stuffed with all of Yasmine's clothes, schoolbooks, bags of pointe shoes, her practice tutu, and all other ballet paraphernalia. She spent some time hugging her classmates – some of them she would see again after the summer holiday, but not all, as others would depart to another ballet school. As Yasmine was saying goodbye to all her teachers, I paused and took a deep breath. I reminisced and gazed over the expansive grounds of the main villa and the surrounding buildings. Six years had passed since that day in June 2002 when ten-year-old Yasmine had resolutely told me, "I want to go home!"

In the end, White Lodge became her "home", the place where she spent four years of her childhood, the place she was now to leave behind. To use a metaphor, the separation from White Lodge and the teachers was like having the "umbilical cord" severed: eight female and eight male students were "delivered" and ready to go to the Upper School. When we finally drove through the gate late that afternoon, we turned several pages in our book, and White Lodge was now to become a memory. A whole new chapter awaited Yasmine and us.

That summer, Yasmine decided to take a complete break from daily ballet classes and to enjoy six weeks of holiday. Before embarking on the next stage of her training at the Upper School, she joined family friends in Los Angeles and travelled through California without a care in the world.

The Royal Ballet School, White Lodge, delivered a group of exquisite young people, beautifully educated, highly self-disciplined, courteous, and well mannered, as well as having achieved high grades in their GCSE exams, all accomplished by growing up in an ultra-disciplined environment under the guidance of dedicated ballet and academic teachers, and House Parents. Whatever path they would eventually choose in future, they had learned valuable skills for life.

Chapter Seven

A Make Year or a Break Year? A Year of Crisis

If you think you are beaten, you are.
If you think that you dare not, you don't.
If you'd like to win, but you think you can't,
It's almost certain you won't.
If you think you'll lose, you've lost.
(Arnold Palmer, golf legend)

The Upper School is located in Covent Garden at No.46 in Floral Street, right opposite the Royal Opera House. This part of the School is where ballet students aged sixteen to nineteen continue the advanced training in classical ballet over a period of three years. After a successful audition, a small number of international students join the former White Lodge students. The four-storey building provides six air-conditioned modern studios, and one doubles up as a performance studio, with retractable seating for 180 guests. There are also separate shower and changing facilities for male and female students, a common room for the students to relax, a healthcare suite with a gym, a Pilates studio, and a physiotherapy treatment room. The academic section comprises four classrooms with computer equipment, an art studio, and an audio-visual room, all located on the fourth floor to take advantage of natural daylight. The studios are linked to the audio-visual room so that classes and rehearsals can be recorded, enabling students to improve their technique and performance quality.

The First Year students were housed at Wolf House, 5-6 Gliddon Road – a red brick, period mansion block situated in West Kensington and a short walking distance to Barons Court tube station. Henceforth, they were to commute daily on the London Underground to Covent Garden.

On the first weekend of September, all the students arrived, including the five new international students. Helped by their parents, they moved in with all their personal belongings. The hectic parental activity on Gliddon Road was quite a sight, as mothers and fathers walking to and from their cars carrying piles of bed sheets, towels, clothes, storage cabinets for their daughter or son's bedroom, cooking pots and pans, plastic food containers, small flower pots and plants, and a week's worth of fresh food supply. They reminded me of a foraging colony of worker ants who are out and about on a mission, marching in a straight line across the kitchen floor.

The students had a common kitchen and a living room where they were free to socialise every evening, watch TV, eat, hang out, and relax together. The House Parents had a bedroom on the ground floor, very well located – especially on Saturday night – in case any student tried to sneak in, or out, past the curfew time. On Saturday evenings, they were permitted to go out, but they had to be back at Wolf House by 10pm. From now on, they had to do their own food shopping and cook their meals, as well as doing their own laundry.

Yasmine grew up in Central London and she was familiar with the area, as we lived only a ten minute-drive away from Wolf House, but for all the other students, living in Central London was a new experience. Yasmine entered her 1st year at the Upper School alongside seven of her former classmates, and five other female students – from USA, New Zealand, and Norway – joined their year group. Brandon Lawrence (now Principal dancer, Birmingham Royal Ballet) and Jacopo Bellussi (Principal dancer, Hamburg Ballet) were two of the fifteen boys in Yasmine's year.

The ballet classes were geared towards the Russian style of training, and during the first week they were given time to adapt.

The first weeks went by without any problems, and Yasmine loved her newly acquired independence. The addition of a few international students in their class contributed to an increased competitive atmosphere and intensity. Coming out of White Lodge, they all felt on top of the world; after all, they had trained at one of the top and most prestigious, world-renowned ballet schools. However, the addition of the international students made them conscious of their new reality: there was now competition from the "outside world". Without any doubt the White Lodge students were exquisitely trained and polished, with clean placement, lovely and expressive use of the upper body and beautifully arched feet. They were all well acquainted with the Ashton style of dancing, displaying gorgeous "épaulement" and fast footwork – some of the many hallmarks of The Royal Ballet School's System of Training that set them apart from their international classmates, who could learn a lot from them. The Royal Ballet School's System of Training is defined on the School's website as: "...to produce dancers with a strong, clean, classical technique with great emphasis on artistry, musicality, purity of line, co-ordination, and a quality of movement, free of mannerisms. Our System of Training has been developed to encompass the eight years of full-time training offered at The Royal Ballet School. It draws upon the valuable traditions from different schools of classical ballet, retaining the best that was created by our predecessors while embracing the demands of classical dance technique as is required of professional artists today. At all times emphasis is placed on natural flow of movement, musicality, the joy of dance, and the development of the dancer as an artist."

The international students, however, possessed an openness of personality; they were more up front, more outspoken, and far less self-conscious, since their personalities had been shaped in a different way as a result of growing up in a different country with a different culture, as well as in a different training environment. Likewise, in that aspect, the former White Lodge students could learn from them.

The pace of training soon intensified, and they realised their current training level was nowhere near that of Year 11. By late October, Yasmine began to remark incessantly that she felt exhausted, although feeling tired had been part and parcel of her White Lodge years. I reminded Yasmine of the words of Miss van Schoor: "If you think you have had it hard in Year 11, you don't know what hard means!" But I also began to question if perhaps her diet might not have been at an optimum, and if the lack of particular essential nutrients was contributing to her physical fatigue. From that moment onwards, I became interested in sports nutrition. I bought a few excellent books to assist me in getting a better understanding of the subject. One of the books I bought was written by Dan Bernardot, PhD, Human Kinetics, 2006, titled *Advanced Sports Nutrition. Fine-tune your food and fluid intake for optimal training and performance.* I wanted to comprehend what a body in high intensity training needed in order to sustain continuous energy, and what exactly created muscle fatigue.

It was a complex subject, particularly as I had never studied the subject of nutrition, and it was an umpteenth eye-opener. The more I understood about sports nutrition, the more I recognised the importance of the right intake of very specific nutrients at specific timings throughout her training day. It is called Nutrient Timing. When Yasmine told me that many of her classmates avoided eating carbohydrates in the evening for fear of putting on weight, I told her this was the wrong thing to do. I reminded her of the fact that there are two groups of carbohydrates, and that in the evening she must eat foods in the complex carbohydrates group. At White Lodge their meals had been carefully prepared for them and great effort had been made to introduce the youngsters to a variety of healthy food. Themed world food feasts were regularly organised by the meal planners to encourage the children to have a healthy relationship with food and to discover new food they usually would not eat at home. It was admirable how the White Lodge staff responsible for healthy meal planning often pulled out all the stops, even paying attention to creating a very inviting visual display of various foods on offer. At the Upper School, however, they had to learn to take care of their own daily meal planning. I could easily imagine that Yasmine, once back at Wolf House after an intense day, would hastily make a salad, open a can of beans or tuna, eat some fruit, and not make sufficient time to properly cook, nor shop, for nutritious food. They were all understandably concerned about keeping their weight under control, and there was intrinsically nothing wrong with that if this was achieved by eating a healthy balanced diet, ensuring that all vital nutrients needed on a daily basis were incorporated in the meals. I wanted Yasmine to realise that it was essential to give her muscles a substantial boost at lunchtime, and to adopt a proper diet. I told her that it was no good to train intensely all day without also paying attention to what she ate in order to re-energise her body and aid rapid repair of her tired muscles.

It is totally wrong for a dance trainee to think that little eating will do them any favors and that it will keep their weight in check: it just wastes away the muscles, and they deprive themselves of vital energy sources needed to sustain their intense daily training. Some people tend to wrongly assume that dancers can't or shouldn't eat much and that they have to carefully control their diet. But if a dancer doesn't eat, or eats too little, she or he will simply have no energy to get through the daily rehearsal schedule and the evening performance. The attitude of dancers and athletes towards their food intake has certainly changed a lot over the past decade and a half, and increased research and knowledge of the nutritional needs of a body in training has significantly benefitted them.

Yasmine, in a way, was lucky as she always had a very fast metabolism and she could (and still can) eat whatever she wanted to, but the issue here was: did or did she not get the appropriate nutrients at the right time throughout the day? Was her vitamin intake adequate enough? It was not about eating when she felt hungry, but about eating the right food at the right time of the day in order to sustain the physical demands of her training, thereby also minimising the risk of injury. Physical breakdown can take place anywhere in the body for a variety of reasons. The key point is that physical fatigue is a limit that lies in the muscles, or in the inability of the brain to activate the muscles. It is all about trying to balance the physical or mental buffer, combined with the desire to perform. That produces a constant need of reaching a balance between the two. Fatigue is not always in the mind. Fatigue and the limits to performing are not simply mental barriers or "mind over matter". It is true that mental strength and willpower are crucial key factors, and are part of the solution, but they never beat physiology.

I urged Yasmine – no later than fifteen minutes after she had finished her last ballet class of the day – to drink cacao powder mixed with milk, eat a double sandwich with turkey (less fat and higher in protein than chicken), a banana and dates, and also one square of 70% dark chocolate, in order to stimulate the insulin needed to kick-start the glycogen recovery of her muscles. That was the optimum timing needed for rapid tissue repair, to prevent muscle soreness and to aid fast recovery from muscle fatigue. The greatest discovery I made was how important it was for her to eat simple carbohydrates together with protein within forty-five minutes after she had finished her training day. That is exactly the time when the body is at its highest capacity to restore glycogen in the muscles, and it is a complex chemical process going on in the body. Drinks, healthy snacks, and fruit were all easy to carry in her ballet bag, so that she could immediately start loading up her body with nutrition instead of waiting ninety minutes or so until she had arrived back at Wolf House. It takes eight to twelve hours for a full micro muscle repair, so the earlier she ate a highly nutritious evening meal, the faster her body could go into recovery mode and be ready for training the next day. The School had always stressed the importance of healthy eating, but in the end, it is up to the individual student to take responsibility for their own health.

I set her on the road to a better understanding of her nutritional needs by putting together suitable and easy recipes to cook in the evening, including an itemised food shopping list for her to use as guidance whenever she went food shopping, specifically with her nutritional needs in mind. As a result, she began to take a great interest in what to eat and when to eat, and it soon became second nature for her to take the nutritional needs of her body-in-training very seriously. Before long, Yasmine told me that she noticed a huge difference in being able to sustain her energy supply levels throughout the day. She had come a long way from being the fussy toddler who only wanted to eat French baguette and pasta.

By early November, I became increasingly aware when Yasmine was at home for the weekend that she looked down in the dumps. She was uncommunicative and remote. She seemed unhappy, and I began to look for possible signs of depression. When I initially queried what was the matter, she was quite evasive, as if she did not want to admit any weakness. All she was prepared to say was that she didn't feel any connection with her teacher. One Saturday evening, I urged her to open up and to tell me more. At long last Yasmine told me that she felt a high degree of acrimony, she felt repeatedly put down and derided for no reason, giving me concrete evidence and contextual examples. She emphasised that she had tried very hard to fight off all those distressing feelings and to not let it get to her, but it wasn't working. Clearly, she was suffering emotionally. Undoubtedly, even if the increased demands of her training could rationalise adverse effects, in the end I could not find any justification for the effect being inflicted on her self-esteem, based on what she had told me.

When Yasmine further divulged that she was every so often reprimanded, and as a consequence had to do press-ups after press-ups on the sideline whilst the others carried on in ballet class, the situation became highly alarming to me. After she had unerringly disclosed what was going on, and what the teacher had said to her, I did not react, nor did I show I was feeling sorry for her. Yet deep down I was greatly concerned to see her joy and enthusiasm for ballet rapidly disappearing. The strong sense of self that Yasmine had built up at White Lodge had steadily diminished and faded away, and eventually it was shattered. At this stage in her growth towards becoming a professional dancer, I was under the impression that the much-needed constructive support was seemingly non-existent. As a consequence, this led to Yasmine dismissing all of her accomplishments, her self-doubt increased, her pure delight in movement progressively lessened, and so did her enthusiasm for her ballet training. Something was clearly going in the wrong direction.

A parent-teacher meeting had been scheduled by the end of November for all the parents to attend, and I hoped to be able to figure out what was wrong. Throughout her training at White Lodge, I had never personally approached a teacher with the intention to complain or question any aspect of her training; I had always had complete trust in her teachers. That Saturday morning, Kamran and I went to the meeting hoping to have a constructive dialogue with her teacher in order to understand, or at least to get more clarity about, what was the matter. We were open for discussion. If we could come to a mutual understanding that the training approach was beneficial to Yasmine, then we could work together in optimising her training and her progress. That's how we saw it.

Instead, it was a cold and distant meeting, without much room to discuss Yasmine's personal issues or needs. I had hoped to be able to shed more light on Yasmine's mind-set with her teacher. Perhaps it was all about her different assimilation of learning and attitude towards her determination to be successful. Yasmine always loved having strict teachers who drove her hard in order to get the best out of her, but that clearly was not the issue here. We did consider the possibility that the teacher might have had the best of intentions and that this was her distinct approach to make Yasmine work harder. However, based on all of Yasmine's feedback, we had reasonable doubts, and we were under the impression that allegedly it wasn't coming from a well-intended place. Her training tactic just wasn't delivering the anticipated result, and this we wished to evaluate, modify, and discuss.

We expected the teacher to be sufficiently open-minded in order for us to examine all the issues, facilitating a better comprehension of Yasmine's disposition as well as drawing her attention to Yasmine's deteriorating state of mind. We felt that our well-intended support would be beneficial in order to ameliorate whatever tension there was between Yasmine and her teacher. Kamran also attempted to enter into a productive conversation, hoping this would aid the teacher to work more positively with Yasmine. We were, however, met with little or no receptiveness. The atmosphere felt very awkward, and we felt ill at ease. It felt more like a one-way dialogue. Her replies were evanescent and shallow, and Kamran and I were under the impression that we were simply wasting her time, as well as ours. We quickly realised that any attempt to have a constructive dialogue was of no use. Maybe we simply expected too much of a teacher-parents meeting.

We left the meeting with more questions than answers, and we had no other choice but to draw our own conclusions. We talked to the other parents, but none of them were confronted with any of our concerns. We simply could not understand, nor accept, her attitude towards Yasmine. It caused Kamran and me a great deal of heartache because we knew how passionate our daughter was about ballet. Her desire to practice was shrinking on a daily basis, no matter how bravely she tried to ignore it all and to get on with it. This should have been a time during which her development into a strong and expressive personality was given room to blossom, and facilitate the growth of her artistry. We were totally exasperated with the situation, and so was Yasmine.

After the unproductive meeting, I realised that the only thing that was within my control was to help Yasmine get through this very negative time in her training, and I wondered, yet again, how I could facilitate this. Yasmine should have been able to focus on her technical and individual progress, not having to be on her guard in ballet class for fear of ramifications. It became very obvious to me that the atmosphere was not going to help Yasmine achieve what she wanted to, and I felt there was just no room to allow her further individual development and contentment. She would simply stagnate and become disillusioned. Daily frustration or tears weren't going to get her very far; she had already tried to suppress them. It would only diminish her energy and become a pointless distraction.

I was very much torn between wanting to ignore it all, or doing something about it. After all, she was in high-level training, and the School was preparing the students for eventual entry into professional life. I was of the opinion that nothing warranted excuses or complaints, that hardiness was the only way to succeed, but on the other hand I vehemently disagreed with the way Yasmine was being treated. I knew that if she had a nurturing teacher who showed strong belief in her, Yasmine would blossom, whereas now her further technical, artistic, and personal development were being impaired. I could have asked for a meeting with Gailene Stock to discuss the situation, but I decided not to, and I held back. Instead, I decided to support Yasmine in figuring a way out of this difficult situation.

One afternoon in December, a few weeks after the parents' meeting, Yasmine was yet again told to go and repeat a string of movements – as well as do press-ups – on the sideline, while the rest of her class continued their normal exercise routines. As soon as Yasmine finished, she was instructed to replicate the same movements all over again until her face turned white from exhaustion. To Yasmine, this felt like a grossly undeserved punishment (a punishment?? what for??) as well as a belittling treatment. She was told in a browbeating manner that she didn't deserve what came her way, and much more.

That evening, Yasmine called me in tears. I could hear she was at breaking point, and every last inch of her self-esteem had completely faded away after being mentally crushed and belittled for the umpteenth time. She didn't seem to have much inner strength left to fight back. Her sense of personal worth and competence – something I had worked so hard to establish when she was fourteen years old – was now totally undone. At that point, I felt the situation was getting out of hand, and I was left to pick up the pieces.

A page in Yasmine's diary reads: "On Monday morning, our teacher came into class in a very bad mood, and she took it out on everybody in our class, but especially on me. I had been performing over the weekend with The Royal Ballet, so I hadn't had much rest, however I was still working just as hard as always, but my teacher thought differently. She said that she could not see any sweat on my leotard and thereby concluded that I wasn't working hard enough. Really? This is so annoying, as I hardly ever sweat! Why is she picking on me using such a useless statement? We later had her again for class in the afternoon, and I got an exercise wrong after misunderstanding what she asked us to do. She ordered me to go to the side and do press-ups as a punishment. During that time my anger was building up. I felt so belittled. It also made me feel embarrassed in front of all my classmates. After the press-ups, I carried on, fighting back my tears, trying to hide them. I thought she could be testing me out to find out just how much toughness I can take, but if this is her way to toughen me up, it just won't work. I am so irritated with what I consider to be undeserved punishments. She wrongly assumes I can't be bothered to work. The tension goes on and on. I guess I must learn to keep all my emotions inside and to not show any! A few weeks ago, she asked me the meaning of my surname. I replied saying that in my father's mother tongue (Farsi) it meant 'cash'. Thereafter she would rarely call me by my first name. She now calls me 'Miss Moneybags'," or she says, 'Moneybags, go and do your exercise in the centre.' I have to deal with the ongoing scorn and belittlements on a daily basis. I have had ENOUGH, and I will NOT take it any LONGER!"

A much-needed and welcome morale boost came from Gailene Stock, who selected Yasmine and William Bracewell to perform at Ivy House, the former home of legendary ballerina Anna Pavlova. After the performance, Kamran and I passed by Gailene in the corridor, and she stopped us. It was the first time Gailene had directly engaged with us. We had never before spoken with her about Yasmine, so we were a little surprised when she addressed us there and then. She smiled and said, "Well, as for Yasmine, she is such a beautiful dancer, she is so gifted and she has amazing facilities. Yasmine will go very far."

Kamran and I really didn't know what to say besides thanking Gailene for her generous remark. Driving back home, we wondered why, if Gailene was thinking so highly of Yasmine, her teacher gave us the impression she seemingly thought otherwise. What was going on? We just could not understand or make any sense of it at all.

Despite the unresolved situation, Yasmine's ballet report at Christmas was very pleasing. Her pirouettes were described as "virtuoso", and she was doing exceptionally well, according to Gailene Stock's written comments. Over the Christmas period, Yasmine and some of her classmates danced with The Royal Ballet's corps de ballet in *The Nutcracker* as Angels and as Snowflakes. Yasmine loved it, and I was relieved to note that her love of performing had not disappeared. In spite of this happy intermezzo, the tension increased at the start of the second term when her year group was preparing for the collaboration with a London Hip-Hop theatre company and a youth dance group, as part of the School's Outreach Programme. Her class was to perform a pas de deux and a group dance choreographed by their teacher. During the afternoon rehearsal preceding the evening performance, the situation quickly deteriorated (again), and it all went rapidly downhill for Yasmine. Tension between her and her teacher intensified, and Yasmine was no longer prepared to put up with it. She had come to the conclusion that whatever she did, no matter how she did it, it repeatedly left her open to disapproval. And that afternoon in mid-February was the last straw for Yasmine. When, straight after the rehearsal, the teacher pulled her aside to express her annoyance, Yasmine really had had enough. After all the preceding, ongoing mentally affecting and soul-destroying remarks, Yasmine unsurprisingly picked a solemn crisis, which is totally normal when someone is already mentally very much on edge, and this was the straw that broke the camel's back. She ran to another studio to cry.

Yasmine became so distressed and cried non-stop, but she only had twenty minutes to compose herself and be ready to go back into the studio to dance. Yasmine asked her closest friend to give her a slap in the face so that she could regain her focus. Her friend, needless to say, resolutely refused, but Yasmine kept insisting. In the end, her poor friend did not have much choice but to slap her in the face. For someone to have to go to such an extreme just shows that Yasmine was under considerable duress and with her dignity totally shattered.

Eventually, she wiped dry her tears, touched up her eye make-up, and twenty minutes later walked into the studio where the performance was about to commence. With her tears barely dried and an artificial smile on her face, she could just about cover up her emotional pain and total despair.

The collaborative performance finished at 7:30pm, and soon after I received a phone call from Yasmine asking me to pick her up at Gloucester Road tube station. Her phone call alarmed me, since she would habitually return to Barons Court. It was highly unusual that she asked me to pick her up midweek, but I did not ask any questions. I knew there must be a serious reason why she had called me. All I said was, "OK. What time?"

"8:15pm," she replied and hung up the phone.

I sensed something was seriously wrong. It was dark, very cold, and it was snowing outside. *Never mind the snow,* I thought. I got into my car and drove to Gloucester Road tube station and waited for Yasmine to come out of the tube station. The street was completely deserted. As I sat in my car waiting for her, I stared at the lamppost right in front of me, watching the snowflakes softly swirl down, and my mind wandered back to the past years and all we had been through just to get Yasmine to this stage in her training. I had a feeling she didn't want it any more; this year had given her little or no joy at all. I reflected on the whole scenario, and I knew all that Yasmine was longing for was to be treated with respect. She yearned for a teacher who unmistakably showed belief in her, and she was no longer prepared to take condescending remarks and distressing insolence. I was absolutely livid, but I had to keep my own distress to myself right now.

Just as I glanced in my rear mirror, I spotted Yasmine walking towards the car with her head down. When she opened the door, I immediately sensed her deep sorrow. She was extremely tense. She literally threw herself into the passenger's seat and started crying inconsolably. I flashed back to when I heard her cry as a little girl, after she had told me, "I want to go home!" that day at the White Lodge Summer Fair.

It was a cry from her heart, a distraught cry, revealing a total breakdown. To see my daughter sitting next to me, shaking, with her head lowered, and with her hands held in front of her eyes, completely shattered me. I so wanted to cry with her, but I had to stay strong. I let her cry and I stayed silent. Words were of no use. I realised that all she needed was this private moment to let it all out, and to be able to release her pent-up stress and anguish.

As the wipers of my car listlessly removed the snow on the front window, I stared out of my side window, with a sobbing Yasmine sitting next to me... and tears started rolling down my cheeks. I suddenly felt totally helpless and very alone in all this.

After a while, Yasmine collected herself, and she looked me straight in the eyes. All I saw was her smudged and run eye make-up. It had been a day filled with tears. She took a deep breath and said, "Take me out of there! Take me to the Paris Ballet School or any other ballet school in the world, but I do not want to continue training with her. She is totally killing my love of dance. I have had enough! I can't stand it any more! I will not take it any longer! Just take me out of there!"

I only just about managed to collect myself, as I didn't want her to see my tears. I asked Yasmine if she wanted to come home with me or to go back to Wolf House. I anticipated that she would want to come home, but instead she asked me to drive her straight back to Wolf House in Barons Court.

"I am too tired, too exhausted, and I have a splitting headache. Please, mum, just take me back to Wolf House for now, and I'll see tomorrow morning how I feel."

It profoundly saddened me to see my daughter in such a state of total distress. How would I be able to sleep tonight? She, who loved ballet with all her heart, had asked me to take her to Paris or anywhere else to continue her ballet training. How could that be? I wanted to cry at the thought of it. I had had enough, too. It had consumed me, and our family life, for too long, and I was about to agree with Yasmine. There was complete silence between us in the car as I drove slowly through the snow to Barons Court.

Suddenly, something inside me gradually altered my thoughts. I don't know what brought it on. Contrary to my maternal instinct of wanting to protect my daughter, hug her, and take her back home with me, I found myself doing the complete opposite. The drive between Gloucester Road and Barons Court had instigated a catharsis in me. It had allowed me to think through the entire scenario and how I was going to deal with Yasmine's distress. Taking her out was to give in; it was to take the easy way out. Encouraging her to stay, to confront and deal with her situation, was to teach her how to fight back, how to be resilient, and how to allow no-one and nothing to come between her and her love of ballet.

I turned into Gliddon Road and parked my car right opposite Wolf House. By now, the snow was falling heavily. Just as I was about to open the door of the car, I suddenly remembered a Shakespeare quote from *Hamlet*: "*I must be cruel only to be kind.*" And it gave me the necessary strength that I needed in order to get myself, and her, through all of this.

I took a deep breath and said to Yasmine, "Let's get out of the car and we'll go for a walk."

Yasmine looked perplexed, but we started walking in the snow in the deserted street. At that moment, it felt as if Yasmine and I were all alone in the world. I felt really miserable walking in the cold with her, but the walk allowed her and me "time-out" from the crisis and tension that had been building up over a period of several months. I walked with my arm around her shoulder, pulling her very close to me, initially without saying a word, taking in the eerie silence.

After walking up and down the street, I stopped under a lamppost and faced Yasmine. I asked her to look me straight into the eyes. Where I found the audacity and the courage to be really tough on her, I just don't know, but I said sternly, "Now listen to me carefully, Yassi. Let me ask you one simple question: are you a loser or are you a winner? You know the choice is yours. You either take charge of your own destiny, or you give in and somebody else will have won, but it will not be you! Are you going to let your love of dance be smashed by one person? Or are you going to rise above it all and come out much stronger and fully in charge of yourself?

"Why would you let a teacher get to you? You should be far above this!" I went on. "You know what? I want you to return to class tomorrow morning with your head held as high as you can. Build a thick wall around you so that nothing can hurt you any more, no matter what she says. Remember, no-one can make you feel inferior. You are your own boss, and all the rest is peripheral. Let all that negativity bounce off you; you simply don't hear it, and do class just for yourself. Rise above all this, Yassi, and come out stronger because of it.

"You have been 'climbing the Himalayas' for so long now, you have reached several base camps, and there are a few more peaks to climb before you can reach the summit. Don't give up midway, and do remember your primary schoolmaster telling you: 'No mountain is too high to climb.' The pain you feel in your heart today will be your strength tomorrow. Return to class tomorrow morning, and instantly forget about today. Put today in a box, tie a ribbon around it, and throw it away as far as you can. Learn to never ever linger on negativity; simply move on, feeling stronger, knowing that you have the capacity to rise above it. You must liberate yourself and stop blaming any external or uncontrollable factors, as these will prevent you from moving forward. They'll keep you imprisoned because of conditions that have previously affected you.

"Evaluate, understand, and discard," I told her. "Make a fundamental change in your thinking pattern, and let go of any emotions that adversely influence your mind; they take up too much energy. Do make those fundamental changes overnight, and fully master and control your state of mind by tomorrow morning. Make it clear that YOU are the winner – and no-one else!"

All of a sudden, a dispirited Yasmine had a revitalised look in her eyes. She was bravely taking it all in, swiftly digesting what I had just told her. She put her mind over matter, knowing that if you want something badly enough, no sacrifice is too great.

There we stood, the two of us, and we gave each other a very long hug. Then Yasmine took a deep breath and let out a huge sigh. Finally, all she said to me was, "I am so sorry, mum, that I had to bother you tonight." Then she crossed both hands on her heart and whispered in my ear, "Thank you, mum, you have just healed me."

She kissed me goodbye, then crossed the road and courageously walked towards Wolf House. At the top of the staircase, just before opening the front door, she turned around, looked in my direction (I will never forget that image), and with a subdued smile on her face she waved goodbye and disappeared inside.

I was finally alone, and now it was my turn to take a very deep breath and to let down my guard. It was my turn to break down, and I did. Months, perhaps years, of quiet frustration and annoyance all came to the surface, and tears rolled down my cheeks. The snow by now was coming down much faster, and I could feel the snowflakes landing on my face, mingling with my tears. There I stood, alone on the pavement, immobilised, as if frozen in time. I remember standing there for quite a while; I must have been in a state of shock about how I had reacted to my daughter, who I loved so much. It had taken all my energy to go against my maternal instinct of wanting to protect her, but I knew that would not do her any favours. Making her stronger would.

Yasmine took my advice, and the next day she returned to the School. She was determined she would not let any adversity during class affect her. She had built a wall around herself overnight, and nothing would get through that wall ever again. She had understood the power that lay within her, and she would not let anything have such adverse control over her. I had made her understand that she must learn to always draw strength out of negativity and setbacks, and to never allow any detrimental situation or circumstances to control her. I had made her accept the fact that she was never going to be able to change the attitude or the teaching method of her teacher, and so she would be better off changing herself. If she wanted to become a professional ballet dancer, she would have to face a lot of hurdles, and she had to equip herself with the relevant mental tools in order to become stronger.

I had used a psychological thought-stopping strategy: her mind had to be "tricked", and by giving her new hope through redirecting her focus, we established some sort of "magic" with the aim to calm her down, and to be able to create her own enthusiastic environment. She needed to free herself from anxiety in order to allow herself greater mental freedom and strength. She needed to find the right balance between her attention to detail and her intensity in concentration, and to be free of adverse class distractions. It was a very depressing battle to fight in order to come out of a corrosive situation as the winner.

Well over a decade later, this episode in her training still remains the saddest one for me personally. It still causes me sadness whenever I remember that chapter, and thinking about it still results in bringing a few tears to my eyes. To have seen my daughter crumble and falling apart, almost losing what she loved doing most in life and what she had worked so hard for over the years, was very hard to process. It could all have been so very different – a year in which she could have blossomed and progressed, as the others did in her class. Instead, it had slowed her down.

In the end, the way I looked at it was that it is always easier to put the blame elsewhere, even when it is fully justified. But letting herself down because of the particular circumstances would have excused Yasmine from moving forward. Enduring the situation enabled her to learn how to be intrepid, but above all to learn how to let go of it all. With great effort, it empowered her in the end. Negativity should never dominate one's thoughts, because it badly conditions and affects a person. By evaluating and understanding her situation, it was possible for Yasmine to free herself, and she created renewed energy in order to deliver the strength to make changes to her inner state of mind. By and large, blaming someone else gives immediate relief from a distressing situation but the ability to take direct control is far more empowering. Sixteen-year-old Yasmine ultimately demonstrated her aptitude to deal with a serious personal crisis.

However, her treatment never deserves any rationalisation or justification whatsoever. Those scars will remain forever – with her as well as with me. The only prolific thing that came out of her mentally "injurious" experience was that it made her so much tougher, and she became more determined than ever before. In the end, we used our disapproval of the circumstances to turn around the various issues so that they worked to Yasmine's advantage. I had shown her how to empower herself through using her adversity, how to take back full control, and to never run away from any difficulty, but to fight back, to face up to, and solve the problem herself.

It is absolutely true that elite-level ballet training necessitates extreme self-discipline and demands an enormous amount of patience and great resilience. Nevertheless, her learning curve – facilitating acquiring those very skills – could have been experienced and achieved in a different way, in a mentally unrestricted and unaffected manner, and without the deep hurt she had to unnecessarily endure. It was not the intense physical demands of the ballet training that had affected her, but the disproportionate, wholly avoidable, negative effects on her mental state that caused her total loss of self-esteem and sense of personal competence – in other words, her sense of self worth.

The beauty of my relationship with Yasmine was that we always felt we were in this together, she knew she was not alone, and we were a team through and through. She would always take every single word of advice and guidance I gave her, and she had complete trust in me. We really were one mind in two different bodies. She realised that every piece of advice I had given her in the past had delivered the required result, and that it had enabled her to grow stronger.

She had fought a tough mental battle, and she would score double victory just one month later by winning the Young British Dancer of the Year 2009 competition. No-one realised what a disheartening time Yasmine had gone through. Remaining optimistic during hard times is not easy, but the most successful people are those who succeed in looking at setbacks as opportunities for a comeback. They are persistent and refuse to succumb to any adversity. Yasmine had understood that the only person who could stop her now was herself. She had conquered her self-doubt, and she stopped being overly harsh on herself. She knew that developing a negative self-image was choosing a path to self-destruction. Yasmine had learned an immensely valuable lesson for life. In addition, she eventually understood that she could never be in control of her performance without being in total control of herself, physically and mentally, and she memorised:

"If you think you are beaten, you are
If you think that you dare not, you don't
If you'd like to win, but you think you can't,
It's almost certain you won't.
If you think you'll lose, you've lost
For out in the world you'll find
Success begins with a fellow's will.
It's all in the state of mind.
Life's battles don't always go
To the stronger or faster woman or man
But sooner or later the woman or man who wins
Is the woman or man who thinks she or he can."

(Arnold Palmer – golfer)

All this had been going on at the same time as she was preparing for the Young British Dancer of the Year 2009 competition. She was working harder than ever before and drew strength out of her difficult situation. She no longer felt any need for tailored feedback from her teacher, as she realised that was never going to come. From now on, she was going to do it by herself.

The Young British Dancer of the Year (YBDY) competition was created in 2000 and was aimed at students in ballet training. The event encouraged the most talented young people in the UK to compete against each other. The year 2009 marked the 10th anniversary of YBDY, and as a result attracted prestigious international judges, including Elisabeth Platel, former Danseuse Etoile of the Paris Opéra Ballet and then Director of the Paris Opéra Ballet School. She was joined by Wayne Eagling (Artistic Director of the English National Ballet), Cynthia Harvey (former Principal ballerina of The Royal Ballet and American Ballet Theatre), Dame Monica Mason (then Director of The Royal Ballet), Steven McRae (Principal dancer, The Royal Ballet), David Nixon (Artistic Director, Northern Ballet), and Monica Zamora (former Principal of Birmingham Royal Ballet).

Yasmine reached the semi-finals on Sunday, 8 March, and she had just one week to prepare for the finals which were taking place the following Sunday. During that week, Principal ballerina of The Royal Ballet Zenaida Yanowsky coached Yasmine, and I remember her telling me how refreshing and stimulating it was to be coached by Zenaida, whose artistry she greatly admired. It is poignant to know that eight years later, Yasmine would be allocated Zenaida's dressing room after Zenaida had danced her retirement performance at the end of Season 2016-2017, coinciding with Yasmine's promotion to Principal ballerina.

By 6:30pm on the evening of the final, people began to arrive at the Linbury Studio Theatre, an adaptable, secondary performance space built below ground level within the Royal Opera House. The bar area was buzzing, and there was a lot of excitement in the air. The last time a female dancer had won the competition was in 2005. Since then, James Hay, Sergei Polunin, and William Bracewell had taken the title. Could Yasmine break the male dancer dominance? By 7pm we were all seated and eager to watch the competition. There were sixteen finalists participating – amongst others were Brandon Lawrence, Teo Dubreuil, Sean Bates, Barry Drummond, Francesca Hayward, and Laura Day. Yasmine was Candidate No. 15, and she first performed the Summer Fairy Variation in *Cinderella* Act 1. We had seen some amazing finalists and beautiful variations, such as Bluebird, Lilac Fairy, Siegfried, and Florestan Variations, and Giselle Act 1 Variation. *How on earth was Yasmine going to impress the judges with her slow flowing, non-virtuoso Summer Fairy Variation?* I pondered. There was neither great technical difficulty nor any display of high extensions or high jumps. This was technically an "easy" variation, but a very hard one to pull off in order to get the necessary mature artistry across. However, applause and cheers followed after her Summer Fairy Variation. *Not bad*, I thought. *Now let's see how she is going to tackle the second one.* Her second was the Female Variation of *La Esmeralda*, which I had been told wasn't a competition favourite because many ballet lovers considered it a rather "brassy" variation, especially when not danced properly.

Again, all the candidates lined up and performed beautiful variations such as the Sugar Plum Fairy, the Silver Fairy in *The Sleeping Beauty*, a Kitri, and another Bluebird Variation. The name of the second last participant "Candidate No.15 – Yasmine Naghdi" was called out to perform her second solo. As she came onto the stage waving her tambourine, she displayed attitude, confidence, and personality. This was technically a much harder solo, and it gave the judges the opportunity to judge her on her technical skills. She danced with great control and never exaggerated her movements for the sake of showing off her technical mastery. It was delicately and confidently danced to perfection, and in full control of the difficulty of all the steps. Huge applause and cheers followed again.

As this was the 10th Anniversary, the audience was treated to individual performances by all the previous winners during the deliberation time of the judges. Lauren Cuthbertson (2001) and Sergei Polunin (2007) danced the pas de deux from *The Nutcracker*, James Hay (2006) danced a Variation from *Paquita*, Jamie Bond (2000) a Variation from *Sylvia*, Aaron Robinson (2004) a Variation from *Diana and Actaeon*, Anniek Soobroy (2002) a Variation pas de six *Laurencia*, Joseph Caley (2003) danced Hamlet's Variation *The Shakespeare Suite*, William Bracewell (2008) the Siegfried Variation *Swan Lake* Act 1, and Ruth Bailey (2005) danced a Variation from *Raymonda*. Seeing the line-up of all the previous winners rightly turned the competition into a prestigious evening. Thereafter followed the Presentation of the Awards by Elisabeth Platel.

Once all the judges and the previous winners had lined up on the stage, the winner was announced. The Sibley-Dowell Award went to Brandon Lawrence; 3rd Place was awarded to Dominic Withbrook; 2nd Place to Sean Bates; and the overall winner was announced as – Yasmine Naghdi. Monica Mason was there to congratulate Yasmine, as well as Gailene Stock and Ricki Gail

Conway, Sponsor of the YBDY competition since its inception in 2000, and all the other esteemed judges.

In total contrast... Yasmine's own ballet teacher was nowhere to be seen.

What a glorious night it was for Yasmine after all that she had been through over the past months, and just reward for having found the courage to carry on. Winning the competition symbolised her double victory: a physical victory as well as a mental one.

Dance critic Deborah Weiss, *Dance Europe* (April 2009) wrote: "...But it was sixteen-year-old Yasmine Naghdi, the winner, who from the moment she stepped on stage in her Summer Fairy Variation really captured my interest. She has that indefinable special quality combined with grace, charm, musicality, and technique. Her stunning Esmeralda Variation raised expectations even further. A bright future? I need shades already!"

Katherine Sorely Walker, *Dance Expression* (May 2009), wrote: "The winner – a decision with which I entirely agreed – was sixteen-year-old Yasmine Naghdi, a product of White Lodge, who is in her first year at the Upper School. Her elegant style and great sensitivity had been apparent in the very difficult Summer Fairy variation from Ashton's *Cinderella* (a role created in 1948 by the lovely Violetta Elvin); she clinched her claim to the title with a delightful account of the tambourine variation from *La Esmeralda*."

Straight after winning YBDY 2009, Yasmine participated in the Ursula Morton Choreographic Award, organised by The Royal Ballet School. She poured all her emotions into it, and she created her own short ballet titled: "*Enough Said!*"

Over the past months, I had reinforced that instead of suppressing what she didn't want to happen, she must focus on what she did want to happen and to focus on neutral thoughts to block out any adversity. It had greatly aided in relieving her tension, but after Easter I pondered what internal battle she continued to fight. She was restless, often agitated, and unfulfilled. Her inner torment and tension reminded me of a pupa trying to wriggle herself out of a cocoon in order to emerge as a butterfly, freeing herself to fly away. Suddenly it all became so clear to me, and I realised the answer was simple and pretty straightforward. Yasmine needed a different environment. She had just turned seventeen, and I felt she needed breathing space. More and more, I became convinced that what she needed was to be able to experience ballet classes and dancing in an entirely new environment, and with new people around her, to stimulate and inspire her. The "corset" didn't suit her any longer; she wanted to set herself free and disjoint herself. I sensed urgency in her, and it felt as if she did not want to lose any time. She was on the "run" again; she was tired of "walking". She was a bird ready to fly the nest, I guess.

I could easily understand how she felt. I had had enough encounters with artists in the past, and I had listened to their frustrations whenever they wanted to create yet another work of art. Exasperation is part and parcel of an artist's life. I began searching for a summer school for advanced students and stumbled on the Prague Summer School, run by Daria Klimentova, who at that time was a Principal ballerina at the English National Ballet. It was April, and acceptance to the Summer School had closed.

Never mind, I thought, and I called up the Registration Office. I spoke to Ian Comer, the Administrator, and I told him that Yasmine was a Royal Ballet School student and about to finish her 1st year at the Upper School. I asked him if it was too late for her to be accepted to attend their 8th International Ballet Masterclasses in Prague from 26 July to 7 August. Without any hesitation, Ian happily accepted Yasmine. The combination of high-profile teaching staff in the wonderful city of Prague would offer a completely new cultural experience for Yasmine, as well as indulging in her passion. I was as enthusiastic about going to Prague for two weeks as she was. I planned to visit all the museums, art collections and galleries, and enjoy the great architecture, while she would attend her daily ballet classes. We both couldn't wait for the school year to end, and were looking forward to our trip.

After the Easter break, preparations for The Royal Ballet School Matinee commenced, and that year the Upper School students performed *The Dream* on the stage of the Royal Opera House. For the performances at the Linbury Studio Theatre, Gailene Stock had cast Yasmine as Princess Aurora in *The Sleeping Beauty*, and she danced the Grand pas de deux, as well as the pas de cinq with classmates Karla Doorbar, Francesca Hayward and Sophie Allnatt as Attendants.

Under the Directorship of Gailene Stock, it had become a tradition to end the Royal Opera House Matinee with the Grand Defile. It really is a spectacle, and a most emotional moment for teachers, students, and parents, as it marks the end of a year of achievements. Each year group has their own colour of uniform: the Lower School pupils wear a leotard and a short skirt; the Upper School female students wear their practice tutu. One by one, the pupils of White Lodge and the students at the Upper School come running onto the stage, year group by year group, and they form neat lines. Seeing Yasmine running on, after this very stressful year, caused a steady stream of tears to run down my cheeks, but I also had a big smile on my face. I was so very proud of her, knowing that she had got through her ordeal thanks to her immense fighting spirit.

It was on a sunny Saturday afternoon in July that Yasmine and I arrived in the centre of Prague. The taxi dropped us off on Jilská, just around the corner from the Old Town Square, and we walked the short distance to the apartment I had rented for two weeks. We entered a charming courtyard, filled from top to bottom with hanging flowerpots. After I had picked up the keys from the concierge, we lugged our suitcase up to the second floor. We loved the apartment, with its interior designed in a quirky 1980s style. I threw open all the windows and I could hear someone nearby playing Chopin on the piano. I instantly felt in heaven! After we unpacked, I handed Yasmine the second set of keys and told her she just had to pretend I was not there at all, that this was to be the start of a new beginning, and she should feel free to come and go, and to do as she liked. We would each go our own way during the day and connect in the evenings, if she wanted to. She had just turned seventeen, and I desperately wanted her to feel unrestricted and free. All I wanted to see was a smile on her face.

Her fellow international students were staying at the nearby YMCA, just across the beautiful historic market place, and I encouraged her to go out in the evenings and to have fun. As far as I was concerned it was "Me, Myself, and Prague", and Yasmine could do whatever she wanted to do. I did urge her to make time to pop into any of the beautiful churches where daily concerts were being played, even if it was only for five minutes. I also encouraged her to enjoy the open-air concerts, or to simply go for a stroll around town and hang out in the park on Kampa Island with her fellow Summer School students. I wanted her to move away from the feeling she was a student, and to feel she was a young professional, in charge of herself.

The Summer School was meant to keep advanced and professional ballet dancers fit during the summer. Yasmine was coached in solo dancing and virtuosity by some of the greatest ballet teachers, such as Elisabeth Maurin, former Etoile at the Ballet de l'Opéra National de Paris, and now teacher at the Paris Ballet School; Cynthia Harvey, former New York City Ballet Principal ballerina; Julio Bocca (former Principal dancer with American Ballet Theatre, and Argentinian superstar); Tamas Solymosi (former Guest Principal with American Ballet Theatre, the Bolshoi, Vienna State Opera, and English National Ballet); Tamara Rojo (then Principal ballerina of The Royal Ballet); and Daria Klimentova.

The following morning, we set out to explore the area. We walked across the Old Town Square and visited the Cubist Museum, followed by a late lunch in the beautiful gardens of the Kempinski Hotel. Yasmine and I always enjoyed being together, and we had so much to talk about. She was very keen to hear what life had been like for me as a university student, and how it had felt living on a campus. We talked about my time in the Middle East, when working there as an archaeologist, and later on about my anthropological research amongst various tribes in Africa. She wanted to know all about my career at Sotheby's that had lasted up until she was born, and she asked if I had any regrets at giving up my international career in order to take care of her, instead of employing a nanny. We had hardly had any mother-daughter time to reminisce over the past five years and to just sit and chitchat about life, nor had she hitherto shown much interest in my life before she was born. My life and hers, at her age, could not have been more different. Our time away from London – and certainly the past year – did us both a lot of good.

Her ballet classes commenced on Monday morning, and she was very much looking forward to her first day. I looked through the open window and watched Yasmine as she walked off to her first ballet class at the National Theatre, a mere three-minute walk away. She turned around and smiled as she waved at me. She looked so happy, and ultimately so was I. The weather was absolutely glorious, and that morning I set off to explore the city. I walked across the Old Town Square – a market place dating from the 12th century, with varied stunning architecture built in the Romanesque, Baroque and Gothic style, each bringing with them stories of wealthy merchants and political intrigues. I continued strolling around in Staré Město, and I passed by a bronze sculpture by the artist Jaroslav Róna of Franz Kafka – a Bohemian novelist and short-story writer whose works I had loved reading as a student. The sculpture was titled "Description of a Struggle".

"How apt is this title," I mumbled to myself.

For a moment, I gazed at the sculpture whose title reminded me of the past year, but I soon moved on. There were more beautiful things to see and to enjoy. In a nearby authentic French bistro that became my go-to place for breakfast, I picked up a few chocolate croissants and headed straight to the Kampa Museum by the river, where I spent the entire day discovering stunning contemporary art by Czech artists, as well as the Frantisek Kupka collection. In Prague, there is art wherever you go, and I was in paradise.

That evening, as I was preparing a meal for myself and listening to my favourite J.S. Bach Cello Suites, Yasmine walked through the door. I had not seen her so bubbly in ages, and we chatted animatedly about our day. By the end of her first week, Yasmine hugged me and said, "You know, mum, I have re-found my love of dancing."

Some days, when she finished ballet classes early, we went for a stroll around the Old Town, popping into art galleries or into one of the many beautiful Baroque churches. In each one of them, a concert would be taking place by Albinoni, Bach, Dvorak, or Smetana. One late afternoon, I took Yasmine to the Kampa Art Gallery, housed in the old Sova's Mills on Kampa Island in Malá Strana, where I introduced her to the Czech and Slovak artworks. Amongst many fascinating works, we both particularly loved those by Jiří Kornatovský and Václav Cigler. Later on, we sat by the Vltava River until sunset and discussed the artworks we had just seen. Those beautiful precious moments are engrained in my mind forever.

On her free Sunday, we climbed Petrin Hill – perfect for a leisurely summer walk away from the hustle and bustle of tourists. We walked through the orchards full of fruit trees, with branches weighing heavily with apples and pears, and enjoyed a far-reaching view over sunny Prague. It was heaven. We settled for lunch in a small family-run restaurant in the middle of the vineyard, and as we sat down, I could sense she was in high spirits. She reminded me of a wilted tulip that had come back to life after dropping a few copper coins into the water. Yasmine was noticeably blossoming again.

Later that afternoon, we strolled around the nearby monastery, so perfectly peaceful, and we chatted non-stop. In the early evening, we returned to our apartment after crossing the illuminated Charles Bridge – a medieval stone arch bridge that crosses the Vltava River, linking the Castle Town with the Old Town. We decided to dress up and treat ourselves to a fancy dinner in a French-Asian fusion restaurant, called Nostress, that I had discovered during one of my daily explorations.

Those two weeks in beautiful Prague provided Yasmine and me with a much-needed breath of fresh air. They were also the happiest days we shared during her entire training. If she had had any reasons to doubt herself, they had now vanished, and she was very much looking forward to a fresh start in the 2nd year at the Upper School. She had now mastered the four Cs of mental strength: control (believe you are in the driving seat); commitment (set your goals and do not distract from achieving them); confidence (cultivate self-belief); and challenge (see challenges, adversity, and change as opportunities rather than as threats).

It had been an emotional rollercoaster of a year – a year in which she had yearned for freedom; a year in which she had wanted to set herself free; a year that could have broken her, but instead had made her so much stronger, and had set her up for what was to come over the following decade. I am so glad to have been able to be there for her, and to help her get through that difficult year, and I am pleased she willingly took my advice on board and followed my guidance. Together, we had overcome her personal crisis, and she had learned how to firmly bounce back from setbacks.

Winners always bounce back faster from setbacks. But we were not there just yet.

Chapter Eight

Seven Months in the Graduate Year

"Learn to control your emotions or they will control you.
We all choke but winners know how to handle choking better than losers."
(Edgar Martinez, American former professional baseball player)

The Second Year and the Graduate Year's accommodation was situated in Covent Garden, at Jebsen House in Mercer Street, a mere two minutes' walk from the School, which was pure bliss after a year of commuting from Barons Court to Covent Garden. On Monday, 7 September, 2009, all the students returned to Floral Street for another year of training, and Miss Young welcomed the female ballet students into their Second Year. The former White Lodge students were familiar with Anita Young, since she had taught them in Year 9 at White Lodge.

However, three days into the start of the Autumn Term, I received a phone call from Yasmine, just after 1pm, to tell me that she had been called into the Director's office that morning. Gailene Stock had informed Yasmine that she would not need to do the Second Year of training, and that she could move up straight away into the Graduate Year.

That morning, Gailene had walked out of her office with Yasmine, and they passed by the studio where her classmates had already begun their ballet class. They surely must have wondered what was going on when they saw Yasmine walk past the studio. The Graduates' class had also commenced when Gailene walked in with Yasmine and announced that she was joining with immediate effect. Glenda Lucena, a former Principal dancer and later assistant to the Artistic Director of Ballet Metropolitano de Caracas, the Ballet Nacional de Venezuela, was their interim teacher. The Graduate teacher Petal Miller Ashmole's husband, David Ashmole (former Principal dancer with The Royal Ballet) had sadly passed away on 3 September, 2009, and she would be absent until January.

As the ballet class progressed from the barre to the centre, Yasmine began hearing sneering remarks such as, "That's another contract less for us." Understandably, she wasn't received with open arms. Competition levels were at their highest in the final year, as they were all desperate to secure a professional contract, and in the first instance a contract with The Royal Ballet. At the end of class, Yasmine sat down in a corner of the studio to take off her pointe shoes when a Japanese student walked up to her and introduced herself as Mari. She hugged Yasmine and welcomed her into the Graduate Year. She was Yasmine's only friend in the year group, and to this day they have remained close friends. Whenever Yasmine is in Tokyo, to dance with The Royal Ballet or dancing in a Gala, Mari and Yasmine always meet up.

Later that afternoon, Gailene called me, and she was interested to hear what had happened to Yasmine over the summer holiday. Initially, I wasn't too sure how to take her question, but I told her that I had taken Yasmine to the Prague Summer School, and that was it. I think Gailene had already noticed well before the summer holiday that Yasmine was ready to fly the nest. She said she would have loved for Yasmine to compete at the Youth America Grand Prix (YAGP), but skipping the Second Year made that now impossible. No doubt, Gailene already knew what was in the pipeline for Yasmine, but we had to wait until the end of January to find out.

In early November, Gailene invited Yasmine to join a small selection of Graduate students to travel to Canada. Over one hundred elite-level ballet students from fourteen major international ballet schools arrived in Toronto for the first ever Assemblée Internationale 2009. Participating ballet schools included the Paris Opera Ballet School (Ecole de Danse de l'Opéra National de Paris), the John Cranko School in Stuttgart, the Royal Danish Ballet School, the San Francisco Ballet School, and the National Ballet School of Cuba. The Assembleé Internationale 2009 was hosted by Canada's National Ballet School as part of its 50th anniversary celebrations, and was the brainchild of Mavis Staines, the School's Artistic Director. The occasion offered an unprecedented opportunity to compare and contrast a wide selection of international talent, as well as a summary of current trends in ballet choreography. Besides a conference, the week-long event included choreographic workshops and performances, providing a rare opportunity for Artistic Directors, ballet teachers, and students to exchange a variety of dance styles and training methods from around the world. This experience forced the students out of their comfort zone: they took daily classes taught by different teachers, and these consisted of a mix of students who had all trained in different styles. It was an eye-opener and an enriching experience for Yasmine. She loved taking ballet classes with the Cuban and Danish ballet students, and she formed an enduring friendship with Robert Binet (Choreographer and Graduate of the National Ballet School of Canada) and Andreas Kaas (Principal dancer, Royal Danish Ballet).

Two evening performances were scheduled during that week, and the second evening was more classically based. The Royal Ballet School presented two works: Liam Scarlett's (then a corps de ballet dancer with The Royal Ballet) *Toccata*, and Kenneth MacMillan's stunning *Concerto* 2nd Movement pas de deux, performed by Yasmine. Gretchen Ward Warren, author of *Classical Ballet Technique*, Professor Emiritus of Dance at the University of South Florida, and former ballet mistress of American Ballet Theatre II, wrote in her lengthy report (*Dance View*, Vol.27, no.1, Winter 2009): "*Toccata* unfortunately offered no surprises to hold our interest in this rather dull, unmusical choreography. The well-rehearsed students, however, showed nice attack. The second Royal Ballet School offering, Kenneth MacMillan's *Concerto*, was an entirely different story. The beautiful, effortless dancing that ensued was cool and mysterious. Full of clean British line and restrained passion revealed many memorable moments. Best of all was the realisation that we were watching a future ballerina. Seventeen-year-old Yasmine Naghdi, with her gorgeous leg line and extensions, remind one of a young Darcey Bussell. Yasmine wove a spell! One sustained lift with her stretched like a bird in flight, balanced on her partner's shoulder, created a stunning image. It was hard to believe she was still a student. She's ready for the big time!"

On their last day, the students were invited to participate and share all of their experiences, thoughts, and opinions on their own training in "Think Tank" sessions for all the ballet schools' Artistic Directors, and in an Ideas Exchange Student Forum. Since childhood, we had always encouraged Yasmine and Tatiana to have a go at public speaking, and often on Sunday evenings after dinner, it became a spontaneous habit for them to select one of my art books, pick any picture they liked, and prepare a short talk about why they had chosen it and what attracted them to the picture. Speaking in front of the classroom had been very much part of my school education in Belgium. On a monthly basis, we had to prepare a talk about a pre-set subject in front of our class. Since this was not done at their school in London, I ensured that it was part of my daughters' home education. We also encouraged them to think "outside the box"; Kamran even stressed for them to think "without a box", and he always urged them to develop their own independent thinking.

Clearly, Yasmine had taken all this on board, and when she had the opportunity to engage for the first time in public speaking during the Ideas Exchange Forum, she addressed the audience, who asked her questions about her training at The Royal Ballet School. Very well intended, she explained that she sometimes felt as if she was living "inside a box". She felt, because of the intensity and inherent nature of the ballet training programme, that there was little time available to explore other art forms, such as going to the theatre to watch a play, attend an opera performance, a dance performance at Sadler's Wells, or an art exhibition. This statement clearly did not go down well with Gailene Stock, who presumed it was a direct criticism of the School, whereas Yasmine's stated observations were merely a generalised comment on the all-consuming nature of ballet training. I guess she hadn't phrased her thoughts in a well-defined manner. Flying back to London, Yasmine could feel that Gailene Stock had not been in the least impressed with her public statement, and she got the cold shoulder treatment. Yasmine couldn't even begin to comprehend why, and nor could we.

After the New Year, Petal Miller Ashmole came back to teach the Graduate students, and Yasmine spent her last three months at the School with her. She was a wonderful teacher, and she treated each one of her students as a young professional, with respect and a great understanding of their mental needs and artistic development. Petal was a real mother figure to her students, allowing them to blossom, and her total objectivity and impartiality as a teacher set her apart. Each and every one of her students was a potential star; she gave them all equal attention, and she never crushed their personalities. There was no partiality provoking unnecessary tension amongst the students, and she guided them most wonderfully towards the end of their eight-year training programme.

All the Graduate Year students had already started the process of auditioning with various companies in the United Kingdom and abroad well before the Christmas holidays, except for Yasmine. October, November, and December had been very busy months for her. Besides flying to Toronto, she had also travelled to Tokyo to perform, and to Hamburg for the 20th Anniversary of the Ballettzentrum Hamburg – John Neumeier, where she performed Kenneth MacMillan's *Concerto* 2nd Movement. Simultaneously, she was also involved in rehearsals with The Royal Ballet's corps de ballet in *The Sleeping Beauty*. I knew from previous years that any available contract with The Royal Ballet was likely to be offered by November, if not December, but those months had passed by without any offer. By mid-January, it suddenly dawned on Yasmine that she hadn't lined up any auditions.

Gailene Stock was at the annual Prix de Lausanne competition, and Yasmine had just started with her new ballet teacher, Petal Miller Ashmole. It was high time to start organising her auditions with various ballet companies, so I wrote an email to Miss Miller asking when Yasmine could be excused from ballet classes. However, by the third week of January, contract offers suddenly started coming in from ballet company directors who had seen her year group at work in a ballet class in October. Yasmine received a phone call from Wayne Eagling, then Director of the English National Ballet, who offered her a contract and implied a fast-track path for her. The Royal Ballet of Sweden also headhunted her, and they offered her a Soloist contract. The San Francisco Ballet also expressed great interest in her, and Birmingham Royal Ballet was also an option.

In her email reply, Miss Miller insisted that Yasmine must wait before embarking on auditioning abroad until Gailene Stock was back from the Prix de Lausanne by the end of January. I took that as a hint, and I waited before organising flights for Yasmine to audition with international ballet companies.

On the morning of Friday, 29 January, Yasmine was called into the Director's office after her ballet class, and Gailene Stock informed her that Dame Monica Mason had offered her a contract with The Royal Ballet to start in eight weeks' time, on 1 April. This meant that Yasmine was not going to be able to complete her Graduate Year, nor perform her scheduled *Concerto* 2nd Movement on the stage of the Royal Opera House for the annual end-of-year Royal Ballet School performances. Life as a student would come to an abrupt end for her, and from one day to the next Yasmine had to make the transition from being a student to being a professional dancer.

In the end, she received five contract offers without having to audition in the UK or abroad. She realised that she was in a very fortunate position. Of course, Yasmine followed her heart and accepted a contract with The Royal Ballet. After all, she had been involved with the Company since her childhood, when she first appeared in *Cinderella* as a Spring Page. She had seen Miyako Yoshida, Alina Cojocaru, Tamara Rojo, Marianela Núñez, Leanne Benjamin, Roberta Marquez, Zenaida Yanowsky, and Mara Galeazzi dance in front of her eyes whenever she performed as a White Lodger in *Swan Lake* and *The Nutcracker*, and as an Upper School student in *Cinderella*, *The Sleeping Beauty*, *The Dream*, and *Romeo and Juliet*.

Joining The Royal Ballet was a natural transition for her, albeit not one taken for granted. That year, she was the only female Graduate to be offered a permanent contract with The Royal Ballet.

Back in those days, the Aud Jebsen Dancers Programme – providing a year of apprenticeship to selected Graduate students, enabling them to work alongside the corps de ballet – did not exist. In Yasmine's day, you were either offered a contract or not. Those Graduate students who were not offered a contract with The Royal Ballet had to audition for a position with other national or international ballet companies.

However, just before Yasmine embarked on her professional career, there was something important to celebrate. 2010 was a monumental year for Birmingham Royal Ballet, marking the 20th anniversary of their move to Birmingham from Sadler's Wells in London. David Bintley, Director of Birmingham Royal Ballet, invited Yasmine to dance Kenneth MacMillan's *Concerto* 2nd Movement, during their Gala on 9 and 10 March. Three weeks before joining The Royal Ballet, Yasmine took the train to Birmingham and danced at the Birmingham Hippodrome. Her first ever public performance review came from dance critic Ismene

Brown of the Arts Desk, who wrote: "What a pity that they can't have the dazzler of last night's show, the student from The Royal Ballet School, Yasmine Naghdi, who made her own compelling, stern beauty of MacMillan's *Concerto* pas de deux. She is off to The Royal Ballet this year, not Birmingham Royal Ballet!"

Nine years later, Yasmine would, for the first time in her career, reprise this role – but now as a Principal ballerina, and her performance was live streamed worldwide.

As she graduated, I graduated, too. She had shared all her tears and successes with me over the past five-and-a-half years, and together we had learned so much. Metaphorically, our journey felt like having crossed the ocean in a sailing boat. Sometimes the winds were strong, and the waves were rough; at times they were high, and they could have potentially wreaked havoc. I looked out for the gusts and the darker patches on the water. I regularly eased the mainsheet in order to de-power the sails for short periods of time, and I maintained the balance between all the sails.

When heavy weather threatened, potentially leading to our boat capsizing, I did not drop the sails to start up the motor and head for the land. Instead, we stayed in the open water, reefed the sails, rode out the storm, and adjusted the sails. Sometimes, we sailed upwind, other times downwind, but together we rode those waves, faced the turbulent winds, as well as the storm. And in the end, we safely crossed, and arrived on the other side of the ocean. When all was said and done, a great sense of satisfaction derived from our successful crossing and winning the race.

A new and exciting chapter waited for both of us. Many new challenges would need to be overcome before Yasmine would finally reach the highest rank in her profession: the rank of Principal ballerina.

Rhapsody. First Season (2010 - 2011) as an Artist with The Royal Ballet. Copyright: Dave Morgan

La Bayadère. Second Season (2011 - 2012) in the corps de ballet. Copyright: Dave Morgan

Jewels. Performing Rubies, partnered by Valentino Zucchetti. Season 2011 - 2012. Copyright: Dave Morgan

Romeo and Juliet. Yasmine and Matthew Ball dancing their debut. October 2015.
Copyright: Dave Morgan

Romeo and Juliet. Backstage post-performance. Yasmine and Kevin O'Hare, Director of The Royal Ballet. October 2015.
Copyright: David Long

Romeo and Juliet. Yasmine and me backstage, after her debut as Juliet. October 2015.
Private photo

La Bayadère. Yasmine as Gamzatti. November 2018.
Copyright: Bill Cooper

La Bayadère. In her dressing room, with Sanja Golubovic, Make-up, Hair and Wigs Artist at the Royal Opera House.
Copyright: Dasa Wharton

La Bayadère. Touching up her make-up before going on stage.
Copyright: Dasa Wharton

La Bayadère. A moment of stillness before going on stage.
Copyright: Dasa Wharton

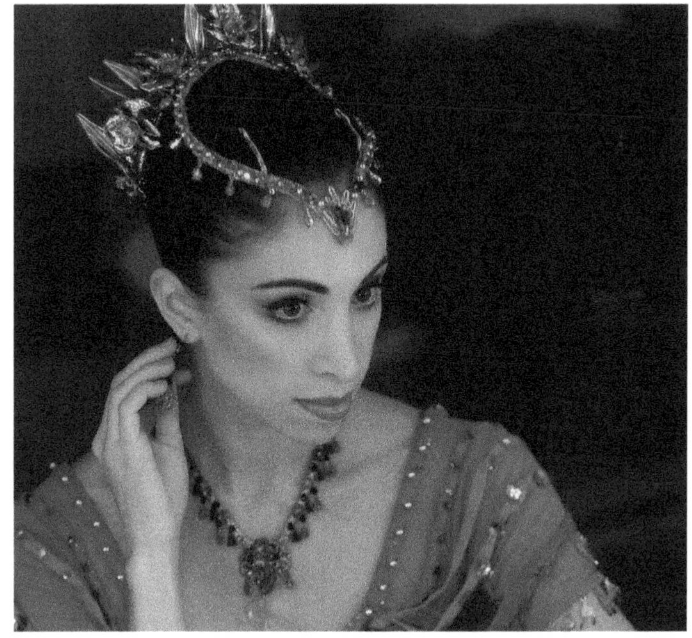

La Bayadère. Yasmine in her dressing room, pre-performance.
Copyright: Dasa Wharton

Back stage, post performance, *La Bayadere.*
L to R: me, Assistant House Manager Salvatore Scalzo, Riccardo, Yasmine, Kamran, Tatiana, a guest.

Swan Lake. Yasmine as Odette. June 2018.
Copyright: Bill Cooper

Swan Lake. Yasmine as Odile, partnered by Federico Bonelli.
Copyright: Bill Cooper

Swan Lake. Getting ready for the performance.
Copyright: Andrej Uspenski

Swan Lake. Yasmine as Odile, before going on stage.
Copyright: Andrej Uspenski

Swan Lake. Odette tutu fitting with John MacFarlane, Scottish designer. Costume department at the Royal Opera House. Copyright: Bill Cooper

Swan Lake. Odile tutu fitting. Copyright: Bill Cooper

Swan Lake. Yasmine and me, backstage post-performance.
Private photo

The Nutcracker. Studio rehearsal. Sugar Plum Fairy with Matthew Ball as the Prince.
November 2020.
Copyright: Andrej Uspenski

The Nutcracker. Backstage. Matthew Ball, Kevin O'Hare, Yasmine and Alexander Agadzahnov, Senior Teacher and Répétitieur to the Principal dancers.
December 2018.
Private photo

Onegin. Yasmine as Tatiana with Bennet Gartside as Prince Gremin.
February 2020.
Copyright: Andrej Uspenski

Onegin. Yasmine and Federico Bonelli, curtain call. February 2020.
Copyright: Rob Sallnow

Onegin. Yasmine, Federico Bonelli, and Bennet Gartside. Curtain call.
Copyright: Rob Sallnow

Onegin. Back stage post performance, Yasmine and Riccardo.
Private photo

The Sleeping Beauty. Yasmine as Princess Aurora and Matthew Ball as the Prince. Opening Night. 7 November 2019. Copyright: Rob Sallnow

The Sleeping Beauty. Curtain call Copyright: Rob Sallnow

The Sleeping Beauty. Back stage post performance with Kevin O'Hare and Dame Monica Mason.
Private photo

Don Quixote. Dancing Kitri. March 2019.
Copyright: Andrej Uspenski

Coppélia. Yasmine as Swanilda and Matthew Ball as Franz. December 2019.
Copyright: Andrej Uspenski

Coppélia. Back stage with Kevin O'Hare and Matthew Ball.
Private photo

Giselle. After the main stage rehearsal, with her coach Leanne Benjamin, former Principal ballerina of The Royal Ballet. February 2018.
Copyright: Dave Morgan

Giselle. Act II - Giselle's grave in the forest. Yasmine and Matthew Ball. February 2018.
Copyright: Dave Morgan

Giselle. Curtain call
Copyright: Rob Sallnow

Giselle. Backstage with Kevin O'Hare, Koen Kessels (Conductor and Music Director of The Royal Ballet) and Dame Monica Mason.
Private photo

Giselle. Yasmine in her dressing room after her performance.
Private photo

Two Pigeons. Back stage post performance with Riccardo, James Hay, and Fumi Kaneko. February 2019.
Private photo

Elite Syncopations. Partnered by Ryoichi Hirano. October 2017.
Copyright: Dave Morgan

Concerto, 2nd Movement. Partnered by Ryoichi Hirano. November 2019.
Copyright: Tristram Kenton

The Firebird. Partnered by Edward Watson. May 2019.
Copyright: Tristram Kenton

Margot Fonteyn: A Celebration. Yasmine as Medora partnered by Vadim Muntagirov as Conrad in Le Corsaire. 8 June 2019. Copyright: Andrej Uspenski

Symphonic Variations. With Vadim Muntagirov. Season 2016 - 2017. Copyright: Dave Morgan

Apollo. Yasmine dancing her debut as Terpsichore with Vadim Muntagirov as Apollo. May 2020.
Copyright: Andrej Uspenski

Ballet Imperial. Yasmine and Friedemann Vogel, Principal dancer of Stuttgart Ballet, in Japan performing with Tokyo Ballet, "Alina Cojocaru Dream Project 2020".
Copyright: Hedemi Seto

Ballet Imperial. Yasmine and Friedemann Vogel at the Orchard Hall of the Bunkamura cultural complex in Shibuya, Tokyo.
Private photo

Attending a Charity Fundraising dinner at Annabel's, Mayfair. June 2019.
Private photo

Yasmine and Riccardo at the Frieze Art Fair Preview, London. October 2019.
Private photo

Palais Garnier. Opening of the Paris Opera Ballet Season 2018 - 2019, with Pat Cleveland and Hedier K. Loubier.
Private photo

Yasmine and her sister Tatiana. 2018.
Private photo

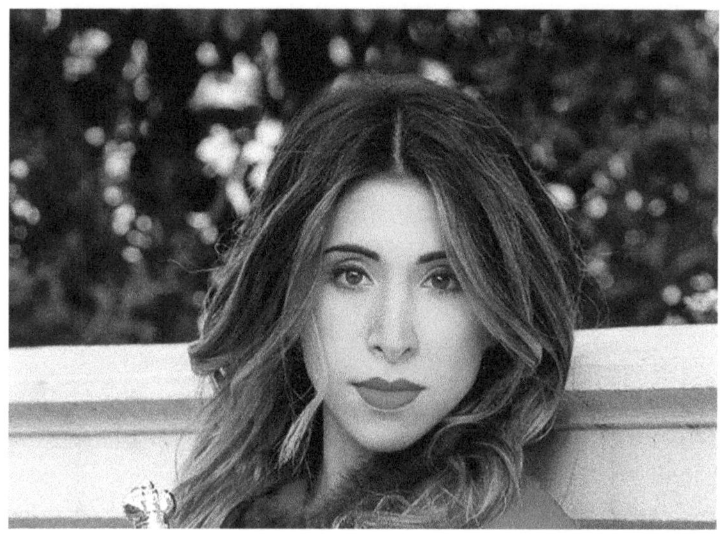

Portrait of Yasmine.
Copyright: Andrej Uspenski, 2020.

Portrait of Yasmine.
Copyright: Andrej Uspenski, 2017.

Chapter Nine

From Corps de Ballet to First Soloist

"Talent alone is just not enough. The best dancers are the hardest workers; they learn from the past whilst preparing for the future, but they perform in the present. They are quick but they never hurry when it counts."

(Unknown)

On Thursday morning, 1 April, 2010, Yasmine walked the short distance from her student accommodation on Balderton Street, just off Long Acre, to Floral Street. Instead of walking up to the entry door of The Royal Ballet School on the left side of the street, she crossed the road and entered the Stage Door of the Royal Opera House. From one day to the other, she had to make the transition from being a student to being a professional dancer, just eighteen months after she had graduated from White Lodge.

For a while, she continued living at the School's accommodation in Mercer Street with the Second and Third Year students, until mid-June when she left on Tour with The Royal Ballet to Japan and to Barcelona. Principals she had so admired during her training at the School were suddenly her colleagues. It felt surreal. When she joined the Company, Tamara Rojo, Carlos Acosta, Alina Cojocaru and Johan Kobborg, Miyako Yoshida, Leanne Benjamin, Roberta Marquez, Ivan Putrov, Rupert Pennefather, Marianela Núñez, Laura Morera, Edward Watson, Zenaida Yanowsky, David Makhateli, Steven McRae, Sarah Lamb, Federico Bonelli, Lauren Cuthbertson,

Thiago Soares, and Mara Galeazzi were the Principal dancers; Sergei Polunin was a First Soloist.

A note had been put onto The Royal Ballet Announcement Board to say that Yasmine Naghdi was joining the Company as a member of the corps de ballet on 1 April, 2010. Joining on April Fools' Day, however, was not a joke. She walked into the corps de ballet dressing room, but she had not been allocated a dressing table. Not sure where she should install herself, she looked around the room and noticed that Romany Pajdak was moving some of her personal belongs to make space for her.

As she entered the large light-filled studio to take Company class that morning, the only available place Yasmine managed to find at the barre was right behind Tamara Rojo. In her days, a corps de ballet dancer would not really engage in a direct conversation with a Principal dancer. A corps de ballet dancer would certainly never position her or himself right next to or behind a Principal dancer during Company class. That was considered a very arrogant thing to do. So, as far as Yasmine was concerned, she couldn't possibly place herself right behind Tamara Rojo, but there was no other place available.

Yasmine dropped her bag at the barre with some hesitation, and just as she started to warm up, Tamara turned around and said, "Just ensure you know the sequence of the exercises."

By 11:45am, Company class finished, and Yasmine had just fifteen minutes to get to the rehearsal studio. With the dancers' energy levels now much higher, the studio rehearsals for *Cinderella* commenced straight away. Some of her former Second Year classmates had joined the rehearsal as covers, and they were standing at the back of the studio to watch. Since Yasmine had already danced with the corps de ballet in *Cinderella* as a Graduate student over the Christmas period, she knew her role as one of the Stars. Once the rehearsal commenced, Yasmine stood amongst the corps de ballet dancers with a big smile on her face. It was her first day, after all, and she just couldn't hide her excitement.

One dancer in front of her turned around and said, "How nice to see someone here with a smile on her face!" But another dancer nearby sneered and said, "Well, let's see how long that will last!"

Earlier that morning, some corps de ballet dancers had questioned Yasmine why she was not wearing her School leotard. They evidently had not read the Director's announcement, and Yasmine explained to them that she was no longer a student but a Company member. Over the coming weeks, her initial excitement was increasingly overshadowed by feelings of loneliness. One day, as she walked through a studio door, right behind a female Soloist, the door was not held open as a matter of courtesy but was left to bounce back into her face. Yasmine quickly realised that new obstacles would need to be overcome and it was not going to be on a bed of roses.

As a student, she had been used to working full out throughout the day, but now she found herself with a lot of spare time. She was not dancing at all, but standing at the back of the studio... as a cover, to watch the corps de ballet rehearse. As a cover, she not only had to ensure she learned her own place, but her eyes had to be on every other dancer's steps and placing. A cover can be asked at any time to stand in and take over from an ill or injured corps de ballet dancer. *Cinderella* was in full swing, and there were just two Triple Bills left to perform before the end of the Season: *Electric Counterpoint/Asphodel Meadows/Carmen* and *Chroma/Tryst/Symphony in C*. Yasmine was only cast in *Symphony in C*, so she had very little to do except stand at the back of the studio and watch the majority of the rehearsals. Welcome to life as a first year corps de ballet dancer!

Of course, it was a most frustrating feeling after so many years of intensive training at the School. Now she either finished straight after Company class in the morning, if she was not involved in any rehearsals that day, or by 6:30pm. Adjusting to life as a young professional dancer, and to the many new circumstances and all that it entails, is not to be underestimated.

Fortunately, there was a wonderful all-female spa on Floral Street, hidden behind an unassuming door. The Sanctuary Spa opened over forty-three years ago to provide a haven and a retreat for The Royal Ballet's dancers. The waiting area was filled with rich, deep shades of purple and burgundy, highlighted with gold and cream accessories. Gentle music flowed around the rooms, and orange scented candles burned and flickered. The Koi Carp Lounge level, located deep underground, was a most relaxing space. There was a sparkling pond in the centre, where gigantic Koi carp leisurely drifted around the orchid pots and the spotlighted bridge leading to the Sleep Retreat. A wooden deck, with over-sized, rounded, wicker seats, overlooked the spectacular water feature. The lights were dimmed, candle flames danced, and soft music played. There was also a small pool, and a swing was attached to the ceiling. Swaying to and fro just above the water was a wonderful and relaxing sensation. It was absolute bliss and the perfect place for Yasmine and me to catch up and relax.

She had asked to meet up with me on one of those free afternoons, and to spend some time together to chat and indulge ourselves at the Sanctuary Spa. When she arrived by the entrance, she looked lost in thought. She was not herself. As we checked in at the reception desk, she told me she missed being busy, and how she would much prefer to be in rehearsals and dancing than going to a Spa. That afternoon, we had a long conversation by the Koi carp pond. I told her that in a way she would need to start all over again, but in a different way, and that she was nowhere yet as a professional dancer. She was simply the graduate who had made it into the Company. That was the easiest part, and the hardest part was still to come! I told her she was only a small fish in a big pond and that she would now need to prove she could be a big fish in that big pond.

She looked at me in disbelief. "What do you mean I am nowhere yet?" she exclaimed.

I repeated to her what my father told me the day I graduated from university. After six years of intense study, field research, and writing my thesis, he said, "You are nowhere yet. Now, go out in the world and prove you can find a job and do well in your newly found profession. Apply all that you have learned and try to make a success of it."

I remember feeling very disappointed by what he had said, as if all my achievements meant nothing to him. At the time, I was very annoyed by my father's remarks, but he was so right. I was nowhere until the moment that I could prove I would be able to apply all that I had learned in my chosen profession and become successful.

I explained to Yasmine that her situation was very similar to the exceptional tennis player who qualifies to enter the Championships at Wimbledon's Grand Slam tournament. Qualifying is one thing, but winning Wimbledon is an entirely different matter. I knew Yasmine could do with a good shake-up and a wake-up call, so that she would get out of her comfort zone and be up and ready for the next challenge.

"Don't let your head hang down, and never ever feel sorry for yourself," I said, knowing that my occasional harshness over the previous years had always worked well for her. Starting out with an inflated ego gets you nowhere. Having confidence in one's abilities, combined with the willingness to work consistently hard, continue to learn, and apply all that one has learned are what really matters. I reminded Yasmine of what I had told her many years before, that each year in training was about reaching another higher-up "base camp". Sometimes she would have to stop and top up her "oxygen supply", and only the fiercest and most determined climbers would reach the top. Those climbers possess an extraordinary inner strength; they never make excuses; they are highly motivated; and they possess total mental control when under the greatest pressure and in the most challenging situations.

That was Yasmine's new reality and, yes, it was hard, but she needed to realise and accept that roles were never going to be served to her on a silver platter. She would need to demonstrate that she had done her "homework", that she had initiated self-learning, and she had to be totally reliable and ready to perform whenever needed. She would have to prove a hell of a lot more before being able to get out of the corps de ballet, which was the first goal she had set herself.

One late afternoon, just a few weeks after she had joined the Company, she received a phone call from Liam Scarlett. Scarlett was preparing the World Premiere of *Asphodel Meadows*, and he asked Yasmine how well she knew the various places in his ballet and if she could replace an injured Soloist at short notice. She had only been able to watch the dancers during a couple of studio rehearsals, but she had not had any opportunity to dance any of those roles. She didn't hesitate, though, and without giving it much thought she answered that she could. She instantly asked Scarlett to give her a pre-recorded DVD and assured him she would be ready for the next day's stage rehearsal. She was ready to leave her "comfort zone", eager to make her mark, and ready to pounce on any given opportunity. This was to be her first chance, and she grabbed it with both hands.

Since Gailene Stock had allowed Yasmine to continue living at the School's accommodation in Mercer Street, Yasmine waited until all the Second and Third Year students had gone to their bedrooms before going into the common kitchen to practise. This is where she taught herself the various places in *Asphodel Meadows*, by watching the DVD Liam Scarlett had given her. At 3am, she finally went to bed, confident that she would be able to deliver later that day.

This provided her with her first taste of life as a young professional dancer, and highlighted how they must be adaptable; be a very fast learner; be confident in their own abilities and talent; control performance nerves and go on stage with minimal rehearsal time, yet perform to the highest possible standard. It was nerve-racking, because she had only one shot at proving her capabilities; messing up this opportunity could mean she would not be asked again.

She danced on the opening night and in all subsequent performances, taking over three different places – not an easy feat for a new and relatively inexperienced corps de ballet dancer, but she did it. At the same time, she had to deal with a certain degree of animosity from established members of the corps de ballet, who understandably weren't very happy that the newcomer was taking over a Soloist's role after having just joined the Company. Establishing oneself as a new member of the corps de ballet is a challenge, as understandably there is a constant competitive undercurrent. The atmosphere can get very tense, especially when the casting for an upcoming ballet is pinned on the casting notice board outside one of the ballet studios. Any corps de ballet dancer is always hopeful to see her or his name on the cast list as a dancer and not as a cover, or they hope to be in the 1st cast, if not in the 2nd cast. Many pray to be given a solo role, or to be singled out as a cover to a Soloist – a big achievement for any corps de ballet dancer. However, competition is absolutely necessary, as it keeps them all striving to continuously better themselves. Yasmine used the competition as a tool to relentlessly drive herself and she never let competition become a hindrance to her own advancement. As a corps de ballet dancer, she managed to keep the fire burning inside – something that can easily be lost if the desired roles aren't coming, or not coming fast enough. They can easily become dispirited.

Two months after she had joined the Company, the dancers left on their annual Tour on 16 June to perform in Tokyo for ten days. *La Fille mal gardée*, *Mayerling*, and *Romeo and Juliet* were scheduled at the Bunka Kaikan theatre; they also performed *Romeo and Juliet* in Osaka on 3 July. One *Romeo and Juliet* performance in Tokyo marked her first experience with a mishap on stage. During Act 1 Scene 4, the Company was dancing all together during the Ballroom scene, and Yasmine stood at the very back, dressed in a long heavy dress and wearing an elaborate Renaissance headdress. As the dancers walked forward and then backward, Yasmine's foot got stuck in her long dress, and she fell down on the stage. As she lay down on the floor, the dancers walked past her to give her room to get up and compose herself. Luckily, as she was at the back, the mishap remained hidden from the view of the audience.

She tried to find her place amongst the established friendship groups, but she was too reserved, and she often set off exploring Tokyo and its museums by herself whenever the dancers had free time. Many of her colleagues were older and at different stages in their lives – some were married, others divorced, and some had children.

During her first full Season (2010-2011), the Company was on stage rehearsing *Voluntaries* by Glenn Tetley. Yasmine was not cast to perform in this ballet, but she had watched the rehearsals at the back of the studio as usual. Since she was not needed for the stage rehearsal that morning, she returned to her dressing room straight after Company class. Just as she was about to take a bite of her banana, she heard her name suddenly being called out over the tannoy loudspeaker system. Dame Monica Mason requested that Yasmine come to the stage immediately.

Yasmine knew what that meant. As she arrived, Monica told her to take over the role from a dancer and proceed on stage straight away. Yasmine could not allow her nerves to show; she could not say that she had never danced the role and had only watched it. She had to deliver. After the stage rehearsal, Monica Mason told Yasmine that she was no longer a cover and that she would dance the role throughout the run of *Voluntaries*, as well as on the opening night. This would become a pattern throughout her two years as an Artist, as well as during the following two years as a First Artist in the corps de ballet.

The demands and pressure on a young professional dancer are huge and unrelenting. They dance well-drilled roles, but they must also be ready to take over at short notice from any other corps de ballet dancer. Very often, Yasmine would not only dance her own roles night after night, but simultaneously take over extra roles from ill or injured dancers. Having a cold, or a raised temperature, or a headache, or being in pain, was never an excuse for her not to dance. She was in a permanent state of total exhaustion, with only Sundays off to recuperate.

In April 2011, midway through her first full season, I was watching Yasmine dance as one of the Harlots in *Manon*, and I began to wonder why some dancers seem to remain in the corps de ballet for many years. What sets one corps de ballet dancer apart from the others? In Act III Scene I, Manon and her fellow convicts arrive in America as prostitutes, after their deportation from France. As they walk off the ramp of the ship, exhausted, broken, and in total dishevelment, I spotted Yasmine, her dress dirty and torn, wearing a short messy wig, and her face smeared with "dirt" make-up.

How on earth does a Harlot become a Manon? I wondered. *How does a Harlot set herself apart from the other Harlots?* It is not a corps de ballet role allowing a dancer to stand out; after all, they are supposed to dance together as one. Yet when looking at all of them, for some hard to define reason, one's eye is spontaneously drawn to some dancers, who have that something extra, an indefinable quality. *They all dance so well*, I thought. *But what special skills or qualities do they really need to possess in order to stand out, besides increasingly mastering higher levels of technique and artistry?*

I began to wonder why relatively few of them become a Soloist, let alone a Principal dancer. Obviously, there are those who naturally stand out and possess distinct qualities that set them effortlessly apart from the others.

The article "British Ballerinas, Now & Then", published on 27 October, 2019, by a group of UK lecturers in Dance History, talks about specific qualities displayed in dancers. In that article, three current British female Principals are discussed and compared:

"The three ballerinas we decided to focus on not only displayed qualities reminiscent of Fonteyn during their performance at the 'Margot Fonteyn, a Celebration' Gala on 8th June, 2019, but they have also on previous occasions all been noted for particular attributes connected to Fonteyn and the English style of performing ballet. Further, all three Principal dancers are of British descent. Our selected ballerinas are Lauren Cuthbertson, Yasmine Naghdi, and Francesca Hayward. All three attended White Lodge and The Royal Ballet Upper School, and joined the Company soon after [both Cuthbertson and Naghdi skipped the 2nd Year at the Upper School; Hayward joined the Company in the midst of the 3rd Year]. All three were promoted to the highest rank of Principal ballerina within five to seven years since graduating into the Company. There were two points that caught our eye: the early evidence and identification of talent, and the particular qualities in their dancing that had an impact on the repertoire they have performed. Cuthbertson is older, thus her repertoire is broader, but all three of them performed Juliet very early on in their careers, and all have danced Principal roles in some of the 19th century classics, which to this day still seem to be the ultimate measure of a ballerina's mettle. However, it is noticeable that Naghdi has been performing Odette/ Odile in *Swan Lake* since the age of twenty-four, but Hayward has not yet danced this crucial role; on the other hand, Hayward has won recognition for her interpretation of Manon, a role that requires sophisticated acting, a role Naghdi still covets. [Naghdi's further [classical] repertoire [to date] also includes Gamzatti in *La Bayadère*, *The Firebird*, Mathilde Kscheshinkaya in *Anastasia*, Princess Aurora in *The Sleeping Beauty* and Kitri in Don *Quixote*, all of which require an impeccable classical technique]. In fact, even the way in which Naghdi performs Juliet accentuates her clarity of line, revealing this way her interpretation of the choreography (*Romeo and Juliet* – Balcony pas de deux.) All three Principals are further associated with a specific school of training and performance style. The notion of English training and performance style, accentuating Cuthbertson's articulation of the English style in his description (2014 review of Lauren Cuthbertson in *The Sleeping Beauty* by Graham Watts) of her poses and lines as 'disciplined', 'refined', 'traditional' and 'elegant'. For Watts, the maintenance of this style is vital for the continuity of the English tradition, which he links to Fonteyn.

References to Fonteyn also appear in writings about Naghdi and Hayward: descriptions of the impact of Naghdi's 'intense dark eyes' (Byrne, 'Royal Ballet'), and her ferocity, her energy and her musicality of her *Firebird* (Gerard Dowler) are reminiscent of both Fonteyn's facial expressions and her quality as a dancer. Hayward has also been compared to Fonteyn (Byrne 'Dancing Queens'; Taylor). The roles that were selected for our three ballerinas for the Fonteyn Celebration capitalised on their particular talents."

Eventually, my question answered itself, once I understood the highly pressurised life of a corps de ballet dancer. Each rank in the Company has its own very different set of pressures. Corps de ballet dancers are likely to be on stage night after night, a Soloist may be on a couple of times a week, and a Principal dancer will only dance the title role twice or three times during the entire run of a particular ballet; their performances can be spaced out over a few weeks or grouped together, in order to accommodate their international guesting schedule. I regarded the life of corps de ballet dancers as unforgiving and gruelling, and at times I felt really sorry for Yasmine and her fellow corps de ballet dancers. When she told me how arduous and painful it is to stand still during those white acts of *Swan Lake*, I couldn't understand why. After all, they were just standing still in a line, weren't they? She explained the effect it has on a dancer's body during those stop-start moments, and how they are at an increased risk of injury. The muscles cool off and become cold as they stand still. The Principals dance for what seems to the corps dancers as an eternity. Afterwards, the audience applauds, and by then the corps de ballet is seriously impatient for the applause to be over so that they can start moving again. They also stand in a turned-out position, night after night, as well as in a lopsided position that puts enormous strain on the body, on their knees and ankles, and this frequently causes painful impingement of their ankle(s). It develops as a result of repeated strain. Let's not forget to mention the sweat dripping off their faces that they cannot wipe off as they stand "frozen in time". They just have to let the perspiration run down their faces. Yasmine said it was pure agony.

When The Royal Ballet restaged Kenneth MacMillan's "*The Prince of the Pagodas*" in June 2012, two years into her career, Yasmine appeared on the stage as one of a pack of monkeys, mimicking monkey-like movements and wearing a hideous monkey face mask. I remember sitting in the Orchestra Stalls, close to the stage, and I had flashbacks of the 1968 movie *Planet of the Apes*. I was only able to identify her from the shape of her arms and legs. I was totally horrified to see her having to behave like a primate, and I pondered, *Is this why she had to train all those years? Is this what she has to do after two years of dancing with the Company?* I felt deeply sorry for her, and I remember it made me feel sad. I really disliked that ballet. Perhaps I invested myself emotionally too much in it all.

At that point, I could not yet comprehend why and how corps de ballet dancers could do what they did, day after day, after day. However, seeing the corps de ballet perform the Shades in *La Bayadère* summed it all up. As a First Artist, and three years into her professional life, Yasmine led the entire corps de ballet of the Shades down that notorious ramp, in every single performance. I don't ever recall shedding continuous tears watching them in such unison, performing with such great beauty.

> *"There is fatigue so great that the body cries, even in its sleep. There are times of complete frustration; there are daily small 'deaths'. Dance is the song of the body. Either of joy or of pain."*
>
> Martha Graham

During her first two years, Yasmine decided she wanted to come back home and live with us. It suited her perfectly well, as she would not have to waste any time shopping for food, cooking a meal, washing her clothes, dealing with utility bills, and all that comes with living on your own. That year, in the depths of winter, she also learned to drive, taking lessons as soon as she had arrived back home from the Royal Opera House, at 7pm. Driving around in Central London during the hectic Christmas shopping period was certainly no easy feat. But then "easy" never did it for Yasmine.

During the time she lived at home, she also became obsessed with baking. On Sundays she would claim the kitchen as her territory, close the door, and bake just about anything, from multi-layered cakes to cupcakes. Yasmine was fast becoming well known for her cake baking talent. She regularly brought cupcakes, or any cake for that matter, into her dressing room, and her reputation even reached the ears of some of the Principal dancers. Curious behaviour, perhaps, but I think it was a way for her to be able to focus her mind on something completely different, and it soothed her, gave her a sense of comfort and contentment, and perhaps also gave her the feeling of being in control. Many Sunday afternoons Kamran and I heard the sound of brisk whisking coming from behind the closed kitchen door, followed by baking smells wafting through our home.

I had often compared Yasmine to a young racehorse, totally impatient to get out on the track and run to win, but that desire had to be reined in or she risked being trampled over and burned out. For Yasmine, it was not a matter of "wanting to dance" but of "having to dance", and dancing somehow had always seemed to be the only way to calm her down. Whenever she could dance, she was calm, and only sheer physical exhaustion would make her happy. She had always been restless, and she was hungry to get her teeth into roles and to master them. Fortunately for her, she did not have to wait too long.

After a while, some corps de ballet dancers will be able to make their way out by being given the opportunity to dance certain short solos in the great classics. For the female dancers, for example, it can be the pas de trois in *Swan Lake*, or as one of the Prologue Fairies in *The Sleeping Beauty*.

By the time Yasmine danced the lead role of Tatiana in John Cranko's beautiful ballet *Onegin* in February 2020, she had danced every single corps de ballet and Soloist role, from the Girl in the Mirror to dancing in the ballroom scene to Olga (the sister of Tatiana). Yasmine's years in the corps de ballet surely made her even tougher, and she began to take more risks, as well as taking on barely rehearsed Soloist roles at short notice. She had found the courage, and she had the self-confidence, to put herself out there in exposing circumstances – something not every dancer is naturally comfortable with. There are dancers who need plenty of time to prepare for a role, and there are others who are risk-takers, who can take on the challenge of going on stage with little preparation. For Yasmine, there was never an excuse not to dance.

I recall during her first season that she had a serious bout of flu just before Christmas, but she had been scheduled to dance every single night because so many dancers were ill or injured, and the Company was very short on corps de ballet dancers. Yasmine wasn't going to give in. Ultimately, it was Romany Pajdak who took pity on her, and she told Yasmine to go home and to give herself a break. She had to insist, and she told Yasmine it was no use "killing" herself.

During that same season, a New Year's Eve performance of *The Nutcracker* was scheduled at 5:30pm and, after having danced at least five different roles in the performance, she walked out of the Stage Door at 7:45pm towards the Covent Garden underground. She found several lines weren't working and many stations were closed, so she set off on foot, walking down The Strand and The Mall, passing by Buckingham Palace, turning into the unlit and totally deserted Constitution Hill towards Wellington Arch. Desperate to get home for our New Year's Eve family dinner, she called her father asking if he could fetch her at the Duke of Wellington Place. Covent Garden and Piccadilly were completely closed to traffic because of the New Year's Eve fireworks.

Kamran sat waiting for her in his car at the top end of Constitution Hill, right by the wall of Buckingham Palace, when a police car suddenly swerved up right next to his car and two policemen jumped out of their patrol car. In a hostile manner, they instructed Kamran to get out of his car.

"Do you know where you are parked?" one of the policemen shouted. "I should be holding a gun to your head!"

Kamran answered that he was only waiting for his daughter, who had just finished performing in *The Nutcracker* at the Royal Opera House.

"Yeh right. Get moving straight away!" the policeman replied in a highly intimidating way.

Poor Kamran circled thrice around Wellington Arch until Yasmine finally appeared on foot out of the dark. She was totally exhausted. After a long day and an evening performance, having to walk from Covent Garden all alone in the cold and the dark along the deserted Mall and Constitution Hill was certainly not inviting to be cheerful and celebrate New Year's Eve.

Towards the end of her first Season, Valentino Zucchetti created a new work for Draft Works called *Trio Sonata*, to be performed at the Linbury Studio Theatre. Draft Works was a programme established to encourage any Royal Ballet dancer to choreograph a work on selected colleagues. Valentino paired Yasmine with then Principal dancer Sergei Polunin. Yasmine was eager to rehearse and to get it all right but that was not easy with Sergei. He would either arrive late and in the midst of a rehearsal, or not turn up at all. She still had to prove herself, whereas Sergei was totally laid-back about the rehearsal process for Draft Works. She would often work alone in the studio with Valentino.

The magic of Sergei was such that when he eventually turned up, he knew what to do instinctively, and he did it with minimal input or effort. As a corps de ballet dancer, Yasmine was totally in awe of Sergei's talent. She could not understand how they all had to work so hard, do their early morning class rigorously, and without any shortcuts in preparation for rehearsals and evening performance, yet Sergei would walk in late afternoon and, without much preparation, go on stage and perform with seeming ease.

Maggie Foyer wrote in her review for *Dance Europe* (July 2011): "Zucchetti's *Trio Sonata* boasted fine performers and benefitted from a strong opening and good finish. Sergei Polunin blazed through an impressive solo that suddenly became a duet as Yasmine Naghdi streaked on to join him, skimming the floor on steely pointes. This young dancer shows a confidence way beyond her years and is definitely one to watch. Even Polunin's slightly under-rehearsed partnering didn't faze her at all."

Dame Monica Mason promoted Yasmine to First Artist in June 2012, just as she was about to retire after ten years as Director of The Royal Ballet. Monica's last programme, "Metamorphosis: Titian 2012", was very ambitious and resulted in a collaboration between The Royal Ballet, several leading contemporary artists, and the National Gallery. I was there on the Opening Night, and I had never seen the House buzzing as it did that evening. There was such an eclectic mix of people coming from diverse backgrounds, young and old, I even saw several 80s-styled punks. There was such tangible excitement, and it felt as if there was going to be one big party. New choreography, great art, combined with the very distinctive qualities of The Royal Ballet, all in co-operation with the National Gallery. It couldn't get any better in presenting a 21st century Gesamtkunstwerk.

Needless to say, I went off again in my time machine, this time back to the early 20th century and the Diaghilev era. The collaboration was inspired by three great artworks in the collection of the National Gallery: "Diana and Actaeon", "The Death by Acteon", and "Diana and Callisto" by Titian. Contemporary artists such as Chris Ofili and Jonathan Dove worked with Will Tuckett and Jonathan Watkins; Conrad Shawcross and Nico Muhly worked with Wayne McGregor and Kim Brandstrup; Alistair Marriott, and Christopher Wheeldon collaborated with Turner Prize-winning artist Mark Wallinger and Mark-Anthony Turnage. It was Monica Mason's wish to focus on the future of ballet and on all the brilliant talents within the Company at that time. The performance was a real feast for the eyes and attracted many youngsters into the Royal Opera House.

It was during her third season that Yasmine had her first big break. She was cast as Olga in John Cranko's *Onegin*, and she danced alongside Dawid Trzensimiech (former Soloist with The Royal Ballet) as her Lensky. By now, she had learned how to give physical substance to the character she was dancing, how to portray the character, how to give substance to lamentation, to celebration, to hate, to passion, to dreams, to fears, and to tragedy. All this had to be revealed through a solid dance technique. That season Yasmine also danced Sir Frederick Ashton's technically difficult *Monotones I* on the opening night – a ballet embodying the very essence of Ashtonian classicism. Ashton's style is truly distinctive in the way the shoulders and the head are carried (*épaulement*) and its fast footwork, resulting in great elegance and often breathtaking execution of the technical demands. From then on, she was dancing all the corps de ballet roles in virtually every scheduled ballet. She was cast in the ballets created by the American choreographer George Balanchine, one of the most influential 20th century choreographers. She danced in *Jewels* as Rubies, Emeralds and Diamonds, as the Two Sisters in his *Apollo*, and in *La Valse* and *Serenade*, as well as in ballets created by multi-award-winning British choreographers Wayne McGregor and Christopher Wheeldon.

Two seasons later, Kevin O'Hare, Director of The Royal Ballet since 2012, promoted her to Soloist in June 2014. She had also received her first invitation to guest abroad that summer, and she flew to Bogota, Colombia, where she performed an excerpt of *Asphodel Meadows* with Valentino Zucchetti on the occasion of the re-opening of the restored Teatro Cristobal Colon, in the presence of the Colombian President Juan Manuel Santos, followed by dinner at the British Embassy in the presence of the British Ambassador. Afterwards, she flew to Bermuda to perform in Matthew Golding's Gala (then Principal at The Royal Ballet) where she danced the *Romeo and Juliet* Balcony Pas de deux with Matthew Ball.

During her first season (2014-2015) as a Soloist, she reprised the role of Olga in *Onegin*, this time with Matthew Ball – who was still in the corps de ballet – as her Lensky, and she repeated various Soloist roles she had danced over the past seasons but now as 1st cast. It was during her second year as a Soloist that Kevin O'Hare cast twenty-three-year-old Yasmine as Juliet in Kenneth MacMillan's *Romeo and Juliet*, partnered by Matthew Ball (aged twenty-one) as her Romeo. Their double debut Matinee was hotly anticipated, and we could all sense the exhilaration at the Royal Opera House. Everyone was thrilled to be able to witness the debut of these two young dancers in this most passionate ballet.

The amorous Balcony pas de deux in Act I swept the audience (and us) off their feet. It felt as if, momentarily, collective breathing had stopped altogether when Romeo and Juliet finally embraced each other, followed by an unhurried kiss. During Act III Scene 4, set in the Capulet family crypt, my eyes focussed on Yasmine's face as she lay on her tomb, slowly waking up, and on her facial expression when she discovers that Romeo had poisoned himself and lay dead on the floor. Yasmine's deeply affecting expressionistic scream was almost too painful to watch, and pierced my heart, and then she finally stabs herself to death, slowly crawling onto her tombstone in agony and in total desperation to touch her Romeo for the very last time. Somebody beautifully described Yasmine's scream to me as "one of the loudest silent screams and the most heart-wrenching" she had ever heard. This was undoubtedly the most passionate role I had seen her dance, and I was an emotional wreck afterwards. A huge crowd was waiting for the performers, not only inside the Stage Door but also outside on Floral Street. According to many present that day, it was unlike anything they had seen for many years. It took Yasmine and Matthew close to an hour to sign programmes as well as having their photos taken with all the waiting fans. In the meantime, Tatiana and Kamran, assisted by Nico Capelle (one of the lovely ushers), were busy taking Yasmine's twenty-three bouquets of flowers out of her dressing room, and kept them all inside the Reception area until the fans had left. We had to order a large taxi to come to the Stage Door and pick up all her bouquets; it was quite a sight as we were basically buried under all the flowers. Thereafter, her career moved really fast, and by the end of that Season she was promoted to First Soloist in June 2016.

During season 2016-2017 the Company was staging Kenneth MacMillan's *Anastasia* – a ballet with which MacMillan broke new grounds, creating strong expressionist movement. One Friday afternoon, Yasmine was called into a meeting with Kevin, and he asked her if she felt she could take over the highly technical role of Mathilde Kschessinska from an injured dancer the following Tuesday. Yasmine had never performed the role before, and she was told she would not get any stage rehearsal. To dance such a technically demanding and exposing role with insufficient rehearsal time felt like a high risk to me. Yasmine had been cast as a cover to Marianela Núñez, but she had been unable to attend most of the rehearsals due to her own conflicting rehearsal schedule, because she was simultaneously cast to dance the role of Grand Duchess Marie in *Anastasia* on the Opening Night. I asked Yasmine how many weeks the other dancers had had in order to prepare for the role of Mathilde Kschessinska. "Several weeks," she answered.

However, she felt it was an amazing opportunity, and she was confident that she would be capable of dealing with the technical challenges, as well as having to dance with someone who was too short to partner her. After having given it sufficient consideration, Yasmine took the plunge. "Rehearsing Mathilde Kschessinska for a few hours on Monday and on Tuesday afternoon will do it for me," she said decisively.

Saying "yes" is the easiest part. Living up to everyone's expectations is a totally different ball game. It all comes down to looking for advantages in every situation, even when conditions are less than favourable, and Yasmine had every reason to feel confident. It took little time to convince herself that she could do it, even with only a few hours of rehearsal time. And her interpretation and technical execution of Mathilde Kschessinska was highly successful.

Dancing her debut as Princess Aurora in *The Sleeping Beauty* followed soon after. Amongst others, Jonathan Gray (*Dancing Times*, March 2017) reviewed her performance: "She seemed born to perform the role, so confidently did she take to the stage. She has an immaculate technique, as well as inherent musicality that she used to bring a wonderful range of nuance to her dancing. Her Rose Adagio was also triumphant, with supported développés given a slow, luxurious, unfurling quality that was as plush as velvet."

Shortly after her Aurora debut, Yasmine danced the role of The Girl in Kenneth MacMillan's *The Invitation*, a role created for Lynn Seymour in 1960. The 60-minute, one-act ballet is set in a tropical country at the start of the twentieth century. It is a most astonishing ballet about the loss of innocence of two young cousins (a young boy and a young girl) as they become entwined with a disenchanted married couple. The girl becomes conscious for the first time of her power, as the married man pursues her; the boy is flattered by the older woman's interest in him. Too naïve to realise the effect she may have on the man, the girl comes to him in her nightgown, and he loses it. An explicit scene of the brutal act of rape follows. The act shows both the physical and psychological realities of rape, aesthetically arranged by MacMillan in a twisting rape scene, expressing lust instead of love. The girl's empty scream cannot but deeply penetrate the bones of any viewer.

This one-act ballet shows MacMillan's most remarkable and all-enveloping choreographic talent at its best, and it is in my opinion his finest psychological ballet. It is extraordinary to see how he was able to depict a terrible act of violence mixed with raw truth and, however painful it is to watch the rape scene, he never turned the art of ballet into sensationalism. *The Invitation* was a comment on the hypocritical moral standards of his time, and I wish in a way that The Royal Ballet would stage it again during this current Covid-19 pandemic. *The Invitation* is a fine work of art, and in my view the rape scene could serve as a stark and pertinent reminder of all the acts of violence continuously being committed on women worldwide, greatly amplified during this pandemic.

I have seen so many wonderful ballets in Covent Garden over the past two decades, but the most awe-inspiring that had real power to transcend any emotion I have ever felt whilst watching ballet, are some of Kenneth MacMillan's one-act ballets, from his absolutely breathtaking *Requiem*, to his powerful *The Rite of Spring*, his daring *The Invitation*, and his plotless *Concerto*, with its pure classicism full of beauty and dreamlike quality in the 2nd Movement. They are all absolute treasures to behold.

By the end of the season, Kevin O'Hare promoted Yasmine to the highest rank of Principal ballerina.

Yasmine at last seemed to have found peace within herself. She was riding high on the waves, controlling them with ease. She had thrived under the greatest of pressures, and she was often at her very best when she herself felt at her worst. She had never wanted to remain in her "comfort-zone", and "easy" never did it for her. Her immense desire, total dedication, steely determination, utter self-discipline, doing what she needed to do whether she wanted to or not, mastering the ability to let things happen under pressure and knowing how to respond to adverse circumstances, had all become her hallmarks. She had become proficient in fast mental recovery from unfortunate events, and she mastered the ability to keep her attention and focus in the here and now.

By now she knew: "If you think you can, or you can't, you are undoubtedly right. The choice is yours."

Chapter Ten

Life as a Principal Ballerina

"It is not what you have achieved but what you had to overcome. That is what defines your career."

(Carlton Fisk)

Ever since Yasmine joined the Company it had become a tradition to meet up after her end-of-season meeting with her Director Kevin O'Hare, to celebrate the success of the season, and at times to also celebrate her promotion. Wednesday, 14 June, 2017, was no different. Her meeting – one of the last ones scheduled – was at 2pm, and just two days before the Company was to leave on their annual tour, this time to Australia. She had had a very demanding season, during which she had danced her debut in the title role of Princess Aurora in the über-classical tutu ballet *The Sleeping Beauty* (three times in one week, if you please), the Sugar Plum Fairy in *The Nutcracker*, Young Virginia Woolf in Wayne McGregor's stunning contemporary ballet *Woolf Works*, the pas de deux and Ensemble in Ashton's serene *Symphonic Variations* – an absolute marathon of a ballet for the dancers and a test of sheer stamina; stamina very few dancers apparently could stand at the time of its creation. She had also danced George Balanchine's neo-classical Emeralds and Diamonds in *Jewels*, showcasing pure dance movement, as well as his explosive and virtuosic showcase *Tarantella*, requiring very fast footwork. She had danced the title role of The Girl in Kenneth MacMillan's *The Invitation* – a role suitable for an actress-ballerina who possesses tender characterisation abilities combined with expressive liquid movement quality – and at short notice she had danced the highly technical and classical ballerina role of Mathilde

Kchessinska in *Anastasia*, as well as the Finale pas de deux in Wayne McGregor's contemporary ballet *Chroma*. Clearly, Yasmine had been put through her paces and to the test on all fronts.

We had agreed to meet up around 2:20pm by the Young Dancer statue – a bronze sculpture by the Italian-born British artist Enzo Plazzotta (1921-1981), on Broad Street, just off Bow Street and right opposite the Royal Opera House. Her meeting took somehow much longer than usual. When I looked at my watch, it was nearly 2:45pm, and there was still no sign of Yasmine coming down Floral Street. Quite how she did it, I couldn't figure it out, but seemingly out of nowhere she all of a sudden jumped in front of us like a Jack-in-the-box. She smiled and in a soft voice, as if wanting to whisper and share a secret with us she said, "I have been promoted to Principal."

It was a hot summer afternoon, and the terrace of the nearby Italian restaurant was packed with patrons tucking into their risotto, pizza, or pasta. I let out an uncustomary, spur-of-the-moment shriek, followed by tears (yes, there they were again!) filling my eyes as I swung my arms around her. The bemused customers all looked in my direction, momentarily pausing putting their forks into their mouths, clearly wondering what on earth was happening there by the ballerina statue. Overcome by the news, we languorously walked towards our favorite Italian restaurant further down the road. Yasmine was walking in front of me, next to her father, who had his arm around her waist. I had a flashback to her first ever stage appearance at the Commonwealth Institute when, as a five-year-old, she had told me, "I don't want to do it!"; to the moment Kamran had been a "tree", around which his young daughter had danced as a nine-year-old; to Kamran's daily evening slog through the rush-hour traffic to fetch her at White Lodge; to the moment I sat in my car waiting for her to come out of Gloucester Road tube station, feeling totally lost; to seeing her smiley face when the two of us sat up in the hills overlooking Prague; and to her calling us to say she had been offered a contract with The Royal Ballet.

On arrival in the restaurant, we ordered a bottle of champagne. It was 3pm and the restaurant was nearly empty, which was just what we needed: a quiet place to sit down, just the three of us. We sat in silence for a while, enjoying our celebratory glass of champagne while the news sank in. The champagne suddenly hit me, as the bubbles on my empty stomach rapidly affected me. Looking at her as she sat there in a contemplative mood, metaphorically it felt like I had "given birth" to her for a second time. I had been an expectant ballet mum for a long time, and "labour" felt like I had had to run a marathon, but typically all the painful and testing moments were swiftly forgotten. They were all replaced by utter happiness and joy.

Congratulations from colleagues, friends and family kept coming in via WhatsApp messages and phone calls. The news, however, had to be kept private until The Royal Ballet Press Office was in a position to officially announce Yasmine's promotion to Principal ballerina – an annual announcement that is highly anticipated by ballet fans, nationally and internationally. It also marks the official end of The Royal Ballet's Season. Family and friends were instructed not to post any congratulations on social media.

Yasmine could not believe that her ultimate dream had come true, and neither could we. She recollected that at the end of her meeting with Kevin, she had had to double-check and ask him again if indeed she had been promoted to Principal ballerina, or whether she had just imagined it. Thirteen years had passed since she first entered White Lodge, since she had performed as a Little Swan with the Company in *Swan Lake*; eleven years had passed by since she had expressed her dream, as a fourteen-year-old in the BBC documentary "The Magic of Swan Lake", to dance *Swan Lake* one day. It takes time to digest when a near-impossible dream is ultimately fulfilled.

From that day onwards, I became a mere spectator, a member of the audience. I had successfully navigated all the potential pitfalls with her during her training at the School, and during her early years in the corps de ballet. I had achieved what I had set out to achieve: to help my twelve-year-old daughter get through her ballet training unscathed. I had achieved my desire for her to grow up in an unaffected manner, to have great mental strength and control, to be mentally balanced and capable of leading a happy life away from the professional demands of her ballet career. I recollect thinking that from now on, my "tears" would solely run during her performances and during her curtain calls. What a relief and a liberating thought that was after all those years.

A few days later, she flew to Australia to dance with the Company in Brisbane, where they performed Wayne McGregor's *Woolf Works* and Christopher Wheeldon's *The Winter's Tale*. At the end of the tour, she travelled to the east coast of Far North Queensland with Kevin O'Hare and a few other dancers, where they performed alongside the indigenous Aboriginals and local youth groups. To round off the experience of a lifetime, they were invited to spend a few days enjoying the underwater beauty of the Great Barrier Reef, after which she flew to Bali for a well-deserved holiday. What a great way to enjoy and celebrate her ultimate promotion.

It was not until a few months into her first season as a Principal that Yasmine moved into her own dressing room. During the first few months she stayed in her First Soloist dressing room, since Principal ballerina Zenaida Yanowsky (who retired from The Royal Ballet at the end of Season 2016-2017, just as Yasmine had been promoted to Principal ballerina) was scheduled to guest as the Queen of Hearts in *Alice in Wonderland*, the ballet that opened Season 2017-2018. Yasmine insisted that Zenaida took as much time as she needed before moving out of the dressing room she had shared with fellow Principal ballerina Laura Morera for so many years. Yasmine felt ill at ease at the thought of Zen (as she is affectionately called by the other dancers) having to pack up in order to make room for her.

At the opening of the season, Yasmine danced her debut in the popular *Elite Syncopations* by Kenneth MacMillan, and she performed the Stop Time Rag and Bethena (Concert Waltz), partnered by fellow Principal Ryoichi Hirano.

In the meantime, she had received an invitation to dance *Romeo and Juliet* in Bahrain on the weekend of 10-12 November, but the dates clashed with her performance dates in Twyla Tharp's *The Illustrated Farewell*. She was due to dance in Covent Garden on the evening of 10 November, so how was she supposed to dance in Bahrain on the same evening?

Her performance schedule was duly adjusted, and after her evening performance on Thursday, 9 November, she dashed out of the Royal Opera House with her luggage in tow and jumped into a waiting taxi to be taken to Heathrow airport. She caught the last overnight flight out to Bahrain, and seven hours later she landed in Manama, the capital, situated on the northeast tip of Bahrain Island. A waiting driver took her directly to the waterfront National Theatre of Bahrain so that she could start rehearsing straight away. That same evening, she had her first performance. However, since Bahrain is a Muslim country, there was an issue with the Balcony pas de deux kiss. Yasmine and Alexander Campbell, who danced Romeo, were told by the organisers that kissing in public was not permitted, and it had to be substituted by an embrace. As their amorousness grew and grew during the magnificent Prokofiev score towards the musical climax, they simply stood still in a quiet embrace.

She was driven straight back to the airport after her last performance on Sunday evening to catch the last flight out back to London, and the plane landed at 7:00am the following morning. She had insisted on flying Business Class so that she would be able to sleep during the overnight flight, as she had scheduled rehearsals all afternoon, as well as an evening performance of *The Illustrated Farewell*. Now, that's what I call a real "*tour de force*": back-to-back performances during the week in Covent Garden, flying to Bahrain overnight, squeezing in two performances of *Romeo and Juliet* over the weekend, and dancing on the stage of the Royal Opera House on Monday evening.

Alongside dancing other roles, Yasmine was also scheduled to dance two major debuts during her first season as a Principal ballerina: Odette/Odile in the Company's new production of *Swan Lake*, and as Giselle in Sir Peter Wright's ballet *Giselle*, a quintessential Romantic ballet. I had seen so many Principal dancers perform Giselle over the past twenty years, and now it was Yasmine's turn. One morning, I attended Yasmine's Giselle main stage rehearsal and I met up with her in her dressing room. About half an hour before the start of her rehearsal, we walked to the stage together. Dressed in her Act I costume, with make-up and hair done, she was deep in thought, focussed, and clearly somewhere else. She was wearing her chunky foot warmers, a thick body warmer, and she had a woolly scarf wrapped around her neck. As I had seen many Giselles coming out of that house, I was childishly curious to have a look inside Giselle's village house.

I waited side stage as Yasmine continued walking onto the stage to check out the props, whilst simultaneously talking to some of the technical staff. There she stood, in the middle of that glorious stage, my once five-year-old, whom I had taken by the hand and walked into her first ballet class. She cracked a joke with some of the technical staff and she chatted with Johanna Adams-Farley, the Senior Stage Manager. Yasmine seemed totally relaxed. She finally made me a sign to follow her, and she showed me the "interior" of the house. It was not as I had imagined it to be... There was just a front panel making up the house, with a chair right behind the panel.

"This is where I sit and wait until the moment comes when I hear the (music) cue, then I open the door and I come out on the stage to dance," she explained, whilst casually pointing at the chair.

"Well, I definitely prefer imagination to reality," I mumbled to myself, as I walked to the Orchestra Stalls to take my seat.

How different is the life of a Principal dancer compared to that of the dancers in the other ranks? When it comes to taking daily Company class, whenever there are multiple teachers, the Principal dancers are at liberty to take class with their preferred teacher; the rest of the Company has to stick to their allocated class. Principal dancers rehearse with their designated *répétiteur* in the privacy of a studio. When the time is reached for the full call (studio rehearsal with the entire Company), the Principal dancers join in with all the others. Principals will usually dance two or three performances in a full-length ballet, and Kevin O'Hare makes the casting decision up to six months in advance; the Principal dancers are the first to be informed of their upcoming roles. Their Covent Garden performance dates may also be discussed if they have international guesting invitation during the season.

The Principals' dressing rooms are situated at stage level, unlike the corps de ballet and Soloists' dressing rooms situated on first floor level. Yasmine's walk from her dressing room to the stage takes less than a minute. Whenever she is performing, she dislikes waiting in the wings for too long, and she prefers to wait in her dressing room until a few minutes before she has to go on. She has caused Johanna Adams-Farley, the Senior Stage Manager, more than a few panicky moments by arriving just before she has to go on stage. The live music, played by the orchestra from the pit, is directly relayed to her dressing room, so she knows exactly which musical cue indicates the right time for her to walk to the stage. Two Principals share one spacious dressing room, in which they have a shower room, a small kitchenette, and a comfortable resting couch. They usually have their dressing room all to themselves, as more often than not only one female Principal will be involved in a ballet (except for Triple Bills).

A Principal dancer is also much more in the public eye and far more exposed on stage for a greater length of time. The responsibility that comes with being at the top is of a very different nature. Dancing a Principal role as a First Soloist still leaves a dancer with marginal room for error or an occasional display of technical weakness, but not so for a Principal dancer. A Principal dancer is expected to perform at a flawless level. Through many years of performance and stage experience, they control their focus, and any encountered difficulty, mistake, slip or fall will not shift their concentration on their performance.

I'll never forget watching Tamara Rojo and Carlos Acosta dancing *Swan Lake*. During Act III, Tamara suddenly slipped and fell badly on the stage. Loud gasps from the audience followed. For several seconds, Tamara sat still on the floor and Carlos stood frozen, giving her plenty of time to recompose herself and allow her to assess any probable injury. After a while, Tamara stood up, and Carlos's eyes spoke volumes, encouraging her, as if he was saying, "You are fine. I am here for you. We can carry on." (At least, that's what I read in his facial expression.) Tamara Rojo stood up, and she carried on even more exquisitely. The way in which Tamara had pulled herself together and carried on performing resulted in rapturous applause and cheers from the audience. A slip or a fall happens to even the greatest dancers, but it is the way in which they carry on that draws the audience's admiration and appreciation.

Under normal circumstances, a Principal dancer will be scheduled to dance one full-length ballet in any given week, but Yasmine once danced three performances as Princess Aurora in *The Sleeping Beauty* in one week, taking over from another Principal dancer. When she danced Juliet in *Romeo and Juliet* during the worldwide live cinema relay in June 2019, she danced *The Firebird* the following night, and a few days later she danced *Le Corsaire* pas de deux and solo with Vadim Muntagirov at the Margot Fonteyn Gala. Only immense stamina and a very strong body can get a dancer through such a gruelling dancing schedule.

Going backstage after Yasmine's performance is always an immeasurable moment of joy and pride. Once the curtains come down and she has received all her flowers, one of the ushers will meet us and accompany us backstage. A security guard stands by the door, and he has the names of pre-cleared and permitted backstage guests. For safety reasons, we wait side-stage during the time Yasmine and her dance partner remain on the stage, usually talking to Kevin and their coach. Sometimes VIPs will also be on the stage to meet them. An usher will in the meantime take all her bouquets to her dressing room, where someone from the wardrobe team will be waiting for Yasmine's return, in order to help her out of her tutu, undo her hair, or take off her wig or crown. She will hang up Yasmine's tutu and carefully store her wig or crown in a wig box. I greatly admire their dedication, and they are part of the group of people who passionately work behind the scenes, enabling a smooth performance run, and taking care of even the smallest of details. Guests are often introduced to us, and they are keen to hear how it all began for Yasmine, how I spotted her talent, and often followed by the question whether or not I had been a ballerina. Once Yasmine comes off the stage, she will meet and greet the waiting guests and pose for photos to be taken with them. We usually stand back and wait for her to finish greeting all the guests before we'll hug her. Once all the guests have left and the stage is empty – except for the hardworking stage crew – we walk with Yasmine to her dressing room where we can share a private moment with her. Sometimes we go for a late lunch or dinner with friends afterwards.

Once she is ready to leave her dressing room, she walks to the Stage Door, as she is conscious that fans are waiting for her; she tries to not let them wait for too long. Post-performance body care will always have to wait. About one hour will have passed between coming off stage and being in a position to return home, if she has danced an evening performance, or she joins us in a restaurant nearby if she has danced a matinee. Arriving back home after an evening performance, her adrenaline level is still high, and she is unable to sleep straight away, however exhausted she may be. She usually checks the cards attached to her bouquets, as she likes to thank her fans for their flowers the same evening. After dancing an evening performance, she is usually ready for bed just before 1am.

To dance the title role of Odette/Odile in *Swan Lake* is a dream come true for any ballerina, and certainly for a newly-promoted Principal dancer. Yasmine had two scheduled performances in Covent Garden of *Swan Lake*, partnered by fellow Principal dancer Nehemiah Kish as her Prince, but she ended up dancing an additional performance to replace an indisposed Lauren Cuthbertson, partnered by Federico Bonelli. After the highly successful premiere in Covent Garden, The Royal Ballet left on their annual summer tour, this time to Madrid, and they presented their new *Swan Lake* to the Spanish audience. Yasmine, being the youngest and newest Odette/Odile, was not cast to dance on tour, as only six performances were scheduled in Madrid. Marianela Núñez would dance the opening night; the following night Lauren Cuthbertson was scheduled; next came Sarah Lamb on Friday evening; Akane Takada was scheduled to dance the Saturday matinee; and Natalia Osipova was to dance the 10pm Saturday evening performance. On Sunday evening, the Tour ended with Marianela Núñez closing the *Swan Lake* performances.

However, five days before leaving on tour, Yasmine was called into a meeting with Kevin O'Hare, and he wanted her to take over two Madrid performances of the indisposed Principal ballerinas Lauren Cuthbertson and Natalia Osipova. Unfortunately, just a few days before catching the plane to Madrid, Yasmine was getting really ill with flu-like symptoms, and she was coughing very badly. By the time she arrived with the Company in Madrid on Monday morning, she had developed a fever and a serious chest infection. She felt really poorly. Nevertheless, she pulled herself together and walked from her hotel to the theatre to take Company class. On arrival, she was asked to immediately return to the hotel and to isolate herself. This is standard practice whenever the dancers are on tour. As soon as a dancer displays any signs of a serious cold or flu, or any other sign of infection, they are immediately instructed to isolate themselves. When The Royal Ballet went on tour to Cuba in 2009, there was an outbreak of Swine Flu, and five dancers were diagnosed as being infected with the H1N1 Swine Flu virus. Among the afflicted were Principal dancers Steven McRae and Marianela Núñez. They had to isolate and were unable to perform.

Yasmine felt devastated as the prospect loomed of not being able to dance her *Swan Lake* performances. If she couldn't take class, she couldn't rehearse, and rehearsal time was vital, especially since she and Matthew Ball had not danced *Swan Lake* together in London. Yasmine called me from her hotel room mid-afternoon to say her chest infection made her feel truly miserable. She had only three days left until her first performance on Thursday evening. I asked her how on earth she thought she could perform *Swan Lake* with a chest infection, as well as being unable to take class and rehearse. And I suggested she should perhaps reconsider and let Kevin know, but I received a firm answer back: "If there is one person who can decide whether I am physically fit to dance or not, it is me. I will dance those two performances and I shall not let the Company down." And that was the end of our conversation.

As soon as she had put down the phone, I booked myself onto the first available flight, and early the next morning I flew out to Madrid. I knew she would be able to handle the situation all by herself, but my maternal instinct was simply far too strong, and I wanted to be there for her. I had booked a hotel room at a short walking distance from where the Company was staying. On arrival in Madrid, I immediately called her to find out how she was feeling. She told me she had had a visit in her hotel room from a Spanish doctor, who had put her on the strongest antibiotics, and he had told her she really should not perform as she had difficulty breathing because of her chest infection. The doctor had given her an inhaler. "Keep it on you, just in case you need it whenever you go off in the wings," he said.

I asked if she was currently resting in her hotel room. "No. I am at the supermarket and about to lug six heavy bottles of water to my hotel room!" she replied in an irritated and drained sounding voice.

I asked if she had eaten anything. "No, I haven't had the time yet," she replied.

I quickly went to my room, dropped off my suitcase, and I ran out to the nearby supermarket to buy all her favourite food, snacks, fruits, and drinks. When I arrived in her hotel, I was so happy to see her, but she was understandably in the worst imaginable mood. She had just two days until her first *Swan Lake* performance, and she was still not able to attend class or rehearsals.

I stayed with her until early in the evening, trying to calm her down, and I ordered dinner to be delivered to her room, after which I left her to rest and have an early night. The following day, she unquestionably needed to take class and rehearse with Federico. I needed to distract myself, and I spent the day enjoying the splendid works of art on display in the collections of the Museo Nacional del Prado and the Museo Nacional Centro de Arte Reina Sofía.

Once Yasmine had finished her rehearsal, she left the theatre and returned to her hotel room. The Company was preparing for the opening night, and her presence was not required. When I joined her in her room, I could see Yasmine looked wretched and weak, and she was also missing the buzz surrounding the Opening Night. At the same time, she was preoccupied, thinking about her own upcoming performance the following night. I knew what she needed the most right now: time-out, total distraction, and a high-energy meal.

I called the Reception Desk and asked them for the name of the best steak restaurant in Madrid. The restaurant "La Cabana Argentina" was the answer. "For well over twenty years, Don Ovidio and Don Fernandez dedicated themselves to offering the best Argentinian steak in Madrid," they told me.

We walked out of her hotel and I hailed a taxi. After navigating through the heavy evening traffic, the driver dropped us off in front of No. 21 on Calla Ventura de la Vega, a narrow street in the old part of Madrid. We were taken to our table in a cosy corner. Yasmine was totally absent-minded, and any attempt on my behalf to distract her with small talk clearly did not work or interest her. I found myself staring at the black & white-framed photos of past guests and famous visitors adorning the walls whilst I was enjoying a nice glass of Argentinian wine and a plate of tapas. I left her with her own thoughts. All she needed was silence. There was a great laid-back atmosphere and lovely Spanish guitar music was playing in the background, but my delight clearly did not rub off on her. It felt strange to sit in front of my daughter in total silence, but I knew there was absolutely nothing I could possibly say to cheer her up right now. My presence was enough for her. We were totally on the same wavelength.

Once our main course had been served, and she had tucked into her steak, she gradually began to relax. She reminded me of a melting ice cube. After our meal, I suggested we'd walk back to her hotel instead of jumping in a taxi. This would give her much needed distraction, and it was a warm summer's night, after all. Close to midnight, we crossed a small historical square and we enjoyed listening to a group of Flamenco players. It visibly relaxed her.

We kissed each other goodnight in front of her hotel, and I returned to mine. I felt happy knowing our evening out had done her a lot of good. *OK*, I thought, *she is back on track*. The next day, I visited the Thyssen-Bornemisza Museum, and I popped into a few art galleries to keep myself occupied until the start of the evening performance. By 6:00pm, I headed to Teatro Real de Madrid, located between Plaza de Espana and Plaza de Isabel II, just in front of the beautiful Royal Palace. Teatro Real – or as it is known colloquially, "El Real" – was founded by King Ferdinand VII in 1818, and it soon became one of the most prestigious opera houses in Europe. There was a bustling atmosphere, and the excitement was palpable. The Spanish audience had all dressed up so elegantly; they were visibly enjoying the balmy evening as they were sipping their champagne or glass of wine and eating tapas pre-performance. The ambiance was truly pleasant.

I tried to relax. I knew I had done all I could to support her. Before treating myself to a well-deserved glass of Mumm champagne (no pun intended), I quickly met up with Yasmine at the Artists' entry door, to hand over her favourite pre-performance meal – a request I had received via WhatsApp late afternoon. She had not made any time to pop out of the theatre to get some food.

By 7:45pm, I took my seat at the theatre to attend the sold-out performance. Before the curtains opened, I had a few minutes to reflect on the past couple of days and on what she had gone through since the beginning of the week. I did not allow myself to get teary, even as the urge was high. I looked around the theatre and at the audience, and I thought, *If only all of you knew... And now she has to give it her all, feeling unwell and taking strong antibiotics.* Any other person would have been lying in bed all week – except for ballet dancers, of course. Barely two weeks after her debut in Covent Garden, she was about to dance Odette/Odile with Matthew Ball as her Prince.

As I sat in the audience, I wondered how she could possibly perform when she felt so weak, but I did not allow myself to become emotionally affected. I knew Yasmine never wanted me to feel sorry for her, and certainly not when she had to perform in less than in optimum condition. She is unforgiving towards herself. Any display of personal, physical or mental weakness is totally unacceptable to her, and it would be misplaced for me to display my maternal weakness. There was no room for any ballet mum tears.

Luckily, I sat next to Lesley Collier (former Principal ballerina of The Royal Ballet, and appointed Répétiteur in 2000). Lesley had taken over as Yasmine's coach in Madrid from Olga Evreinoff, who had coached her in London. Lesley assured me that Yasmine would be fine and that she would be able to get through this long ballet, even if she wasn't feeling 100%.

Two days later, and without much time to recuperate from her Thursday evening show (rehearsals took up her recovery time), her second performance – partnered by Principal dancer Federico Bonelli – started, but this time at 10pm. Yasmine was very much under the weather, she was weakened and still on antibiotics, but there was no stopping her. She was on a roll, she was fearless, she was in her zone, she was on fire, she lived in the moment, she was self-assured, she had prepared herself as much as she could. And above all, she trusted herself. *After all, she is doing what she loves doing most*, I told myself with a sigh.

At fifteen minutes past midnight, with Act III in full swing, Yasmine was about to tackle the highly anticipated Coda and the thirty-two fouettés. I was nervous, knowing that the antibiotics would affect her inner-ear balance, and she had never danced that late at night. Applause followed the tour-de-force fouettés, but I overheard a woman sitting right behind me saying to her neighbour "*...oh, but she 'travelled'* (meaning Yasmine did not stay on the axiomatic "head-of-the-needle" spot*) doing her thirty-two fouettés.*"

I had to seriously rein myself in from turning around and saying, "Well, dear, you try doing this being ill, as well as dancing two performances of *Swan Lake* within the space of forty-eight hours." Luckily, I managed to zip my mouth shut!

The performance finished at 1am, and a large crowd had gathered at the Stage Door by the time I arrived there. When Yasmine ultimately walked through the Stage Door, I could see she was totally drained but she kept smiling, as dancers do whenever they are confronted with the public. She posed willingly for photos to be taken of her. There were many mothers with their young daughters or sons, keen to have their photo taken with Yasmine, as a souvenir. It was nearly 2am by the time the crowd had left.

I finally hailed a taxi, her physiotherapist joined us, and we returned to her hotel. Back in her room, I asked if I should order some food from the restaurant, but she was already preparing her bath so I knew it was time to leave her alone. I wanted nothing more than to stay by her side. It had been a tough week for her, as well as for me, but I knew I had to give her space now to be alone. I was content knowing that I had done whatever I could do to help her, to have been there for her. I left her room at 2:30am and I walked back to my hotel on a deserted Calle de la Princesa.

With the Madrid tour coming to an end, she could turn the page on her first season as a Principal ballerina. The following day, she flew out to the South of France to perform in an open-air Gala, and from there she flew to Denmark to dance in various open-air locations all over the country. On my flight back to London, I thought, *How much must she love dancing for her to do what she has just done*? Her love for ballet goes far beyond mere love, and for mere mortals like me, it is sometimes difficult to fully comprehend this.

> *"It is no exaggeration to say that, apart from talent, intelligence, physical capability and beauty, ballet calls for the devotion of a nun, the willpower of a mountaineer, the bodily strength of a lion, the endurance of a long-distance runner, the memory of an elephant, the industry of a bee and the self-discipline of a soldier."*
>
> (Maria Fay, *Mind Over Body*)

Yasmine had much to look forward to the following Season (2018-2019). She was dancing her debut as Gamzatti in *La Bayadère*; Kitri in Carlos Acosta's *Don Quixote*; Fokine's *The Firebird*, partnered by Edward Watson; Ashton's *Two Pigeons*; and she would also reprise several other roles as well as dancing Juliet in *Romeo and Juliet*, and *Symphony in C* for the worldwide live cinema relay.

In the midst of preparing for her debut as Kitri in Covent Garden, she had been invited by Helgi Thomasson, the Director of San Francisco Ballet, to dance Aurora in his version of *The Sleeping Beauty*, with Principal dancer Joseph Walsh as her Prince. Any free time she had rehearsing her role of Kitri at the Royal Opera House was filled by teaching herself Helgi Thomasson's version of *The Sleeping Beauty*, and without a coach. After dancing her debut as Kitri in Covent Garden, she flew out to San Francisco early the following morning. On arrival at the San Francisco Opera House, she was told she could take the day off to get over her jetlag, but she insisted they start rehearsals straight away. The San Francisco Opera House was just across the road from the apartment where she was staying. Her only "flatmate" was a mouse that just wouldn't leave her alone, and I received several photos from across the Atlantic Ocean of Yasmine chasing the mouse that kept her up all night. The presence of the mouse was reported to her contact at San Francisco Ballet, and a Pest Control team was promptly sent to her apartment. Multiple mousetraps were placed all over her flat. That night, I received a photo of the mouse being trapped by the tip of her tail. Yasmine took pity on the mouse, and she set her free...

Soon after her return to London, Yasmine started preparing for her debut in the title role in Mikhail Fokine's *The Firebird*. Years before, during Yasmine's first year as an Artist in the corps de ballet, Dame Monica Mason (then Director of The Royal Ballet) had selected Yasmine as a cover to Lauren Cuthbertson, in preparation for a "Partnership and Access" performance at the Royal Opera House. Monica herself had danced the title role in *The Firebird*, and she in turn had learned the role from Margot Fonteyn; Tamara Karsavina, who had created the role of *The Firebird*, had rehearsed Fonteyn.

Dancing the role of *The Firebird* requires immense stamina, besides possessing an impeccable technique. The ballerina has to become savage, untamed, wild, and authoritative. It is a killer role unlike any other. There is no human emotion on display. The ballerina needs grandeur, elevation, and she must be able to dance on a grand scale; she must become an insubordinate and a hard-to-manage bird. Yasmine was in awe of Monica's extensive knowledge, and she felt deeply honoured to have such a wealth of historical knowledge being passed down, from Tamara Karsavina to Margot Fonteyn to Monica Mason, and now to herself.

Shortly afterwards, Yasmine flew to Japan on Tour with the Company to dance Kitri in Carlos Acosta's *Don Quixote*. She returned to Japan in August at the invitation of Miyako Yoshida, much loved former Royal Ballet Principal ballerina who retired at the end of Season 2009-2010. The Sugar Plum Fairy was Miyako's signature role with The Royal Ballet, and she danced her last Sugar Plum Fairy in December 2009 when Yasmine was still a Graduate student. Yasmine danced in all of Miyako Yoshida's shows as a Snowflake. Ten years later, Miyako Yoshida invited Yasmine to dance The Sugar Plum Fairy in her Farewell Gala, "The Last Dance", performed in Tokyo on 7 and 8 August, 2019.

At the start of season 2019-2020, her tenth season, she had been invited to dance the title role Odette/Odile in *Swan Lake* at the VIII World Classical Ballet Kremlin Festival, held at Kremlin Palace in Moscow, with Isaac Hernandez (Principal dancer, English National Ballet) as her Prince. Sadly, she had to cancel those performances due to an ankle injury. When on holiday in Mallorca with her fiancé Riccardo, she seriously sprained her ankle whilst they were climbing the Serra de Tramuntana mountain range. By the time they had reached the road and Riccardo had found a taxi to take her to the nearest hospital, her ankle had swollen up to the size of a grapefruit. She spent the remainder of their holiday on crutches, lying by the pool. She was beyond furious with herself, but I told her an accident is just that: an accident.

The Royal ballet opened the season with *Manon*, and Yasmine was cast as Mistress – a role she had danced since she was a Soloist – with Marianela Nuñez and Roberto Bolle dancing the title roles. But she had not recovered in time after her fall. Her first comeback role was *Concerto* – 2nd Movement, partnered by fellow Principal Ryoichi Hirano. Her performance in *Concerto* was filmed for the worldwide live cinema relay, and it was the perfect short ballet to come back to: lyrical, slow, and controlled.

On Thursday, 7 November, the honour of dancing Princess Aurora on the opening night of *The Sleeping Beauty* fell to Yasmine, partnered by Principal dancer Matthew Ball. Dance critic Gerald Dowler wrote in his review: "First night Aurora was Yasmine Naghdi, a Principal who combines pin-point technical accuracy with meltingly beautiful arms. Her Princess was generously danced, with noticeable use of her eyes, which darted around to each of her four suitors in the Rose Adagio with a mixture of excitement and curiosity. Throughout, her dancing was characterised by fine musicality, which allowed her to 'ride' Tchaikovsky's music and to phrase the choreography in great arcs of movement. Her solo in Act II was danced with the purest classical proportion, grace, and poise. In Act III she brought a new found regality to her dancing as she celebrated her marriage to Florimund, her movements expansive yet always aristocratic."

Vera Liber, *British Theatre Guide*, 7 November, 2019, wrote: "Three hours (including two intervals) of five-star pleasure, the first night of *The Sleeping Beauty* is a glorious opening to the festive season. Impeccable dancing from Yasmine Naghdi as Princess Aurora, sweetness itself, I am in love. She alone is worth the price of the ticket. Their romantic pas de deux are in another realm, but the focus is on the ballerina, it is her ballet after all, his very much the supporting role. Technique strong, balances strong, acting charming, expressive face, one that bears some similarity to Margot Fonteyn's in the 1946 production that reopened the House after the Second World War."

Five days after dancing the opening night of *The Sleeping Beauty*, Yasmine went home after the half an hour call had passed, as she was not scheduled to dance Aurora that night; fellow Principal dancer Akane Takada was. Yasmine had checked on her colleague during the half an hour call, had been assured that all was fine, and that Akane would be able to dance the evening performance. Just as Yasmine had her dinner and was about to take a bath, her mobile phone rang. As soon as she heard Kevin's voice, she knew what was up. He asked her how quickly she could get to the Royal Opera House. She said it would take her about half hour.

Yasmine ran out of her flat to grab a cab, knowing the audience was made to wait for her arrival before the performance could proceed. The taxi driver must have thought she had gone mad, as she constantly urged him to drive faster and faster, just like a jockey urging his horse to race faster. She instructed the driver not to follow his GPS but to follow her shortcut directions. Act II was eventually cut out, and the Interval was extended until Yasmine arrived at the Royal Opera House. Kevin went on stage to announce Yasmine's arrival and to inform the audience that *The Sleeping Beauty* was about to resume. She literally ran to her dressing room, where staff were waiting to do her make-up and hair, and to assist her in putting on her tutu.

The Prince that night was Alexander Campbell. They had never before danced Princess Aurora and Prince Florimund together, and they had only five minutes in the wings to quickly practise their fish dive before going on stage to finish the ballet. Yasmine felt like she had finished running a marathon.

Hari Mountford, in "The Ballet That Actually Went Wrong But Had A Happy Ending", *The Londonist*, 15 November, 2019, described the atmosphere: "...minutes before it began, Director of The Royal Ballet, Kevin O'Hare comes on the stage to announce that due to an injury, Ryoichi Hirano (Prince) will not be dancing this evening: Alexander Campbell, another of the Company's Principals, will take his place. After all the show must go on... After the second interval, however, there is a delay. Everyone is seated yet Act II is running ten minutes behind schedule. Kevin O'Hare graces the stage for a second time and informs us that Takada was injured during the previous act and cannot continue with the performance. Gasps circulate. The shock ripples through the audience. Suddenly this real-life drama feels tenser than *The Sleeping Beauty* itself. We are assured, though, that another ballerina is on her way to dance the second and third acts: the show must, once again, go on. The theatre empties out as people head to the bar or they go home (staying for some would have meant missing their last train home).

Forty-five minutes later the warning bell sounds to let us know that the ballet will recommence, as the ballerina has arrived. Kevin O'Hare (his third appearance) lets us all know that the ballerina who has come to save the day is Yasmine Naghdi, who danced the production's opening night. Act II is cut short, but we are treated to the full Act III. In all honesty we were utterly spoiled with Naghdi, and her flawless technique and her beautiful lines are exquisite."

Just before Christmas, she danced her debut as Swanilda in *Coppélia*, simultaneously preparing to dance her debut as Tatiana in John Cranko's *Onegin*. Her much anticipated debut was scheduled on 24 January. It was a dream come true to be given the role of Tatiana. She had artistically grown up in this ballet, as she had danced all the other roles. She had watched and admired many Tatianas in the past, and she had always wondered how she would eventually portray her. It is definitely her outright favourite role to date.

"I can live the story on stage with so many outpourings of emotions. It's the same as with Juliet. I can go deep within the character and the story, and I feel emotionally totally drained afterwards in a very beautiful way. Each time I danced this role, I matured and grew artistically as a dancer, and throughout each performance," she said.

Immediately following her debut, she flew out to Japan to dance in a Gala organised by Hikaru Kobayashi (former First Soloist of The Royal Ballet), from 28 January until 3 February. Yasmine danced the *Swan Lake* – Black Swan pas de deux, Solo, and the Coda – with Vadim Muntagirov as her partner; also Juliet in the Balcony scene from *Romeo and Juliet*; as well as *La Sylphide* pas de deux with William Bracewell. They danced three performances in Tokyo.

Two days before she was due to return to London, she received a phone call from Alina Cojocaru, asking Yasmine if she could take over from her and dance *Ballet Imperial* with Friedemann Vogel in the "Alina Cojocaru Dream Project 2020", from 2 to 6 February. Yasmine said yes before realising what she was getting herself into. She had never danced this ballet before. Additionally, on arrival in Tokyo, she had come down with the flu and a chest infection, and she was really unwell (she somehow always seems to catch a bug whenever taking a long-haul flight). She had felt perfectly fine flying out to Tokyo.

On the other hand, I began to seriously worry about the Coronavirus, as the media were reporting numerous cases of infected passengers on board the *Diamond Princess* cruise ship, anchored at the Yokohama port in Japan since February 3. *If the virus is circulating on that ship, it surely must be circulating in Tokyo, too*, I concluded. Yasmine could just not afford to get ill, and promptly made an appointment with her trusted Japanese medical doctor, who put her on an hour-long intravenous vitamin drip. The next morning, she felt much better and, in a matter of two days – with the "help" of a DVD – she taught herself *Ballet Imperial* in her hotel room. On the third day, Yasmine and Friedemann Vogel had their one and only stage call with Tokyo Ballet, in the Orchard Hall of the Bunkamura cultural complex in Shibuya. Yasmine absolutely adored dancing with Vogel, and they danced two performances of *Ballet Imperial*.

She flew back to London on 6 February, very much looking forward to dancing Tatiana in *Onegin* on 24th February, and to start rehearsing Odette/Odile for her upcoming *Swan Lake* performances in Covent Garden... but that was not to be.

This is the intense, supposedly glamorous, life of a Principal ballerina.

"*Chapeau. Il faut le faire!*" as the French say.

Chapter Eleven

And Down Came the Curtains at the Royal Opera House

Onegin
24 February, 2020

Act III, Scene 2: Tatiana's boudoir

Federico Bonelli (Eugene Onegin) and Yasmine (Tatiana) are dancing their third pas de deux in one of the most effective story ballets of our time. Tatiana's internal struggle is translated into her physical scuffle between her and Onegin. Federico desperately whirls around Yasmine, pulls her towards him, and lifts her. Her resistance gradually diminishes, and she eventually runs towards him and jumps into his arms. Regardless of her emotional upheaval, Tatiana realises that Onegin's change of heart has come far too late. She tears up his letter before his eyes, and she orders him to leave her forever. The crimson curtains slowly lower after what was to be Yasmine's last full-length performance that season. Yasmine and Federico's "red runner" (when the front of the curtain is pulled back centrally, providing a backdrop for them to take their "curtain call") gave the audience another chance to clap and cheer for Tatiana and Eugene Onegin. When the applause gradually faded and they both disappeared behind the curtain, little did we all realise what a "tsunami" was about to hit us, and that we would not see Yasmine dance a full-length ballet again for at least another year-and-a-half. We were all still happily mingling backstage, unaware that our lives were about to change.

The first warning signs came two weeks before the first lockdown on 23 March, 2020. No-one was allowed to wait by the Stage Door any longer, nor to go backstage after a performance. By the end of the following week, all the dancers received a Company email on Sunday 15 March, instructing them not to come into the Royal Opera House the following morning, until further notice. It was a swift and sensible decision, a week before the Government ordered a total lockdown of the entire country.

Yasmine had just started rehearsing her role of Odette/Odile, and she was very much looking forward to performing *Swan Lake* again later on in the Season. Two years had passed since she danced her debut in June 2018. Then, from one day to the other, there were no more rehearsals and no more performances, and Yasmine's three *Swan Lake* performances in May and June were cancelled. On Tuesday, 24 March, 2020, precisely one month after her last performance in *Onegin* and one day before her 28th birthday, the United Kingdom went into its first lockdown.

As I write, the world is engulfed in a pandemic. Everything closed down, apart from food shops, pharmacies, and banks; airports closed and planes stopped flying; people stopped driving their cars; the roads and skies emptied; theatres, cinemas, bars, nightclubs, hotels, and restaurants all closed their doors. London went eerily quiet. Except for the birds... they were singing their hearts out.

The beginning of this pandemic reminds me of the story of *The Sleeping Beauty*, when Princess Aurora is joyfully dancing without a care in the world, then Carabosse (the Wicked Fairy) interrupts her by giving her a spindle, and Aurora pricks her finger and collapses in a dead faint. Carabosse laughingly reminds everyone of the spell she had cast at the christening of Princess Aurora, that she would die on her sixteenth birthday. The Lilac Fairy intervenes to ensure Aurora will not die, but fall into a hundred-year-long sleep and that a prince would reawaken her. The entire palace falls asleep, thick forest starts growing, branches, and roots engulf the entire palace. *The Sleeping Beauty* has a most distinctive place in The Royal Ballet's repertoire, as the Company reopened the House after World War II in 1946 with *The Sleeping Beauty*. But to me, the story serves as an affecting metaphor of the current situation The Royal Ballet finds itself in, and in this case no-one knows for how long the Royal Opera House and The Royal Ballet will be in a deep "sleep". All we can do for now is wait for the Prince to arrive...

Initially, Yasmine thought the dancers would all keep going, no matter what. But one morning, Philip Mosley called her to say that her Odette/Odile rehearsal was cancelled that day, and that she would be updated as soon as possible. The dancers were still allowed into the building, so she quickly went to the Royal Opera House that morning to grab a few pairs of pointe shoes and some dancewear, just in case they went into lockdown. They all felt they might be off for a maximum of three to four weeks. She was convinced the Triple Bill might be cancelled, but she had high hopes she would be able to dance *Swan Lake*.

Yasmine ensured she kept fit and in peak condition by doing daily Company classes at her home via Zoom, Pilates, yoga, and strength training. At first, the dancers enjoyed their welcome break from rehearsing and performing, but the four weeks' break soon became six weeks. Following a Company Zoom meeting, it was announced that the situation would last for much longer. It was a heart-breaking feeling, and any likely light at the end of the tunnel completely faded away. They just didn't know when they would be able to go back to performing. It soon became obvious that the dancers would not be required to be back any time soon, and the long summer months lay ahead of them. Yasmine had several international invitations lined up to perform abroad, but that was now no longer possible.

When on 3 June, 2020, Italy reopened its borders, Yasmine and Riccardo didn't wait, and they immediately flew to Milan. They spent all of June on the Italian Riviera, in a house by the sea – her favourite place to be. Away from the familiar ballet studios and all her colleagues, Yasmine tried to keep up with her daily ballet class via Zoom. Self-motivation was hard to keep going, and inevitably it gradually started to fade. The daily Company class had only one purpose now – attempting to stay fit and flexible. But working on stamina and doing centre work was impossible. Yasmine would go for long afternoon walks by the sea, whilst Riccardo was able to continue working remotely. A performer she was no more, and it felt like she had lost not only her job but also her identity, and the ambiguity surrounding the reopening date of the Royal Opera House wasn't helping either. She realised she had to keep herself engaged, and to channel her energy into a new project in order to keep going mentally.

Walking by the sea one afternoon, the idea grew to make a dance film. She had always felt a great connection with the sea since her childhood. She loved the smell of the salty air, and the energy and the sound of the waves inspired her. One evening, after returning from their evening walk, and encouraged by Riccardo, Yasmine decided to create a short film aimed at all young dance students, to inspire them to feelings of hope and to give them the comforting thought that they would be able to come back stronger after these difficult times. She contacted a ballet school near Genoa and found four young ballet students eager to collaborate. She met up with Lorenzo Rapetti – a filmmaker who had never worked with ballet dancers before – and Yasmine directed the filming in Italian.

The project allowed her to make good use of her energy, it took her mind off the dreadful situation, and it offered an interesting learning curve. She contacted Paolo Buonvino, the world-renowned composer of the music for *Medici: The Magnificent* – a striking Netflix historical drama series set in Florence, which she had enjoyed watching during lockdown. She approached his agent and explained that the music would be used in a charitable video with the sole purpose to inspire young dancers during this difficult time. He instantly waived the copyright fee.

By the end of June, the dancers were informed they would not be required to be back at the Royal Opera House until early September. Yasmine had no choice but to accept that the possibility of performing for an audience in the near future now seemed to be non-existent. Riccardo suggested they stay put in Italy for the entire summer, and to go on a once-in-a-lifetime road trip. After all, there was no reason for them to return to London, and it would positively distract her.

They spent time on the island of Sardinia, with its many white sandy beaches, rugged coves, and spectacular dunes, and on Sicily's east coast in beautiful Val di Noto, where many towns are listed on Unesco's World Heritage List. The beautiful architecture in the area represents the culmination and final blossoming of Baroque art in Europe. As the sun sets every evening on the sumptuous, honeyed limestone buildings and reaches out with painterly warmth as the hot air cooled down, Yasmine and Riccardo joined in the nightly irresistible social stroll called the *passeggiata*, whilst enjoying many enticing places to consume an *aperitivo* or a *gelato*.

For the first time in well over a decade, Yasmine was able to totally free herself from the daily self-discipline of practice and performing. Never before in her life had she been able to feel so free. In August, they drove from Sicily to mainland Puglia, with its breathtaking landscapes, rugged coastline with crystal clear waters, fascinating caves and small coves, wild small beaches, pine and eucalyptus forests, and charming old towns. It was an area she fell head over heels in love with. Their road trip ended in Tuscany, known for its romantic images of idyllic hill towns with medieval towers, flowering green hills, and fields full of flowers, and for its turbulent history and unsurpassed artistic legacy.

It was an inspiring, truly unique, enriching, and soul-healing time for Yasmine during this dreadful pandemic. It aided her in leaving behind any concerns she had about her career being on halt – and where better to leave it all behind than in beautiful Italy.

The return to a new reality after the summer of 2020, however, felt strange to say the least. Once all the dancers returned to the Royal Opera House, at the start of season 2020-2021, they commenced straight away with their daily Company class, but they needed to adjust to their altered working environment: there were allocated timed studio slots with marked squares on the floor, allowing only eight to ten dancers in at one time, and they all had to wear face masks. Doing intense physical exercises with a face mask on was not only physically restricting but also took its toll mentally. At the entrance to the Stage Door, there were now hand sanitizer dispensers, one dancer at a time was beeped in, their temperature was measured, and they were required to go straight into the studio, into their allocated square. No socialising was allowed with colleagues, nor hanging out in the corridors or rest areas or staff canteen. They had about four to five weeks to get fit, and eventually they were told about the upcoming repertoire and their roles.

The few real-life couples would automatically be able to dance with each other without having to implement social distancing measures, so they were the easiest to schedule for the upcoming performances. The other dancers, of course, objected as they felt they would lose out on any opportunity to dance simply because they were not in a relationship with a fellow dancer. In order to resolve this issue, management realised they would have to do regular testing on all the dancers, and that meant unpleasant deep nose swabs twice a week. The dancers also had to be in a "bubble", and could only dance with their "bubble" partner. Yasmine was "bubbled-up" with Nicol Edmonds, and they danced the Stop Time Rag and Bethena (Concert Waltz) in *Elite Syncopations*, which was a great Season opener. Everyone was over the moon to be back on stage and to be able to dance again, albeit for a socially distanced audience. The excitement didn't last long, though, and another lockdown soon followed in November.

Yasmine was scheduled to dance the Sugar Plum Fairy in *The Nutcracker* on 19 December, 2020, and her performance on

22 December was to be filmed for the worldwide live cinema relay. Both her performances were cancelled, and the live filming never took place, due to London entering into Tier 5 two days prior to her scheduled performance. Two weeks later, right in the midst of winter, the UK went into its third lockdown. That took a further mental toll on her, especially as she had worked so hard to get back to peak performance level. The long winter months lay ahead of her, with no performances to look forward to.

24 February, 2021, was a painful reminder of the day when she last danced the full-length ballet *Onegin* at the Royal Opera House the previous year.

Chapter Twelve

The End of My Journey

My journey as a ballet mum effectively came to an end eight years after Yasmine had started her training at White Lodge. I have learned so much along the way. Her journey has truly enriched me. I connected with all her challenges, and I made them mine. Right from the outset, I was very keen to understand what elite-level ballet training, and all that it entails, was all about. It fascinated me.

What Yasmine has achieved is entirely hers. She merits every inch of her success. She is the one who fought back when things were tough; she battled it out; she worked incredibly hard; she was at times in physical or mental pain – but she never gave up. She did it all.

People every so often ask me what I think or feel whenever I watch Yasmine perform on the stage at the Royal Opera House. It is hard to describe, but it is as if I become one with her; it is a most magical feeling. We have this inexplicable telepathy between us. She knows what I think even when I haven't said a word to her, and I often know what's going on inside her mind without her telling me anything. I have the greatest admiration for her because I know what it took her to get to where she is now, and only I know all of her veiled suffering.

Purposely, I consider it to be her world and not mine. I solely and intentionally existed, and still exist, on the periphery.

I really do not feel any sense of entitlement to enter her world, and Kamran and I will never go backstage after her performance without asking Yasmine beforehand if she is happy for us to be there. Whenever we attend one of her performances, we feel very privileged to sit in the glorious Royal Opera House, and we do not want to ever take that very special feeling for granted.

I, too, was told many years ago to "enjoy the ride". But did I? I suffered at times, knowing how hard her training was. She has achieved what she set out to achieve, and when the crimson curtains open and I see her standing on the stage as Odette or Juliet or Tatiana or Kitri or Giselle, I know what it took her to reach the very top of her profession. To me, professional success is about achieving a healthy work-life balance, to have a fulfilling life away from the stage, and to have other interests to focus on. Yasmine certainly ensured she did, and I am not at all surprised she does not want any performance photographs of herself on display in her home. When on a few occasions I have placed some framed performance photographs of her in her living room, they always disappeared soon after. "Home is home. Stage is stage," she says.

When I reflect on the past seventeen years since Yasmine started training at White Lodge in 2004, on all those students who trained at White Lodge, on those who were subsequently able to progress into the Upper School, and the select Graduates who were offered a contract with The Royal Ballet, four former White Lodgers reached the top rank of Principal dancer of The Royal Ballet: Yasmine, Francesca Hayward, Matthew Ball, and the youngest recently promoted Anna Rose O'Sullivan. (Former White Lodgers and current Principal dancers Laura Morera and Lauren Cuthbertson pre-date 2004.) This is by no means intended to diminish in any way the achievement of other dancers who have trained at the School and became a Principal dancer, First Soloist, Soloist, or corps de ballet dancer in a UK or in an international ballet company. It solely serves to highlight how near impossible it is to reach the highest rank of Principal dancer of The Royal Ballet, one of the foremost ballet companies in the world. Yasmine's journey has highlighted various skills that a ballet student needs to be able to develop throughout their training, as well as skills needed to become a successful professional ballet dancer. Clearly, it is not sufficient to just possess a body that can cope as well as withstand the intense training or the professional demands. It is also necessary to be extremely self-disciplined, possess fast learning skills, have the ability to process and apply corrections fast, working around "criticism" and using it as a learning tool, have a very high degree of wanting to achieve absolute excellence, be consistent and driving oneself continuously forward, have a high degree of focus and a strong memorising ability, have the aptitude to work as a team, and ultimately possess an engaging personality as they eventually need to become veritable artists. Where it "stops" for elite-sports women and men (high-level mastering of the technique in their chosen sport enabling them to win Grand Slams, Tournaments or Games), it only begins for the professional ballet dancer: once she or he fully masters the technique of dancing ballet after many years of training, they need to be able to add an extra layer if they want to reach the top, because they must become a true artist. Technique alone will not get them to the top of their profession. In a way, ballet dancers are artistic athletes, and they are unquestionably in a league of their own. Footballers Cristiano Ronaldo and Lionel Messi, tennis players Novak Djokovic, Rafael Nadal, Roger Federer, and Serena Williams, and golfer Tiger Woods, did not need to become an artist in order to reach the top of their profession.

Many years ago, I invited an acquaintance of mine to the Royal Opera House, as I wanted to introduce her to The Royal Ballet. She had never attended a ballet performance. Before the curtains went up, I tried to enlighten her about the demands of a dancer's life and what it takes to prepare for a role, adding that dancers are nonetheless human beings. They may have just broken up with their partner, or they may be ill or in pain, or have a loved one who passed away, yet "the show must go on" and they will perform. She replied emotionlessly, "You know what? I don't want to know about their problems. I don't want to know if they are ill or sad or upset or unwell or in pain. When I come to see a performance, I expect to see dancers at their best."

Needless to say, I was very taken back by her unforgiving reply, and I felt really hurt by her complete lack of empathy with the dancers. How could she be so cruel, so harsh, so inconsiderate, and so insensitive? But in a way, she was right. People go to the ballet to be entertained and to see dancers perform at their very best. When the audience settles in their seats, they want to be transported into another reality, they want to be moved by the ballet's story and by the technical and artistic skills of the dancers. Of course, the audience has no idea what goes on behind the scenes, or what goes on in a dancer's private life, or even the pain they are in, or anything that might affect their performance. The dancers are experts in leaving their personal issues behind them the moment they step onto the stage. Their adrenaline numbs everything. The human "drama" – inherent to the career of a ballet dancer – is of no importance or of any relevance. Depending on which side of the curtain one takes their "seat", the world of ballet is either a beautiful world or an unforgiving and highly demanding one.

To me, ballet dancers are, beyond any doubt, the most astonishing individuals. We know that in order to become a highly accomplished dancer they must have an unfaltering belief in themselves and in their talent, have downright dedication and total concentration, and they must have the ability to let go of losses and failures and look forward, day after day, to new challenges. They are to be admired and looked upon as some of the greatest role models in our society. As far as I am concerned, there is no other profession as highly demanding as that of a ballet dancer for the many reasons mentioned throughout this book. But there is another side to the coin. On the surface, it is all very magical, it is glamorous, it transports the audience to another planet, and ballet offers us great visual pleasure in tandem with gorgeous orchestral music. It assists many to fleetingly forget about life's problems or hardship. To the audience, the dancers are otherworldly creatures; not really human. In fact, they hardly are like any other normal human being, but behind that magic lies the uncompromising and demanding life of the ballerina and the male dancer. There is the incessant preoccupation with the body, the daily Company class, followed by afternoon rehearsals and the evening performance, adding in early morning Pilates before class or gym workouts to their daily workload in order to fine-tune their muscles. There is the injury management and revalidation for some. They don't really have much power over their career path and the roles they are cast in. A director or a choreographer shapes it. They are the ones who make the artistic choices.

I recollect reading about Lynn Seymour's ordeal in Jann Parry's *Different Drummer: The Life of Kenneth MacMillan* (2009). Lynn Seymour (who joined The Royal Ballet in 1958, and was promoted to Principal in 1959) was Kenneth MacMillan's muse when he created the role of Juliet on her, and Romeo on Christopher Gable. Margot Fonteyn and Rudolf Nureyev, however, danced the Opening Night on 9 February, 1965. Seymour and Gable had been relegated to dance their debut as the fourth cast at the fifth performance. It was pure public humiliation for Seymour and Gable. It must have been beyond devastating for Lynn Seymour, and all the more painful since she had arranged to abort her unborn child in order to be able to perform the role of Juliet. In those days, it was unacceptable for a dancer to get pregnant.

It is a most intriguing part of the book, shedding light on protocol and Company politics, attitudes of the powers-that-be, as well as the ego battles, in the middle of which – to their own detriment – dancers were trapped. Empathy and respect for dancers, treating them as human beings who had feelings, let alone having a voice, was seemingly non-existent back in those days. As a result, Kenneth MacMillan and his muse Lynn Seymour left The Royal Ballet for Berlin a year later. Christopher Gable retired from dancing in favour of acting.

There is also the audience. Each and every one of them has their own favourite(s) according to their individual taste, and some connect with dancer X, whilst others connect better with dancer Y. Some have an extensive knowledge of ballet and of the technical demands of ballet dancing, aiding a deeper appreciation of the art form; others are content to enjoy a pleasant evening out, watching dancers perform on stage.

There are also the opinions of various dance critics. We only have to read the reviews after an opening night to note how one critic will give the performance two stars while another one will give it three, or four, or five stars. Some critics will rave about a dancer's performance; another one will floor her or him, or even the entire performance. I do miss the reviews of those highly knowledgeable and well-informed dance critics such as Clement Crisp, Judith Mackrell, Alistair Macaulay, and Ismene Brown. They were all contributory to being able to increase a better and deeper understanding of all the ballets I had seen, and I learned so much just by reading their erudite reviews. Sadly, they have now all stepped down.

Laura Cappelle (*Dance Magazine*, August 08, 2019) writes: "...In one fell swoop, dance criticism has lost decades of experience and memories, and these writers won't be easily replaced... Together they made up a rich fabric of perspectives. There was always something to learn from Mackrell's clear-eyed elegance, Jennings tough-love straightforwardness, or Macaulay's unravelling of historical and choreographic structures. ...The balance is now shifting further toward freelancers who juggle writing with other occupations... Few young writers have the means to see hundreds of performances, much less hundreds of Swan Lakes."

Clement Crisp once famously quipped: "I want to hear from someone who has been to 500 Swan Lakes before they lift a pen." And I entirely agree with him. Crisp was such a knowledgeable critic, with a very rich dance vocabulary and a unique sense of humour, who with great economy of words could say it all in just a few short paragraphs. Now, unfortunately, some reviews seem to have been written in haste by freelance writers, and some reviews are rather formulaic; more often than not, very little of substance is said in a few short paragraphs. The absence of those truly knowledgeable and professional dance critics can undoubtedly be felt, and they are a great loss to the dance world.

When one has gone through this extraordinary journey, words absolutely fail me to express the highest respect I have for ballet dancers. It is a world that demands the uppermost veneration of anybody who is involved, in order to give us, the audience, an astonishing experience. From the Director of The Royal Ballet, Kevin O'Hare, and his Artistic and Administrative staff, to the Music Director of The Royal Ballet Koen Kessels, and the Orchestra, to the formidable Senior Stage Manager Johanna Adams-Farley, as well as all the technical and backstage crew and staff, and those who dismantle the stage late at night, to all the dressers, make-up artists, and the staff in the Costume Department, to every single freelancer and all the ushers, the dedicated Box Office and Stage Door staff, from the charismatic and charming Front of House Manager Salvatore Scalzo, to Nicolas Capelle, one of many ushers, who is always lovely and generous with his time whenever he carries Yasmine's bouquets to her dressing room, often assisting us in getting them all into a taxi, to the affable Eugene at the Stage Door, whom I have known since Yasmine was eleven years old, as well as all the teachers who tirelessly train so many enthusiastic and devoted young students. They are all part of this magical world that makes up The Royal Ballet and the Royal Opera House. They enrich the life of so many people, including ours. They all cannot get enough praise, admiration, and appreciation for what they do. In the end, I can only agree with Albert Einstein who said:

"Dancers are the athletes of God."

Chapter Thirteen

A *Tête-à-Tête* with My Daughter

When I embarked on writing *Tears of a Ballet Mum*, it meant having to relive the past twenty-nine years.

One evening during lockdown, Yasmine and I took out the photo albums relating to her years at The Royal Ballet School. We had not looked at them for well over a decade. The first photos showed her Junior Associates' audition photos and eleven-year-old Yasmine attending the White Lodge Summer Fair as a Junior Associate. Some showed her standing all by herself in a pensive mood, followed by photos of Yasmine dressed as a Spring Page and a Coach Boy in *Cinderella* dating back to December 2003, of twelve-year-old Yasmine as a Little Swan when she danced in *Swan Lake* with The Royal Ballet, of pyjama parties and pillow fights in her dormitory at White Lodge, of a Saturday evening 60s' costume party, and other fancy dress disco parties, photos of various White Lodge Summer Fairs, some showing her dancing as a Chicken in The Chicken Dance in *La Fille mal gardée*, Year 11 Graduation photos showing Yasmine in her long gown coming down the staircase at the back of White Lodge, of Gailene Stock giving Yasmine a rose at the bottom of the staircase, Young British Dancer of the Year 2007, 2008, and 2009 competition photos, photos of seventeen-year-old Yasmine talking to Dame Monica Mason, and photos of Gailene Stock and Zenaida Yanowsky coaching her, photos of Yasmine with Lauren Cuthbertson, Sergei Polunin, and other previous YBDY winners, as well as photos of her last day in the Graduate Year with her teacher Petal Miller Ashmole.

As we browsed through the albums, I asked Yasmine if she could change one thing about her younger self during the time she was in training at White Lodge what she would do differently. She replied without any hesitation: "To worry less. I definitely worried far too much, more than I needed to, but that is easier said than done! It is part of the process you have to go through, with all the doubts and questions you have as a child. As the brain evolves and grows, it hands you the tools to be able to deal with your fears, doubts, and insecurities. I would certainly tell myself to worry less and instead focus on the task at hand. I would concentrate more on my personal journey and not be distracted by what others are doing and saying."

This brought us to the subject of current social media use by young dance trainees.

"Yes, social media has such a heavy presence in our lives right now. I think social media can be a distraction from what is the true essence of ballet and ballet training. It is absolutely vital to stay laser-focussed on what you want to achieve, on who you are, and to draw out all the trivial 'noise'. One has to concentrate on one's own journey and progress, work on self-improvement, on mental strength and control, and on mental wellbeing. It is absolutely vital to stay grounded and focus on what really matters. When I started training at White Lodge, Facebook was still in its very infancy and Instagram and TikTok didn't exist yet, thus comparing myself to others did not distract me. I could concentrate on my progress, and I only had my classmates to measure myself against. I reduced many distractions in my training environment so that I could solely focus on my own advancement."

Looking at a photo of twelve-year-old Yasmine posing in her new school uniform, taken on the morning I drove her to White Lodge to start her first day, I asked her if she had been conscious of what was waiting for her.

"Definitely not," she said. "No child can ever have an idea what awaits them at the start of their training. However, I always had a feeling that it would all work out for me in some way or another, and it felt as if I had a 'guardian angel' sitting on my right shoulder, telling me everything would be all right and fall into place. Of course, I also had a little 'devil' sitting on my other shoulder, trying to tell me otherwise. That's when doubt sets in, but also when dreams are made, and having strength of character comes in handy. Teachers, friends, parents, or carers are all helpful when obstacles are thrown at you from left, right, and centre, in order to develop into the professional dancer you eventually want to become. Most people have absolutely no idea what a student dancer or a professional dancer has to go through on a daily basis."

"You know that throughout your training years I was very conscious of the fact that I did not want to give you the feeling I was overly present in your life," I replied. "Did you ever feel I was?"

"Well, one thing I know for sure is that I could have never done it without you, and that I wouldn't be where I am today without your phenomenal support and your level-headed advice. Of course, it very much depends on a child's personality. I believe if I had had a different personality, I could have rebelled against you, but I was an obedient, gentle natured, and highly sensitive child, and I always felt reassured by you. I needed that. I feel very lucky and fortunate that you were able to invest so much time in me. I had complete trust in every word you said. I accepted your advice and all your guidance. We had, and we still have, such a lovely and close relationship," she told me. "To have had a knowledgeable and informed parent paving the way for me, so that I could grab the tools, was absolutely amazing. Teenagers usually rebel against their parents and teachers, and they will do the opposite of what's being asked of them; they are dealing with changes in their personality, and changes in their physical and mental development. We had a very harmonious partnership in the sense that we worked together, you never suffocated me, and you always left the final action or decision up to me, so in the end I always felt that I was the one in charge.

"There was never any wrong guidance, and I am so grateful to have had you as my guardian angel, or fairy godmother as I like to call you," Yasmine went on. "As a child, you really need someone to be there for you, to look out for you, and to get an adult perspective on issues you are confronted with. You need a trusted person right next to you to give you the assurance, or reassurance, that you are doing all right. Good communication is key. You just got the balance right: you knew when to merely listen to me and not say anything; you also knew when I needed advice and what precisely to say to help me; you also knew when to be tough on me. And there were certainly times you were really tough, and there were also times you just wouldn't take any of my moaning or complaining. It all rightly toughened me up. I would not change it for anything in the world. Mollycoddling just has no place at all in elite-level ballet or sports training; it only weakens you. It will never set anyone up in order to be able to deal with the harsh demands of a professional career in ballet."

I reminded her of that weekend she came home, having just started the first Term in Year 9, when I told her that she could change course whenever she felt like it. Looking back at it now, I wanted to know if she had ever questioned her chosen path.

"Yes, of course I did," she admitted. "Doubt was, and still is, present almost every day. It is human nature to doubt what you do, but that should be seen as a positive in order to drive you in the right direction. Particularly as a child in training, you are always faced with doubt about your own abilities; you are faced with your peers, and you will always wonder if you are as good as the others, and you will always wonder if you will get a good grade, good results, dance well at the end-of-year performances. When things don't go like you want them to go, your doubt will get amplified. That's where a strong personality has to come in, so that you are able to keep yourself going and to keep pushing yourself in the right direction. You need to tell yourself: 'Well, I didn't get a satisfying result this time, but next year I will be better.' Even when dancing with a ballet company as corps de ballet member or as a Soloist, you'll go to the casting board and you will see the name of someone else or you'll see the names of two people in front of you, and you are only down as a cover. You will feel it is not fair, or you will doubt your capabilities. Doubt is poisonous for your mind and your self-esteem. You need to be very strong to keep going and to work hard every day, and use that to drive yourself forward rather than to allow yourself to give in, to feel sorry for yourself, and to get upset and spiral down. But one never loses doubt. It's part of being human. Anyone who doesn't doubt her or himself is incredibly lucky."

Looking at the photos of her trip to St Petersburg, where she is standing next to her ballet teacher Miss van Schoor in front of the Hermitage Winter Palace on the snow-covered square, wearing a white Cossack faux fur hat, our conversation moved on to the topic of the good and the bad moments, and I asked her what her best and worst memories were.

"Well, we always tend to push away our bad memories and I do have several, but my worst memories are of those moments when teachers were dismissive, or when I felt disrespected or belittled. As a young student, you seek appreciation and you seek the attention of your teachers, and when you don't get that your doubts will be augmented and you will feel worthless, not good enough, not appreciated, and this often leads to low self-esteem or, worse, self-destruction. My best memories are when Christopher Carr grabbed me as an eleven-year-old saying, '*This one will do*!' resulting in my first appearance on the stage of the Royal Opera House. When Gailene Stock selected me, alongside a few other students, to go to the Mariinsky Ballet School in St Petersburg to take classes with the Russian students and to perform. It was the pivotal moment when I decided I wanted to become a ballerina. My two weeks at the Prague Summer School, where I felt totally free from any restrictions whatsoever, and my joy of dancing came back. When Gailene Stock fast-tracked me into the Graduate Year, thus gaining a year to accustom myself to being a young professional dancer in the corps de ballet. And the final five minutes I spent with my Graduate teacher Petal Miller Ashmole on my last day at The Royal Ballet School. Her advice to me was priceless."

Of course, we could not avoid recalling that evening when we walked together in the cold and the snow. It is a time she really is not keen to talk about at all, because "the past is the past", she says. Since then, we have hardly ever mentioned that challenging year.

I hesitantly touched on the subject, because I wanted to know if she could remember how she felt when I picked her up at Gloucester Road tube station, and when we went for a walk in the snow. There was silence between us for a moment, and she took quite a while before she replied.

"Oh, I felt totally broken and lost. You really saved me. I was ready to pack my bags and leave. For a moment, I even contemplated giving it all up. I had reached a point where I could no longer take what was going on and I had totally lost my motivation. You provided me with a strong shoulder to cry on, and you managed to show me the bigger picture. You encouraged me to rise above it all, to make myself mentally stronger, to solely focus on my mental well-being and on myself, and to completely ignore what had become a corrosive atmosphere. That moment we stood in the snow, you were incredibly tough on me, but that precisely aided me to make a complete U-turn and to come out so much stronger. It's not when things are easy that one learns how to fight back; it's when things are really tough. Your empathy and support, combined with your profound understanding of my distressed state at that time, persuaded me to continue and to never give up when things are tough. It made me into who I am today."

"So, what do you ultimately consider are the factors that have contributed to you reaching the highest rank of Principal ballerina?" I asked her.

"Oh, there are many. Firstly, I am blessed with a strong body that could take the intense training, and as a young dancer in the corps de ballet and at Soloist level. I could take on physically and technically demanding roles, and often at short notice. I also recover fast post-performance, as well as from an occasional physical niggle. I am also lucky to have a very fast metabolism. As a student, I could eat whatever my body asked for. I never had to diet or restrict my diet, and that goes hand-in-hand with a healthy body. My mind is also very much like a sponge. I am a fast learner, and I adapt like a chameleon. I have also been injury-free throughout the entire decade I have been dancing with The Royal Ballet, so I never had to stop dancing because of an injury, thus my career progression was never slowed down. I was able to complete every season, reaching my goals in each rank. Once I became a professional dancer, I invested every bit of my dream, hopes, and energy in defining myself. Up until I became a Soloist, I had no life outside my daily involvement with my profession, and I gave it my all – day after day. My only day off was on a Sunday, my only resting day in a week. Looking back now, it feels as if I was running inside a tunnel, all I wanted was to run towards that 'light', that 'exit', which for me was reaching the top. Excellence in ballet, and dance on the whole, demands a lifestyle of profound and true commitment, as does the training during your childhood. There is no short cut, no room for excuses, or any display of weakness. As you know 'Easy' never did it for me; the tougher it all became, the more I thrived. You need a fighting spirit, and a strong and balanced mind, and that needs to be set up in childhood. I also feel timing and luck are crucial factors. Entering the Company at the right time, when there are shifts in dancers leaving ranks, or when a higher injury rate opens up places and you can take over a role at short notice and grab those opportunities. I would say my height, small to medium, has also been an advantage, because I could/can dance with shorter as well as taller partners, and this makes a dancer very versatile. Another factor is that I always did, and still do, my 'homework'. I always researched my roles, and as a dancer in the corps de ballet I had my eyes just about everywhere, so that I was at all times ready to go on stage at short notice, and also being adaptable to the various repertoire, from the contemporary to the classics."

"As you are well aware, I realised very early on in your training that your mental health was first and foremost of utmost importance to me," I told Yasmine. "And it was my hope that assisting you to develop strong mental skills would facilitate getting through your training with greater ease."

"It certainly did," Yasmine replied. "Firstly, the initial and main thought mechanisms that helped me as a child were learning to firmly believe in myself and my abilities, to learn from my setbacks and to see them in a positive light, to control external distractions, to achieve inner silence, and certainly to have the ability to cut out all the unnecessary 'noise', as I call it. And there can be a lot of it. You showed me the way, and I committed myself early on in my training to prioritise my personal and mental development, and this helped me greatly to ease the hurt that I felt at times. That resulted in being able to fully focus on what really mattered. I was a highly sensitive child, and thanks to you I toughened up. I ensured that I was doing the right thing under the most demanding circumstances, and ultimately, I avoided distractions on a daily basis. I eventually learned to avoid wasting my energy on issues that were beyond my control. I learned how to control what was in my control, and to let go what was not. Developing such a thought process and self-confidence took time. After our walk in the snow that notorious evening, I never lost perspective ever again, and from then on I knew where my priorities lay."

Our conversation moved on to her years as a professional, and I asked her to pick out one moment when she was the most emotional after a performance.

"Ah, that has to be after my performance of Tatiana in John Cranko's *Onegin*. I had dreamed for years of dancing the role of Tatiana. When I joined the Company, I did the most basic role in this ballet, that of the reflection of Tatiana when she goes to the mirror. It is a non-dancing role. Then I danced all the corps de ballet roles. As a First Artist, I danced Olga, and again as a Soloist. I danced every female role in this ballet, and when I was told I was cast as Tatiana, it really was a dream coming true. I had watched so many great ballerinas dance Tatiana, and I was eager to stamp my own mark on the role. The ballet *Onegin* is so real, so natural, and so raw. Becoming Tatiana is an indescribable feeling. I had never experienced anything like it before. I could pour so many of my own emotions into her character. It is very hard to let go of Tatiana when the curtain comes down, and I still sobbed once my performance was over and I walked back to my dressing room. It is really hard to come away from her character. It is hard to go back to being Yasmine after having been Tatiana. Of all the roles I have danced over the past decade, this is the character I have connected with the most, and I so enjoyed living her journey. It has been the greatest moment in my career so far, and a great memory that I will always keep very close to my heart. It was an immense honour to have been chosen by Reid Anderson (Artistic Director of the Stuttgart Ballet from 1996-2018, who stages John Cranko's masterpieces with renowned ballet companies all over the world), and to work so closely with him. I learned so much from working with Reid in preparation of my debut. It was, and will always remain, very unique to me."

"You are about to start your 12th Season with The Royal Ballet, but what does professional success and excellence really mean to you?" I queried.

"Success to me is fundamentally to be happy with who I am and with what I have achieved, and to be able to live a balanced life. My personal happiness paves the way to being a happy and a healthy dancer, and it allows me to rehearse, focus, and work towards what I want to achieve, and to create a positive working environment for myself. If you don't do it for yourself, nobody else will! Happiness is never served on a silver plate, and as a professional dancer there is always a plethora of distractions and dissatisfactions, but I refuse to be preoccupied by them. I refuse to be distracted by any unconstructiveness, as well as by issues potentially preventing me to get the very best out of myself."

She went on, "I regularly debrief myself, because I have a deep-rooted desire to be in a constant state of improvement; it is a fundamental and vital part of the joy I find in my profession, of wanting to achieve excellence and perfection. If I am not happy with my performance, I will always analyse why, but I also take a positive out of it. Why criticise yourself after you have given it your all? Try approving of yourself, too, and see what happens! What I consider to be a moment of technical failure is an opportunity to learn. It assists me to correct what went wrong, adjust, and to avoid it in the future. People may naturally assume you always believe in yourself, but when the results aren't there, the first thing that can shatter is your self-belief and confidence. The key to my success is that over the years I have also developed a self-determining belief without feeling the need for any external approval."

Within this context, I told Yasmine that I had recently watched tennis star Venus Williams being interviewed. Upfront as Williams is, her reply to a journalist asking her how she deals with questions and criticism from the media after having played a match, or winning or losing a tournament, was: "To every single person in the media asking me a question, I say: you can't play as well as I can and you never will, so no matter what you say or write, you'll never light a candle to me. That's how I deal with it."

Yasmine replied, "Well, external appreciation and validation of the arts, sports, and ballet is, and will always be, totally subjective. To me, self-confidence is not about 'they like me'. Self confidence is 'I'll be fine if they don't'."

So, what exactly does "having success" mean to you? I asked.

"Success is having reached the highest rank in my profession, but success is an ongoing process. You can never rest on your laurels. Dreams and goals never end, and this keeps the fire inside me burning. The work is never over, but once in a while you must take stock and be happy with your achievements, however small or big.

Gratitude also contributes to my feeling of having achieved success. Life as a ballerina is being in constant pursuit of excellence, and I relish its intensity and cherish the beautiful moments that come with success. It is a life of passionate absorption, giving it personal meaning. That 'charged-up' feeling I get when I walk out of my dressing room towards the stage, the flow of adrenaline I get when waiting in the wings just before I start dancing, my mind telling my body: You are the master of your own instrument. Together we are ready... let's go! That's a very powerful feeling unlike anything else."

She went on, "I used to think that the path to excellence and success was to work, work, work, and shut out the rest of my life, and only live for the future. I was so wrong. I really do love working extremely hard, but I no longer shut out the rest of my life, nor do I live any longer in the future. I want to live life on my own terms and in my own way, reach the goals I have set out for myself, and to be the one I want to be. The way I look at achieving excellence as a ballerina, or what defines excellence for me, was perfectly summed up by the Ancient Greek philosopher Aristotle: 'Excellence is an art won by training and habituation. We do not act rightly because we have virtue or excellence, but we rather have those because we acted rightly. We are what we repeatedly do. Excellence, then, is not an act but a habit. Excellence is never an accident. It is always the result of high intention, sincere effort, and intelligent execution; it represents the wise choice of many alternatives – choice, not chance, determines your destiny.'

"Nothing comes instantly, and genuine success should never be envied. There is always a long and tough process behind someone's success. However, stardom in the world of ballet does not come overnight, because a ballet dancer needs to work very hard, every single day of her or his career, in order to maintain their technique and to continuously improve. Ballet is not Hollywood or Broadway, where stardom can easily be achieved overnight!"

"Seventeen years have passed since you started your ballet training at White Lodge. You are now into your second decade of dancing with the Company. Looking back, what do you consider to be your happiest moments so far in your career?" I asked.

"Oh, my ultimate happiest moment was certainly when our Director Kevin O'Hare promoted me to Principal ballerina. My ultimate dream came true. All the sacrifices I had made were worth it when I reached this high point in my career. Exceptionally happy moments were also when I was cast in dream roles such as Juliet in *Romeo and Juliet*, Odette/Odile in *Swan Lake*, Tatiana in *Onegin*, *Giselle*, Swanilda in *Coppélia*, and as Kitri in *Don Quixote*. I hope in the not-too-distant future to add to my list of happy career moments the roles of *Manon* and Mary Vetsera in *Mayerling* – two major roles I am longing to perform. Dancing all those roles are unique, ecstatic moments. To be able to step into the shoes of past great ballerinas who danced those roles is simply the most amazing feeling. I have a great attachment to The Royal Ballet, because I grew up alongside the Company. And having trained at The Royal Ballet School, its history, as well as the style of English Ballet, is firmly implanted in my veins, and its roots can be seen in the way I dance."

Looking through one of her early albums, there is a photo of her father carrying her as a baby during one of our regular walks in Richmond Park, dated 20 September, 1992. Twelve years later, I added underneath the photo: *"Little did she know what was awaiting her..."*

"What if you ever have a daughter who tells you that she wants to become a ballerina? What will you say to her?" I asked.

"I think I will support her and try to do the same as you did with me, and pass on my knowledge, but the child of a ballerina will always be looked upon differently. I would not want to be too involved and would allow her space, because I would want her to find her own path, enabling her to figure it out by herself," she told me. "Perhaps I would try to sway her towards a different profession, because I know how hard the whole process of becoming a professional dancer is, as is the profession itself. But ultimately, if she felt really strongly about pursuing a career in ballet, I would be there for her. Ballet training has the potential to set you up for life, certainly when great care and attention is given to mental health. The self-discipline a child needs to develop from a young age, the focus, the ambition to achieve, the push for excellence, and so much more, are all valuable, transferable, and useful life skills to possess."

"One day your career will inevitably come to an end and some people have asked me if I think it is gloomy prospect that a career of a ballerina is so short," I told Yasmine. "My reply has always been: 'Short? Yasmine started her vocational training aged twelve, she became a professional dancer aged eighteen, and she will likely have danced for over two decades. That's a long time to have your feet in pointe shoes.' So, what will you take away with you once your career is over?" I wondered.

"A path is only a path. Ballet is a path I chose and followed as a child, and this resulted in having a career as a ballerina. It will be a journey from which I will only take the beautiful moments with me; a journey that ultimately made me very strong; a journey that totally absorbed me and enriched my life," she said. "I'll take all my mental skills and life perspectives with me in order to give myself renewed energy to do other great things, allowing me to expand my horizons in meaningful ways. Being a ballerina is just one aspect of who I am. My private persona is entirely separate from who I am professionally. It often surprises me when people meet me and say: 'But you are so... normal. I would have never thought you are a ballerina!'"

Yasmine paused for a moment and quietly reflected. "It is not what will be gone but what is left that will count for me, and whenever that moment arrives, I will have prepared myself well beforehand."

After Six Months of an Empty Royal Opera House

The Royal Opera House finally reopened on 17 May 2021, and The Royal Ballet dancers were finally able to perform again for a live audience – for the first time since November 2020.

We have been able to watch Yasmine dance the stunning pas de deux with fellow Principal dancer Ryoichi Hirano in Christopher Wheeldon's *Within the Golden Hour*. We had the pleasure of watching her dance Terpsichore in *Apollo* – one of George Balanchine's masterpieces – on the opening night, partnered by Principal dancer Vadim Muntagirov as the young god Apollo, as well as her debut as the Pink Girl in Jerome Robbins' *Dances at a Gathering*.

Yasmine closed The Royal Ballet Season 2020-2021, and danced Princess Aurora in *The Sleeping Beauty* – Act III, with Principal dancer Federico Bonelli as her Prince.

One can say that her Prince did come in the end.

"Ballet is full of mysteries. Before Company class starts every day at 10:30, they straggle in, drawn and ashen-faced. They line the studio with bags and bundles that disgorge a cargo of bandages and woollies, plasters and cotton wool. It is less a dance studio and more a casualty ward as they pad and plaster bruised feet, bruised toenails, tie scarves like tourniquets around their heads and waists, heave themselves in plastic trousers. As they hobble about, I wonder how these invalids will ever bear the rigours of the barre. Then, against all reason, a daily miracle takes place. As the first notes of the piano are struck, far from wilting they begin to shimmer with well-being, their eyes open wider, their hair starts to shine, their skin glows and, as the time for centre work arrives, the general radiance is dazzling. The miracle is that they are drawing strength from the very act of dancing itself, living off it, and nourished by it. As a long day of rehearsals passes, the energy drawn from the dance seems to grow until the accumulated vitality is offered to their evening audience as an incomparable gift."

Donald Hamilton Fraser, from *Dancers*

Milton Keynes UK
Ingram Content Group UK Ltd.
UKHW051709240324
439787UK00006BA/127/J